To Lotti

Happy Cooking!

ESSEX FEAST

ONE COUNTY, TWENTY CHEFS

cookbook & food lovers' guide

Stephanie Mackentyre

Published by Feast Publishing
E: office@feastpublishing.co.uk
W: www.feastpublishing.co.uk

First published in paperback in 2017
ISBN (paperback): 978-0-9933601-2-1

Editorial: Stephanie Mackentyre, Tessa Allingham and Glyn Williams
Design: Mark Shreeve
Photography: Phil Morley

All accolades or guide listings refer to 2017 unless otherwise stated. Carte average refers to the average cost of a three-course meal from the à la carte menu, without wine.

Recipes listed in this book have been tested and provided to the publishers in good faith. Feast Publishing cannot be held responsible for any loss or damage, caused by any omissions or errors therein.

Contents

In England's green and pleasant land, Essex has charm and appeal by the spade-load. It's a county packed with variety, with the busy, urban chic of our market towns rolling into the lush countryside and farmland that stretches into Suffolk in the north, or gives way to the call of the coast and the lapping North Sea with its unique inlets, creeks and estuaries in the east. If it's the high life you want, Essex can provide it joyfully; if it's isolated pastoral solace you need, then it can give you that too.

Its near-perfect climate for agriculture, with fertile soils and mild maritime temperatures makes farming a key part of the county's economy. For food-lovers, this translates into tasty ingredients and abundant artisan products; it really does offer a wonderfully rich world of food.

Essex is a cook's paradise! The county is blessed with incredible produce, packed with field-to-fork deliciousness and freshness, and countless farmers' markets, farm shops, delis and independent food stores that sell a cornucopia of edible delights. It scores pretty highly on the drinks front too with excellence in brewing, wine-making and distilling offering an alcoholic alternative to some of the fantastic cordials and juices being made from local orchard and hedgerow fruits. What's in the glass seems to be becoming just as important to food-lovers as what's on the plate, and if it's a local tipple then all the better!

Fancy eating out? Then you're in the right place. The Essex dining scene is vibrant, there's a tremendous array of fantastic restaurants with passionate, hard-working chefs at the stoves, and warmly welcoming front of house teams at every door. We've brought just twenty of them together here in this book, asked each one to tell their own Essex story and share the love they have for the region and for a particular local ingredient. I hope every chapter gives you a flavour of what this wonderful county can give whether to those lucky enough to live in these parts year-round, or to visitors dipping into its delights all too briefly.

Essex has always had a special place in my heart. I remember the annual Sunday School outing to Walton-on-the-Naze (always a magical day for a little girl!) which is a place that still sparks nostalgia whenever I go there! With two children of my own, we've enjoyed many happy weekends over the years exploring the Essex countryside – Mersea Island and Thorpe le Soken remain perennial favourites – with our border collie, Bonnie, who adores Bulhus Woods in particular. If I want some retail therapy, I love the vibrancy of Colchester and Chelmsford, especially when shopping is punctuated with a delicious lunch of course.

My professional life has been quite Essex-centric ever since I started some 15 years ago writing the food and drink pages for *Essex Life* magazine. When the magazine launched its annual Fine Food & Drink Awards, I was flattered to be asked to be a judge, and have reviewed contenders for the Restaurant of the Year title ever since. Meeting the chefs, producers and the county's food community when I help present the awards is a joy, as is co-hosting the event with David Whiteley from BBC *Look East*. Add in regular slots on BBC Radio Essex talking about foodie matters with Ronnie Barbour on his mid-morning show and you might be fooled into thinking my life as a food writer is a glamorous one, but to be honest you're more likely to find me in a muddy field, perhaps sheltering from blustery wind in order to get the plough-to-plate story straight from the farmer's mouth! On days like those it doesn't quite feel that glitzy, I promise you! It goes without saying that I am expected to try every food that's put in front of me, and I do enjoy pretty much everything, though I have to admit I draw the line at black pudding which can be tricky these days given that it has become such a popular ingredient.

I'm privileged to have a job with food at its heart, and I am extremely lucky to be plying my trade here in Essex. I cannot think of any other place where I would rather work and play than right here in this glorious county.

I hope you enjoy feasting Essex-style as much as I have enjoyed putting this book together.

Steph

Stephanie Mackentyre, Editor

Welcome

Cooking notes

We want you to enjoy the exciting, original recipes from some of our favourite Essex chefs, that are included in this book. To ensure you get the best out of the dishes, please take time to read the following tips and a few words of caution. Much of it will be second nature to many home cooks, but if in doubt, do refer to these notes.

WELFARE IN THE KITCHEN

Sharp tools, high temperatures and close proximity to humans and pets make the kitchen a potentially dangerous place. Accidents can happen when cooking, so please minimise the risk by applying appropriate caution, care and common sense.

COOKING TEMPERATURES AND TIMINGS

Cookers, and especially ovens, can be fickle pieces of equipment. Please treat all temperatures and times as a general guide and adjust to suit your own cooker.

Temperatures and timings are based on the use of a domestic, electric, non-fan oven so please adjust to the appropriate equivalent level, if you have a different cooker type.

MEASUREMENTS

- General cookery rules and common sense apply
- Spoonfuls are measured level
- Handfuls and pinches are based on an 'average' woman's hand and fingers (apologies if that's non-PC!)
- Bunches for herbs are standard retail sizes
- Eggs are large and free range from a local, happy farm flock preferably
- Milk used is full fat unless otherwise stated

SEASONING

Recipe seasoning instructions refer to adding salt and pepper to taste. We choose to use local Maldon sea salt flakes, crushed between clean fingers or milled for fineness, and black peppercorns, freshly-ground to order. Some dishes may taste or look better on the plate with the alternative use of white peppercorns, eg fish dishes and cream sauces.

GENERAL TIPS

- Rapeseed oil should be cold-pressed, good quality and local where possible.
- Keep warm plates to hand both for storing cooked elements of dishes hot while finishing recipes and then to serve up on as required.
- Recipes call for standard preparation of ingredients ie the kitchen 'norm' such as all produce being washed before use and trimmed, peeled, cored, deseeded etc if needs be. Any need to the contrary will be indicated. Meat and fish to be oven-ready and if required to be skinless or boneless, this will be stated accordingly.
- To rest food, leave somewhere hot on a warm plate, loosely covered with foil if your kitchen is cool or draughty, until required.

FOOD SAFETY

It goes without saying that ensuring the health and well-being of the people eating your food is vital! Use your common sense backed up with a bit of research and advice from reputable books and online sources.

Please do pay particular attention to:

- Quality and freshness of ingredients – check expiry and best-before dates
- Storage of produce and ingredients in the kitchen
- Use of raw and partly-cooked eggs
- Allergen risks
- Cooling and refrigeration where dishes are stored mid-preparation before finishing
- Fridge temperature – are they low enough for safe storage?
- Oven temperatures – is it hot enough before you start cooking?
- Core temperature of cooked dishes – has the food reached the right temperature before consumption?
- Finished dishes, not consumed immediately after preparation – are they stored at appropriate temperatures and consumed within safe time limits?

If in doubt, consult the Government's own online health and nutrition website for food safety advice at www.nhs.uk/livewell

MISTLEY THORN
SHERRI SINGLETON

THE CRICKETERS ARMS
PATRICK LIVIC

HAYWARDS RESTAURANT
JAHDRE HAYWARD

THE SUN INN
JACK LEVINE

Meet the chefs

It's quite a line-up, isn't it! Our twenty talented chefs take some of the best ingredients Essex has to offer, and prepare them creatively and innovatively in kitchens from coastal Manningtree to riverside Dedham and rural Chigborough via historic Colchester and Epping Forest.

Why not pay them a visit? Eat some of the county's most delicious food with seductive views of rolling countryside or gentle waterways, maybe overlooking peaceful village greens or in characterful spots in buzzy town centres. Choose from award-winning fine dining restaurants, relaxed pubs, or informal neighbourhood favourites. There's something for every taste in these pages, and while each restaurant has its own unique personality, every one of them determinedly champions the fantastic produce on its doorstep.

Above all, wherever you find yourself, enjoy your meal – and maybe raise a glass to the people who produced the ingredients, and the hard-working chefs who created the food on your table.

THE MAGIC MUSHROOM
DARREN BENNETT

THE BULL & WILLOW ROOM
SAM BAXTER

BOATHOUSE RESTAURANT
CAMERON MARSHALL

THE CREEK
TERENCE HOWARD

THE SQUARE AND COMPASSES
CRAIG LOVERIDGE

RUBINO KITCHEN
ROB HORTON

LUCCA ENOTECA
MICHAEL BONACCORSI

THE SPOTTED DOG
SIMON EDWARDS

THE WHITE HART INN
KAREN STEELE

CHURCH STREET TAVERN
EWAN NAYLON

THE ANCHOR RIVERSIDE
DANIEL WATKINS

THE GREEN MAN
RICHARD LEWIS

THE HOOP
PHIL UTZ

GRAIN
PAUL WENDHOLT & JORDAN 'SID' SIDWELL

THE VINE
STEPHEN MANN

PIG & WHISTLE RESTAURANT
MATTHEW COURT

THE MISTLEY THORN, MISTLEY
SHERRI SINGLETON

Wild at heart

Pungent wild garlic, foraged in Wrabness woodland, is a favourite ingredient for chef-restaurateur Sherri Singleton

Sherri Singleton stipulated three criteria when her husband David McKay, who is from Essex, persuaded her to move from her sunny, native southern California to set up a home and restaurant in the UK: a Georgian house, to be no more than an hour from London, and to have views of the water. She got the lot.

Her (Georgian) home is in Mistley – a snappy hour into London Liverpool Street – and is a stone's throw from the river Stour. The 18th century house that the couple bought in 2000 is adjacent to The Mistley Thorn, the restaurant with rooms that she and her husband have nurtured since 2004, and the Mistley Kitchen cookery school, while their third enterprise, Lucca Enoteca is a few minutes down the road in Manningtree. "I love this area because of the wealth of local produce available right on our doorstep," Sherri says. She regularly has pheasants or bags of courgettes brought to the kitchen door by locals. "It's wonderful; I would happily offer them something in return, but quite often they just leave them and go." This very natural bounty fits Sherri's approach to food, and her roots in seasonal, simple Californian-style cooking; it's not surprising to hear that she loves working with foraged local ingredients such as wild garlic and nettles too.

Much of her fresh produce and interesting salad leaves come from Pete Thompson, who specialises in supplying wholesale markets and the catering sector from his family business at Brook Farm in Great Oakley, north-east Essex. Founded in 1948 by Pete's grandfather George Thompson, the business has expanded through the decades to corner the market for oriental vegetables and herbs for Chinese restaurants – the likes of collard used to make Chinese 'seaweed', and jumbo spring onions whose green stems are softer than the English variety and therefore dissolve more easily in the wok. The company's innovations have also stretched to creating the UK's first outdoor fig orchard. But our visit was outside the farm's boundaries in the great Essex countryside to gather freshly sprouted wild garlic from the hedgerows to use as a zingy accompaniment with its fresh zestiness enhancing a spring fish dish.

"Seafood is a speciality of our restaurants," says Sherri as we head to Wrabness with Pete, whose huntsman's knife possibly qualifies him to be Essex's answer to Bear Grylls! "Mersea oysters are available year-round and we'll have Colchester natives when they're in season, and plenty of locally landed fish and shellfish. But I love using foraged ingredients like wild garlic and nettle tops in our pasta and pasta fillings or to flavour potato gnocchi; and they of course work well in aioli, or great as a soup along with asparagus spears."

The woodland in Wrabness is a carpet of bluebells and wild garlic, the pungent scent as heavenly as the setting with its river Stour views. Sherri and Pete pick the garlic and nettles gingerly, gloves sadly forgotten, the bristly, smarting tips stinging fingertips even with the clearly inadequate protection of two plastic bags wrapped around their hands. Garlic and nettles gathered, we drop into The Mistley Thorn to deliver a crate of produce, some of it from Pete's other business, Clear Water Farms, which grows herbs on water in vast polytunnels. Thai basil, water spinach, and even fruit juice from Pete's Tendring Fruit orchards are welcomed by the busy Thorn chefs.

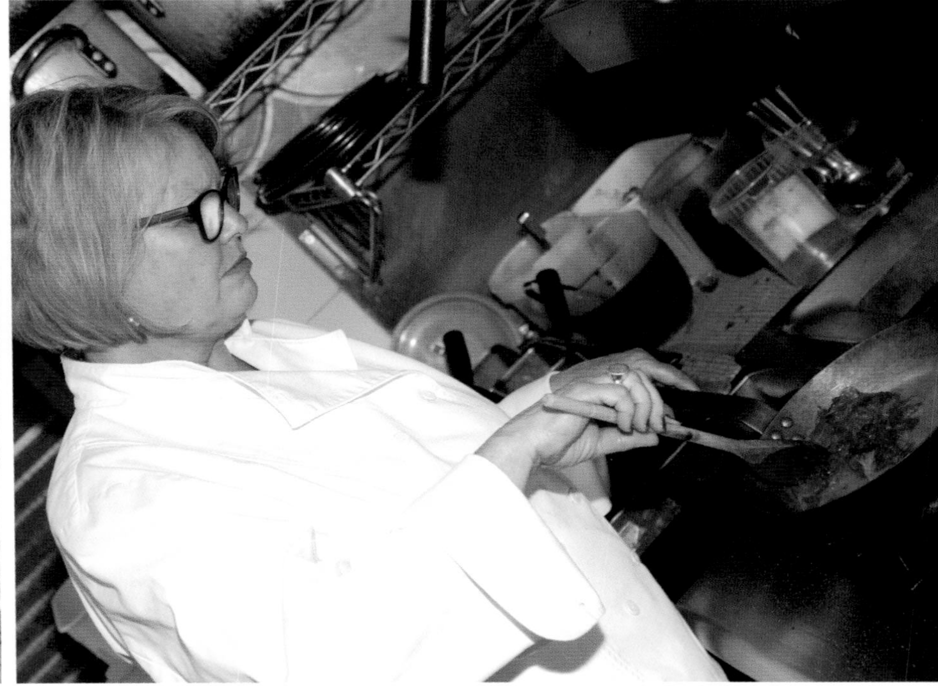

Sherri pops from there next door to drop off more local goodies for The Mistley Kitchen. Part purpose-built cookery school and part well-stocked cookshop, there she works with guest chef-instructors like Italian food writer Ursula Ferrigno, master baker Sue Hudson and preserver Kylee Newton who take turns in hosting a variety of culinary workshops for enthusiastic amateur cooks, with cookery course themes such as 'quick and easy Thai food', knife skills, or 'fish and seafood the Italian way'.

In all three of her kitchens, Sherri champions plenty more local produce, using a plethora of interesting farmed, foraged and bartered ingredients. "We also make a pesto from wild garlic, and in the past, we've made beetroot pasta and a beetroot base for pizza which, believe it or not, goes down brilliantly. Of course, all our dishes, whether here at the Thorn or at Lucca, are made by hand. Our pizza recipe there is still the original one we learnt in Naples, with just a few alterations to make it work with the temperature and humidity here in Manningtree!"

The relaxed, informal style of the very natural cuisine belies the skilful kitchen craft and attention to detail put in the kitchen and on to the plate for each and every dish at the Thorn. Taking the wild garlic harvested earlier, Sherri sets to work picking it over, shredding the stems and leaves ready to be wilted for her colourful fish main course of grilled fish and wild spring greens, soon served up with earthy Jerusalem artichoke roots and a zesty, rich orange, tomato and basil butter sauce.

Watching such an insightful chef clearly relishing the quality and excitement of new season ingredients, harvested for free from a wild hedgerow, is a joy.

The simplicity that Sherri espouses in the pan and on the plate in allowing the essence of her quality, local produce to sing by gilding it with as much exuberance or restraint as is warranted, is the product of an evolved palate and sensitive approach; hers clearly born out of a familiarity with and appreciation of the best seasonal ingredients that have been garnered from working hard in kitchens, spending precious days off and holidays dining out and travelling the world. The likes of seared south coast fillet of bream with seaweed crushed new potatoes, naturally salty samphire and a shellfish bisque, or organic courgette and broad bean salad with feta and mint dressing demonstrate her incisive, produce-led cooking clearly. Senses are further spoilt with soulful comfort desserts to finish, perhaps rich Chocolat St Emilion with mascarpone cream and amaretti, lemon tart with pine nut crust or butterscotch budino.

Wood-grilled fish fillets with wild spring greens, jerusalem artichokes and tomato, orange & basil butter sauce

For this smoky, interesting fish main course, we like to cook local fish from the Essex coast, such as wild sea bass, cod or sole fillets. If you don't have access to a wood-fired grill, a charcoal barbecue works well and alternatively, you can of course use a conventional cast iron char-grill pan on your hob.

Be sure to cook the jerusalem artichokes before the fish fillets; you can also roast them instead of grilling, for about 15 minutes in a hot oven and they will hold up well. You can then finish them by reheating on the grill while the fish and greens cook. The sauce is best prepared ahead, kept warm and ready to go, stored in a hot vacuum flask (pre-heated with boiling water and drained). (serves 4)

Butter sauce

30g shallots, very finely chopped
30ml white wine vinegar
45ml dry white wine
1 tbsp double cream
120g unsalted butter, cubed and chilled
Ground cayenne pepper, to taste
Zest and juice of an orange
2 tomatoes, peeled, seeded and diced
Small bunch of fresh basil, leaves picked and shredded

Place the shallots, vinegar, white wine and 30ml cold water in a small heavy-bottomed saucepan over a medium heat, bring to a boil and reduce until just over a quarter of the liquid remains. Whisk in the cream and simmer again for one minute. Add the butter, one cube at a time, whisking continuously until each piece has melted before adding the next. Do not allow to boil. The sauce should be shiny and thickened. Season to taste with sea salt, black pepper and cayenne. Stir in the zest and 1tbsp of orange juice, followed by the tomatoes and basil. Keep warm in a hot vacuum flask.

Roasted jerusalem artichokes

500g jerusalem artichokes, skin-on, scrubbed and peeled (optionally)l if very knobbly
Local rapeseed oil

Before grilling the fish, slice the artichokes into medium-sized chunks or slices and lightly oil. Season generously with salt and pepper. Place on the hot grill and cook for about 10-15 minutes, turning as needed until the artichokes are well marked and caramelised. They are ready to serve when they are easily pierced.

To serve

8 skin-on white fish fillets, around 125g, scaled and pin-boned
600g wild greens such as wild garlic and nettle tops (or grown alternatives such as asparagus tips or water spinach)
2 tbsp local rapeseed oil

Pre-heat your chosen grill until very hot. If using a wood oven or barbecue, add a handful of water-soaked hickory chips for flavouring the smoke. Lightly season the fish and place on the grill skin-side down. Leave the fish to cook for several minutes without moving, otherwise the skin may tear. Once you see a caramelised edge, carefully flip the fillets over, using a large spatula or fish slice.

Cook for a further 1-3 minutes, depending on the thickness of the fish. To test the fish, carefully give it a gentle press with your finger; it should still be a bit springy in the middle. Remove the fish to a warmed plate and allow to rest somewhere hot whilst you prepare the greens.

Heat a deep sauté pan or wok over a high heat. Pour in the oil, add the greens, stir well and pour in 3tbsp of water. Stir-fry with tongs until the liquid has evaporated. Remove from heat and season to taste.

To serve, divide the wilted greens and grilled artichokes between hot plates, top with the fish fillets and spoon over the butter sauce.

Brodetto fisherman's stew

We flavour our fish stock with leeks, shallots, bay, thyme, parsley, white wine and fresh tomatoes. It's best to use a good mix of tasty seafood, skinless fish fillets, firmer round white fish and softer flatfish cut into chunks, as well as crab claws, raw scallop meats, cooked mussels and cleaned squid in rings. (serves 6+)

125ml good olive oil
2 onions, peeled and chopped
6 garlic cloves, chopped
800g passata
125ml dry white wine
1 litre of good fish stock
Large pinch of chilli flakes
Large pinch of saffron
2kg fish in chunks and shellfish
Handful of flat parsley

In a large hobproof casserole dish, gently fry the onion in the oil until soft and translucent. Add the garlic and cook for another two minutes. Add the tomatoes, cover, turn up heat and cook over a moderate heat for 20 minutes, stirring occasionally. Stir in the wine and bring to a boil, then simmer for two minutes. Pour in the fish stock, return to the boil and simmer for 15 minutes. Add the chilli and saffron. Season lightly and gently stir in firmer fish before simmering for three minutes.

Lightly mix in any raw seafood and softer fish, bring to a simmer and cook for about three minutes. Fold through any cooked shellfish and heat through. Adjust the seasoning and stir in most of the parsley leaves, chopped. Scatter remaining leaves on top before serving.

Beetroot gazpacho

A sweet, zingy alternative to the classic Spanish recipe. In the picture, the soup is finished with diced tomato, cucumber, red onion, mixed peppers, citrus juice, shredded herbs and more wine vinegar. (serves 6)

3 medium beetroot, some stem left on
½ tsp Maldon sea salt
2 tsp red wine or sherry vinegar
1 tbsp caster sugar
4 ripe tomatoes
1 large cucumber
A handful of coriander leaves
1 tsp fresh thyme leaves
4 cloves garlic, crushed
500ml tomato juice
½ tsp crushed red chilli flakes
Pinch of cayenne or a dash of Tabasco sauce
3 tbsp lime juice

Bring the beetroot, vinegar and sugar to the boil in a snug, lidded, non-reactive saucepan with enough cold water to cover. Simmer until tender, about 30 minutes. Remove the beetroot, reserving 250ml of the cooking liquid. When cool, peel the beetroot and cut into small dice for garnish.

Halve, seed and dice the tomatoes and cucumber. Stir with the chopped herbs, remaining ingredients and reserved juice in a large bowl. Refrigerate for up to 24 hours. Strain the base, reserving both solids and juice. Process the solids, stopping as soon as it becomes a coarse purée. Strain this through a fine sieve into the juice. Stir, cover and refrigerate until chilled (for up to 3 hours). Season to taste before serving very cold in chilled bowls.

Dead-easy chocolate cake

This dead-easy chocolate cake recipe is my 'go-to' dessert for any occasion and stores or freezes well. Glam it up with ganache icing or seasonal fruit, or enjoy it just with good ice cream or mascarpone. Rice flour is gluten-free and creates a moist texture, but you can use plain flour or ground almonds. The cake will sink and crack as it cools. (serves 6+)

250g salted butter, plus more for greasing
250g good plain chocolate (70% cocoa), chopped small
6 eggs, separated, at room temperature
250g granulated sugar
6 tbsp rice flour, plus extra for dusting the pan

Preheat the oven to 180c. Butter and line a 22cm cake tin pan with a circle of buttered baking paper before dusting with rice flour and shaking out. Place the butter in a mixing bowl over a saucepan of barely simmering water.

Add the chocolate to the melted butter and stir occasionally until a smooth mixture. Remove the bowl and cool slightly. Whisk the egg yolks lightly with the sugar until just mixed. Add to the warm chocolate mixture and fold in the flour. Separately beat the egg whites until soft peaks form. Fold these gently into the chocolate bowl until just mixed.

Pour the batter into the pan and bake for 45 to 50 minutes. The cake is done when the sides are set but the centre of the cake is still soft. Remove and allow to cool in the pan.

FAVOURITE KITCHEN GADGET?

It's not really a gadget, but I have a wood oven here at Mistley, and also in my home kitchen which I love. I really had to badger my husband for them but it was worth it! Failing that, I use my Microplane grater every day - we stock them in The Mistley Kitchen shop.

BEST RESTAURANT EVER EATEN IN?

The River Café in Hammersmith. Last time I visited I had char-grilled turbot on white beans with Capezzana olive oil and lemon; it was just the most delicious thing I've tasted in ages, but so simple. That first meal at Chez Panisse takes some beating as well!

FAVOURITE PART OF ESSEX?

Walking the Essex Way. I love this coastal northern part of Essex especially the stretch between Mistley and Harwich and having a nice pint and dressed crab at The Alma!

MIDNIGHT FEAST?

I love guacamole and tortilla chips – home-made of course, and using my mom's recipe!

SHERRI ON HER...

SIGNATURE DISHES

Starters

Smoked haddock chowder

Wood-grilled squid or octopus, chilli, lime, garlic

Grilled Mersea oysters, smoked tomato butter, sourdough crumbs

Mains

Brodetto, our stew of local fish and shellfish in tomato, saffron & fennel broth

Wood-grilled cuttlefish, Alison's Organic leaves, chilli, garlic & coriander Amano olive oil, hand-cut skin-on fries

Haloumi, pepper, courgette & aubergine skewers, parmentier potatoes, romesco sauce

Puddings

My Mom's famous cheesecake, toffee sauce, praline

Meyer lemon tart, pinenut crust

Lemon sorbet, homemade limoncello

MUSIC IN THE KITCHEN?

I like to listen to jazz. We went to Cuba last year, and I got really into Cuban Son music which is great fun and really gets you moving.

COOK'S TIP OR CHEF'S CHEAT?

We use loads of garlic in the restaurants and workshops, and the best way to peel them is to break the whole head into cloves and place them into a bowl with a fitted lid. Shake the bowl furiously for a minute or so and all the cloves should peel themselves!

DISH OF MY CHILDHOOD?

Globe artichokes with butter and lemon. I lived near a field of artichokes as a child and we used to have to pick the artichokes and bring them back for my mom to boil. Talk about child labour!

PERFECT DAY OFF?

Going to London, seeing an exhibition, having a nice meal and engaging in a bit of retail therapy with my daughter Isla, an expert shopper!

WHERE DOES FOOD TAKE YOU?

I travel widely. I was in Amsterdam last week and I leave for Bordeaux tomorrow. I have travelled around South East Asia and I adore Japan, Mexico and Italy. I love the freshness and immediate cooking styles of Vietnamese or Thai as their food is all focused simply on flavour and quality of ingredients.

MADE ME LAUGH...

We've had the occasional diner who has asked us to 'heat up their gazpacho'. We do pretty much whatever people want; after all we are in the business of trying to please people!

Thorn of plenty

The charming, welcoming Mistley Thorn – or the Thorn as it's affectionately known – is at the heart of the historic port village of Mistley on the river Stour. Once a coaching inn, it can still offer a very comfortable bed for the night as well as a good meal, with four of the 12 individually designed bedrooms upstairs overlooking the stunning estuary. Step inside the ground floor to find a relaxed welcoming dining space, bare wooden tables and exposed brickwork with a central bar and views of Mistley Quay.

It was a meal at Alice Waters' legendary Berkeley restaurant, Chez Panisse, that set Sherri on her career path. "I went there for my 20th birthday back in the 80s. I was at uni studying design and I was also working in a restaurant front of house at the time. When I ate at Chez Panisse, I realised right then and there that I wanted to jack it all in and make my life in restaurants."

On moving to Essex in 1989, she and her husband David opened The Stour Bay Café in Manningtree to rave reviews. The property is now home to Lucca Enoteca, the couple's neighbourhood trattoria, while The Mistley Thorn and the cookery school and cookware shop, Mistley Kitchen, are just down the road. As much as the right location and well thought out offerings, the secret to their success is firmly put down to their loyal staff. At the Thorn, general manager Rowan Hunter works alongside Karl Burnside (head chef for seven years), while at Lucca Enoteca, a long-standing team includes head chef Jonathan 'Wiggy' Whitfield and pizzaiolo Michael Bonaccorsi. "Things are going really nicely," says Sherri. "We've recently added a two-storey cottage here at the Thorn as well as an extension on the kitchen. We are looking possibly to open another Lucca – if we find the right location."

The Mistley Thorn
High St, Mistley CO11 1HE
W: mistleythorn.co.uk
T: 01206 392821 E: info@themistleythorn.co.uk
/TheMistleyThorn
@TheMistleyThorn
/themistleythorn

Accolades: AA two rosettes; Waitrose *Good Food Guide*; *Michelin*; *Sawday's*; *Good Hotel Guide*; runner-up, Best Restaurant, *Observer Food Monthly* Awards 2016, 2015, 2014

Covers: 85

Cost: carte average £25; wine from £15.95; pint from £3.70

Open: Mon-Sun B 8-10.30; Mon-Sat L 12-3, D 6-9.30 (10 Fri & Sat); Sun L 12-4.30

Details: 12 en suite rooms, four with river views; wheelchair access; dogs welcome in some rooms; free WiFi; some parking

No kidding

A breed of old English goat, thought to be extinct, is being reared and bred at Thorndon Country Park to graze the land and supply delicious meat for chefs like Patrick Livic, head chef at The Cricketers Arms.

Goat meat may account for some ten per cent of the world's red meat consumption – it's a fragrant staple in Caribbean cuisine, tastes delicious in middle eastern pilaf or kofte, and slow-cooked in a curry it is tender and sweet – but for a French chef like Patrick Livic, steeped in his country's classical cooking tradition, it is a step into the unknown. Goats' cheese is a familiar part of the French repertoire – but goat meat is new territory for him.

"I'm a chef, so I am constantly trying new ingredients," Patrick says. "I wasn't fazed by trying goat meat, but it was good of Roger to drop some off a week before for me to experiment with!" Roger Beecroft is herd manager at the Essex Grazing Project, and is part of a team responsible for saving and looking after a herd of purebred Old English goats that now live in Thorndon Country Park in Brentwood. The animals were rehomed from the Cheviot Hills where their numbers had made them a nuisance to the forestry plantations. "This breed was originally a cottager's goat with a distinctive beard," says Roger, "but over the years they were crossed with something else so that today only a few purebred animals remain. We brought 60 of them here, and they will be bred carefully and given to other sites around the country with a similar approach to conservation and breeding as ours."

Roger is keen to develop relationships with local chefs who want to put goat meat on their menus even though the project is around 18 months away from having commercial supply volumes. He is convinced that the meat from his animals will be quite different from existing product – born in the spring, the animals will spend almost two years grazing the natural scrubby grassland of Thorndon (it's a diet that makes the meat particularly tasty, he says) before they are slaughtered at nearby Burnham. "They will graze alongside the herd of Red Poll cattle that we also manage, and whose meat we supply to Essex butchers."

The goats were shy at first, nowhere to be seen, but the sound of Roger shaking a bucket of dry feed soon tempted one brave chap, with an endearing bearded face, to poke his head round the shrubbery. He stepped gingerly forward into the open to snaffle some of the food, his herd-mates following suit so that before we knew it we were surrounded by grey and white shaggy-haired goats perfectly happy to eat while Patrick and Roger discussed the animals' new habitat and lifestyle. Before we left even the Red Poll cattle, who graze the same land, had joined in the impromptu afternoon snack. The arrival of the bull, however, brass ring through his nose, was the cue for us to make our excuses and head back to the safety of Patrick's kitchen.

Patrick decides on cooking the meat three ways. Tender confit leg meat is pulled off the bone and turned into a croquette, coated in fresh breadcrumbs and fried till crisp and golden; the breast is braised in a rich beef stock for 12 hours; the loin he cuts deftly from the carcass before seasoning it simply with Maldon salt and freshly-ground black pepper, and pan-frying it in plenty of butter. The meat is lean but succulent – for Patrick the flavour is somewhere between beef and hare, less fatty and milder-tasting than lamb. He plates the cuts up with courgette flower in a light, puffy, tempura batter, heritage carrots and pea shoots.

Cooking goat wasn't too far from Patrick's comfort zone, though he's happiest working with rabbit, hare and venison supplied in season often by gamekeeper friends. Dishes like wild rabbit ravioli with butternut squash velouté and basil oil, or venison loin pan-fried with dauphinoise potatoes and a red wine jus are popular at certain times of the year. Grazing boards, overflowing with charcuterie, cheese and chutney, or fish and seafood, go down well, as do locally-made sausages served with mash, or 28-day aged steaks and maybe a homemade chocolate parfait or vanilla pannacotta to finish. "I'd say my style of cooking is mainly classic French," Patrick says, "but it's probably best described as continental with a bit of British thrown in for good measure!"

Patrick is proud of his homemade dessert menu with its mix of continental and British influences. The red fruit sabayon served with frozen yoghurt, a crisp ginger biscuit crumb and baby meringues sells readily, as does a vanilla pannacotta served with plump local strawberries that have been marinated in balsamic vinegar and the aniseed flavour of pastis. A rich, dark Belgian chocolate parfait is universally popular, as is the cheeseboard with its array of artisan cheeses served with homemade quince jelly.

Patrick was brought up not far from the Champagne region in northern France, but has lived in the UK for over 15 years. "My mum taught me how to cook, and then I went to catering school in Paris and worked in France for 10 years. I came to England to learn the language, but I ended up staying! I might go back to France one day but I'm happy here in Essex; I have no plans to move just yet."

Now that he has cooked with goat, he's keen to do more. "Roger and I are going to keep in touch," Patrick says. "He's going to let me know once he has more meat available, and I'm going to try his Red Poll beef in the not too distant future too. Another new ingredient to try!"

Trio of kid goat – crisp shoulder croquette, slow-braised leg and pink loin

A popular special when we can get free-range goat, this elegant trio of rather unusual meat combines a crisp croquette of the confit shoulder, pink-seared loin and the slow-braised leg. We add colour and texture with crunchy tempura-battered courgette flower, and sweet slow-baked whole heritage carrots. You will have lots of lovely leftovers for delicious suppers from the shoulder and leg preparation. (serves 4+)

Shoulder croquette

1kg goat shoulder
3 garlic cloves, sliced
2 tbsp chopped, fresh thyme
Maldon sea salt
500g duck fat
2 onions, finely diced
1 garlic clove, finely chopped
1 tbsp thyme, finely chopped
1 tbsp local honey
Few tbsp of seasoned plain flour
1 large free-range egg, beaten
250g fresh breadcrumbs

Place the shoulder in a snug container and rub it with the garlic, thyme and a good handful of salt, then press down with a tray and heavy weights for 6 hours in the fridge.

Pre-heat the oven to 140c. Rinse the goat off quickly under cold water and pat dry with clean tea towels.

Place in a snug ovenproof dish, melt the fat and pour over. Cover with foil and bake for 6 hours or until tender.

Remove from the oven and set aside till the meat is cool enough to handle. Carefully drain off the fat and while still warm, shred the meat into a bowl. Stir in the onion, garlic, thyme and honey. Roll the mixture into thumb-width cylinders and clingfilm each tightly before chilling overnight.

Pre-heat the deep fat fryer with oil to 180c. Unwrap the cylinders, cut into croquettes and then roll separately in flour, egg and then crumbs. Deep-fry until golden and keep warm.

Braised leg

Rapeseed oil
1 leg of goat
2 onions, sliced
4 carrots, sliced
100g flour
1 tbsp tomato purée
approx. 1 litre good beef stock, simmering

Pre-heat the oven to 180c. Heat up a heavy casserole dish on a high heat, add a little oil and brown the goat quickly on all sides. Remove the meat and keep warm. Brown the carrots and onions in the same pan until light-golden. Add the flour and cook while scraping the pan for a further minute before stirring in the purée. Return the goat leg and pour in the stock, bring to a simmer, cover tightly with foil and bake for 3 hours. Remove from the oven, cool and refrigerate. Remove the leg from the dish and set aside. Put the liquor into a pan and boil to reduce down to a thick glaze texture. Shred the leg meat off the bone and fold into the jus. Set aside and keep warm.

Pan-fried loin

300g goat loin
Rapeseed oil

Pre-heat the oven to 180c. Season the loin to your liking. Heat up a heavy oiled frying pan on a high heat, brown the loin on all sides and then transfer the pan to the oven for 3 minutes. Remove and rest somewhere warm.

To serve

Carve the loin and arrange on warm plates with the braised leg meat, a croquette and a swirl of the jus.

Sea bass bouillabaisse-style

In the restaurant, this rich fish starter brings a classic Gallic flavour to the menu. We add opened mussels and clams as a garnish. (serves 4)

200g king prawns in the shell
1 onion, finely chopped
1 garlic clove, sliced
1 tsp fennel seeds
1 tsp cumin seeds
2 star anise
Olive oil
200g chopped tomatoes
1 tbsp fresh parsley, chopped
1 egg white
40ml double cream
2 sea bass fillets

Shell the prawns and refrigerate both. Soften the onion, garlic and spices in a splash of olive oil in a saucepan on a low heat. Add the tomatoes and the shells, simmering for 20 minutes. Push through a sieve and reduce on a high heat back in the pan until thickened to a sauce. Cool and chill.

Process the prawns, parsley, egg white and cream until smooth. Lay a fish fillet skin-side down on a large double layer of clingfilm, top with the prawn cream and then the other fillet. Wrap up tightly and then enclose in another clingfilm sheet and refrigerate for 15 minutes. Place into a steamer over boiling water, cover and cook for 20 minutes.

Unwrap, cut into four and serve with the reheated sauce in soup plates.

Lamb's sweetbread and wild mushroom millefeuille

One of my favourite offal, sweetbreads are much like a firm chicken mousse in texture and very delicious, perfect paired with fungi. They need poaching for 2 minutes, cooling and peeling before use. (serves 4)

1 packet good puff pastry
1 egg yolk
Rapeseed oil
1 shallot, finely diced
1 garlic clove, finely chopped
1 tbsp parsley, shredded
150g wild mushrooms, cleaned and chopped
150g lamb's sweetbreads, cooked
100ml beef stock
100ml double cream

Pre-heat the oven to 180c. Roll out the pastry between clingfilm to 5mm thickness. Cut out discs with a 5cm cutter. Place onto a baking tray and brush with egg yolk. Bake for 15 minutes and allow to cool.

Gently cook the shallots with the garlic and parsley in a hot oiled saucepan over a low heat until softened. Turn up to medium, add the bite-size mushrooms, cover and cook for 2 more minutes, then add the sweetbreads, cover and cook for another 5 minutes. Pour in the stock and the cream and simmer for 5 minutes. Season to taste.

Layer the discs with some of the hot filling on warm plates until you have three layers deep. Pour a little sauce around.

Dark chocolate parfait

This is the richest bittersweet chocolate ice cream you could imagine. I add to the indulgence and interest with a zingy, fragrant ice cream shake, blended with melon liqueur and fresh passion fruit. (serves 4+)

500ml whipping cream
2 egg yolks
1 egg
75g of sugar
150g best dark chocolate, grated

Whisk the cream in a chilled bowl with a handwhisk until soft peaks and chill.

In a large glass bowl set over a half-full saucepan of simmering water, whisk the yolks, egg and sugar together. Continue whisking until thickened into a custard. Remove the bowl and set aside.

Place another bowl over the pan and melt the chocolate. Fold this into the custard and cool for 5 minutes. Whisk half of the cream into this mixture, then lightly fold back into the remaining cream until fully combined. Transfer to a snug lidded plastic container and freeze overnight.

To serve, carefully dip the container into boiling water briefly, unmould and slice into portions.

PATRICK ON HIS...

CHEF'S TIP?

Just keep it simple but do it well. An omelette can be incredible if cooked well and with the right ingredients.

FAVOURITE KITCHEN GADGET?

I'd love to have an ice cream maker here in the pub. I'm hoping that by putting it in this book the owner might buy me one!

FUNNY CULINARY MOMENT?

In my first job I remember I was trying to truss a chicken. I just couldn't do it, I was so stressed I just couldn't seem to memorise what the head chef was telling me to do. I can laugh about it now, but at the time it felt like the worst day of my life.

BEST DISH I'VE EVER EATEN?

My first ever fondue when I was much younger. I remember I was in the Pyrenees and it was just so simple but delicious – hot, sticky cheese – and as cheese is my favourite thing to eat, it tasted amazing to me.

SIGNATURE DISHES

Starters

Wild rabbit ravioli, butternut squash velouté, basil oil

Vintage tomato confit, green pesto

Pork rillettes, house pickles, crusty bread

Mains

Poached lobster Bellevue, caviar & gin Marie Rose, chunky chips

Roast duck supreme, honey, lime, wild garlic, marinated summer vegetables, pommes paille

Chicken ballotine, potato & pea croquette, aubergine, caviar, madeira jus

Puddings

Patrick Chichi – peach Melba baked Alaska

Blueberry sabayon, iced yoghurt, ginger crumb, baby meringue

Black and white chocolate delice

CULINARY MENTOR?

Mainly my mum because she encouraged me to cook and to stick with it as a trade. Regrettably, I only see my parents twice a year as they live in Mauritius. I go over to them once a year and then they come over to Essex once a year. Other chefs have influenced my professional career too, people like Marco Pierre White especially. I like his vision of food and his food styling.

BIGGEST EXTRAVAGANCE?

I like it when I have a free hand and the budget to make something amazing for a customer, perhaps for a wedding or a particular dish, like for example a croquembouche as a table centrepiece; I really love to be able to stretch my creativity and imagination.

SOMEWHERE I'D STILL LIKE TO EAT?

Hôtel de Crillon in Paris. I worked there for six months and it's very expensive, but I'd like to go back as a customer.

DISH OF MY CHILDHOOD?

My mum is Mauritian and my dad is from Normandy, so we enjoyed lots of dishes made from cream and Calvados with a spicy twist from my mum's side.

French cricket

Cricket has been played on the green outside The Cricketers Arms since 1850, though it is a moot point whether French-born chef Patrick Livic has played – let alone absorbed any of the sport's obscure rules – in the 15 years he has spent in the UK, and the six months he has worked in this kitchen.

Local cricket fans will be the first to grab a seat in the small courtyard at the front of the red-brick building to enjoy a summer's afternoon of leather on willow, but the main event is inside the pub, where the spacious dining room and bar is spread across three distinct areas. Stone floors and plenty of original beams add to the rural atmosphere, as do open fires in winter, and armchairs that invite lingering, whether over Patrick's food or a drink and simple bar snacks.

The pub, owned by Punch Taverns since 2012 and sister to the Eight Bells in Saffron Walden, is just a 12-minute drive from Stansted airport. It has two function rooms, and regularly hosts wedding receptions with the village green used as an attractive location for pictures. The 10 en suite bedrooms, including family rooms, are all individually decorated either in contemporary or traditional style.

Wines are supplied by Berkshire-based Milton Sandford Wines, who have put together a list offering everything from a simple George Kinross Chenin Blanc 2016, a Gavi di Gavi 2015 from Piedmont, or a cru Beaujolais Pavillon des Perrets Morgon 2014.

The Cricketers Arms
Rickling Green, near Stansted CB11 3YG
W: thecricketersarmsricklinggreen.co.uk
T: 01799 543210
E: info@thecricketersarmsricklinggreen.co.uk
/TheCricketersArmsRicklingGn
@CricketersArms_
@thecricketersarmsrickling

Covers: 60

Cost: carte average £30; wine from £17.65; beers from £4.10

Open: Mon-Fri B 7.30-9.30, Sat-Sun B 8-10; Mon-Sat L 12-3, D 6-10; Sun L 12-6

Details: private dining for up to 40; private hire of entire pub possible; 10 en suite bedrooms; parking

The sweet stuff

Jahdre Hayward doesn't let a bee allergy stop him having productive hives in the kitchen garden behind his Epping restaurant – or from making delicious desserts with their honey

For someone allergic to bees willingly to keep hives a stone's throw from their workplace seems bizarre; for Jahdre then willingly to lift out some of the swarming frames for closer inspection for the sake of a photograph or two, is extraordinary.

Jahdre Hayward discards the beekeeper's protective clothing as soon as he can, far more comfortable in his chef's jacket and back behind his familiar stove where he works carefully to turn the honey from his bees into a delicious dessert. Honeycomb is first, Jahdre heating the honey, sugar, water and glucose to a deep amber colour before adding bicarbonate of soda and letting the molten mixture seemingly take on a life of its own, bubbling and heaving in the tray as it cools and hardens before being snapped into chunks. He serves the sweet shards with a honey parfait, churning a simple mixture including more honey, cream and sugar in his Thermomix before pouring into silicone moulds and leaving them to set in the freezer. He serves the parfaits with honey purée, yoghurt mousse and a vivid green dill ice cream to give a refreshing balance to the sweetness of the rest of the plate.

"I love using our honey," says Jahdre. "We make honey and oat bread, use it to glaze duck breasts and we'll do honey roast parsnips at Christmas. It's in many different desserts – of course – and we even use it in our palate cleansers and cocktails."

Jahdre and his wife Amanda have run Haywards for four and a half years, he in the kitchen, she (also a trained chef) managing the front of house team. The property shares a sizeable plot with Amanda's parents' pub, the Forest Gate Inn, and it's at the end of this plot that the kitchen garden is to be found. Here, the family grows a wide variety of fruit, vegetables, herbs, micro herbs and edible flowers including strawberries, rhubarb, onions, potatoes, courgettes, tomatoes, wild garlic and beetroot, many of which feature on the menu.

A popular asparagus starter comes with a salad of green and white asparagus teamed with an egg yolk emulsion, lemon, hazelnuts and sundried tomatoes. Then there is one of Jahdre's signature dishes, breast of duck garnished with confit duck leg cannelloni, pear and a celeriac purée using home grown celeriac. The garden's prolific rhubarb is also well-utilised, often featuring in a dessert. Jahdre uses it to make sorbet and ice cream as well as purées to be used in cocktails and palate cleansers.

This plot is also where the three hives, each home to some 40,000 bees, are looked after by expert beekeeper, Robin Harman of the Epping Forest Honey Company. "As long as you don't stand opposite their entrance you'll be fine," Robin explains as we approach, all of us – photographer included – clad in protective suits and Robin armed with a smoker to calm the bees. "Oh and they don't like cheap perfume or the scent of bananas! By the way," he adds, "Jahdre is allergic to the Africanised honey bee, not these which are Essex Mongrels!"

Despite our reservations, we are met with dappled sunlight under the shade of trees, and bees more intent on making honey than bothering

"I love using our honey... we make honey and oat bread, use it to glaze duck breasts and we'll do honey roast parsnips at Christmas."

us. "Bees do best in their own environment," Robin explains. "People think you go and get a box of bees like you go out and get a cat. There's quite a lot more than that involved in bee-keeping!" Through his company, he offers beginners' courses to teach people the basics of beekeeping and encourage them to put a few hives in their gardens.

Each hive is home to one queen who lays around 2,000 eggs a day and is cared for by thousands of female worker bees, and male drones whose purpose in life is to mate with the queen. It's a complex and industrious community – but the end result for Amanda and Jahdre is up to 50 jars of honey a week during the summer months, much of which they sell in the restaurant or pub. "It's been really well received," says Amanda, pregnant with her first child at the time of our visit, "perhaps due to the health benefits, helping hay fever sufferers and boosting general well-being. I had a spoon of our honey with lemon every day throughout the winter and I felt really well despite working full time since I fell pregnant."

Before opening Haywards, Jahdre and Amanda lived and worked in Melbourne, Australia. "We'd love to go back to Australia one day, maybe when we've retired," says Jahdre. "It's an amazing country, with an incredible food scene and we have some great friends there, but we returned to the UK to open our dream restaurant. I'm classically trained [The Savoy under Anton Edelmann, Rules restaurant, Hanbury Manor, and The Ritz are all on his CV] and this opportunity would never have arisen in Australia, as we have been lucky enough to have the support of Amanda's parents to convert one of the buildings on their land into Haywards."

It's not surprising to see reflections of Jahdre's Australian experience on Haywards' modern European menu – he uses less butter and cream, preferring lighter, punchier flavours and often an Asian twist to dishes. He'll serve roast monkfish with a prawn boudin and dashi and ginger broth; cured and torched mackerel with dill purée and oyster velouté; or white chocolate and strawberry cannelloni with a yuzu curd.

Honey parfait, yoghurt mousse, honeycomb and almonds

A celebration of our very own honey, this dish is enhanced at the restaurant when we serve it with honey meringues and a scattering of bee pollen as well as dill sorbet, almond nougatine and purée. This is a real treat of a dessert! (serves 4)

Honey parfait

1½ leaves gelatine
30g honey
160ml milk
2 egg yolks
100g caster sugar
175g double cream

Soften the gelatine in cold water. Warm the honey and milk and allow to cool. Whisk the egg yolks and sugar in a glass bowl over a saucepan of simmering water until pale and fluffy before removing the bowl. Whisk the slightly cooled milk mixture into the egg mixture and cook again over the water until it coats the back of the spoon. Remove the bowl from the heat and whisk in the drained gelatine. Cool in fridge for 90 minutes. Whisk the double cream to soft peaks and fold into the chilled mixture. Refrigerate until set, preferably overnight. Whisk again and then place in a container or pipe decoratively onto a tray, before freezing until set.

Yoghurt mousse

1 gelatine leaf
25ml milk, warmed
25g caster sugar
100g double cream, softly whipped
115g natural full fat yoghurt

Soften the gelatine in cold water for 15 minutes. Dissolve the sugar in the milk and whisk in the drained gelatine. Set aside to cool.

Whisk the milk mixture with the yoghurt in a separate bowl and then fold in the cream. Place into a container or fill a piping bag and pipe into desired shapes on a tray, freezing until set.

Honeycomb

200g sugar
30g glucose
40g honey
30ml water
10g bicarbonate of soda

Cook the sugar, glucose, honey and water over a high heat in a large heavy based saucepan. Stir until it turns a light caramel colour. Carefully whisk in the bicarbonate, which will make it froth, and then remove from the heat. Slowly pour into a deep tin, lined with baking parchment. Once cold, break up into shards.

Honey purée

150g honey
150ml water
6g agar agar

Simmer the honey and water together, whisk in the agar agar, then boil for 5 minutes. Pour into a container, cool and refrigerate. Once set, liquidise until smooth, adding warm water to bring it to a purée consistency.

To serve

3 tbsp ground almonds

Chill plates and spoon purée decoratively. Take the honey parfait from the freezer and roll in ground almonds. Add to the plates with the mousse and honeycomb.

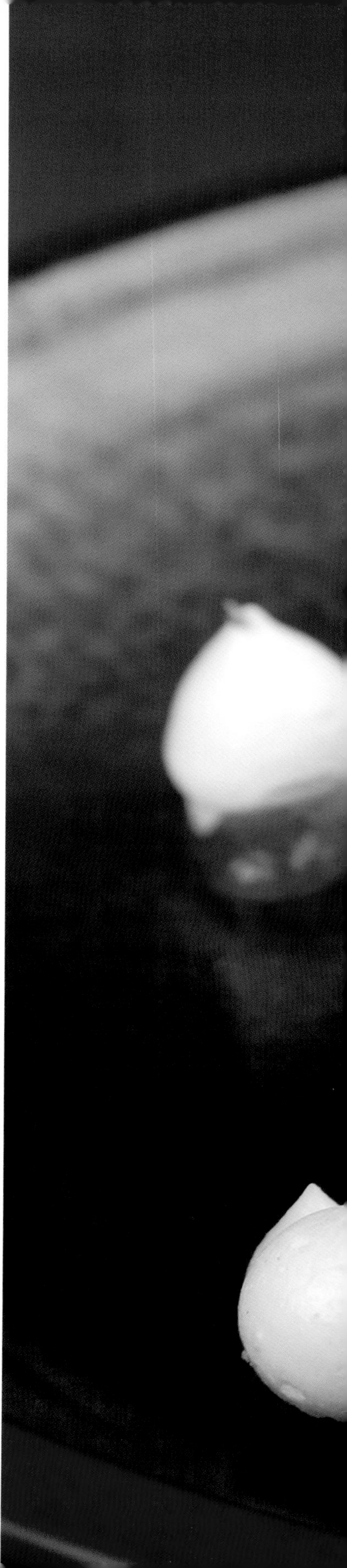

Olive oil-poached trout with horseradish cream

Trout is beautiful in this dish, but you can use salmon if you prefer. At Haywards we serve this at room temperature as a starter with avocado and vibrant red cabbage gazpacho. (serves 4)

100g grated horseradish root
1 tbsp horseradish cream
250g whole milk
Pinch of salt
3g agar agar
4 approx. 160g skinless trout fillets
1 garlic clove, peeled and crushed
1 sprig of thyme
200ml good olive oil

In a heavy saucepan, simmer the horseradish root, cream and milk with a pinch of salt. Remove from the stove and leave to cool. Sieve into a clean pan, whisking in the agar agar and stirring for 2-3 minutes over a medium heat. Place in a container, cool and chill. Once cold, blend with some warm water until smooth.

Pre-heat your oven to 55c or its lowest setting. Lay the trout out in a small, deep roasting tray on a bed of garlic, thyme and a good pinch of sea salt. Warm the oil and pour over enough to cover the fish. Poach in the oven for 12 minutes until the fish is just flaking. Remove the fish from the oil and dry off on a clean tea towel.

To serve, spread a little purée on to plates, topped with the trout and chosen garnishes.

Chicken wellington

We serve this alongside roast chicken breast with a mushroom purée and spring vegetable fricassée. (serves 4)

2 chicken legs and 1 breast
Duck fat to cover
2 long shallots, diced
2 cloves garlic, diced
3 flat mushrooms, chopped
50ml madeira
180ml double cream
2 egg whites
Tarragon leaves, chopped
1 sheet puff pastry
Egg wash of yolk and milk
Thyme leaves

Pre-heat the oven to 125c.
In a deep tray, cover the legs with duck fat and bake for 1 hour. Remove, cool and flake the meat.

In a hot frying pan on a medium heat, soften the shallots and garlic, add the mushrooms and cook for 10 minutes. Add the madeira, simmer and stir until dry. Stir in 2 tbsp of the cream and a little salt, cool and chop to a coarse mix, before chilling.

Pulse the diced skinless breast in a processor and blend in the egg whites, the remaining cream and a pinch of salt.
Put the mixture into a bowl, and fold in the leg meat, mushroom mix and tarragon before chilling. Lay the pastry onto a parchment-lined baking tray. Leaving a wide margin, place the mixture down one half of the length. Brush the pastry with egg wash and fold over, crimping well to seal. Trim and refrigerate while the oven pre-heats to 170c. Brush top with egg wash and sprinkle with thyme leaves. Bake for approx. 25 minutes. Slice to serve.

Thank you for your
support - hope you
enjoy the Book
Hayward

Vanilla cheesecake with a rhubarb glaze

A simple yet delicious dessert, complemented at the restaurant with apple sorbet and a shortbread crumb. (serves 4+)

75g digestive biscuits, crushed
15g caster sugar
25g unsalted butter, melted
2 leaves of gelatine
40ml full fat milk
1 vanilla pod, split open
200g full fat cream cheese
60g caster sugar
130ml double cream
1½ gelatine leaves
100g rhubarb purée

Pre-heat the oven to 160c. Stir the biscuits and 15g sugar together and mix well with the melted butter. Press into a greased loose-bottomed cake tin and bake for 5 minutes. Cool and refrigerate.

Soften 2 leaves of gelatine in cold water for 15 minutes. Warm the milk in a pan, add the vanilla and the drained gelatine. Blend the cream cheese and remaining sugar, remove vanilla pod, then mix into the milk mixture. Whip the cream to soft peaks and fold into the mixture. Pour onto the biscuit base, smooth the top and refrigerate until set.

Soften the remaining gelatine leaves in cold water for 15 minutes. Warm the rhubarb, whisk in the drained gelatine, allow to cool and pour over the cheesecake. Chill well before slicing and serving.

JAHDRE ON HIS...

FAVOURITE COOKBOOKS?

I have too many, at least 300. My latest is by Dan Hunter an Australian chef who has a restaurant called Brae just outside Melbourne.

FAVOURITE PART OF ESSEX

I love walking in Epping Forest and spending time in our favourite coffee shops in Epping – Dada and Fred & Doug's. I also like to visit different parts of Essex to try new restaurants.

FUNNY CULINARY MOMENT?

My closest friend and I used to work together at the Savoy hotel in London. One day we were working on potage making all these soups and the gazpacho which takes two days to prepare. Someone dropped the gazpacho and I was madly scooping it off the floor in such a panic because in those days you would get in so much trouble if you made a mistake. Thankfully, there was some in the fridge which we used instead so we didn't have to tell the head chef. We still laugh now about how scared I was!

ULTIMATE DREAM?

I am still working hard to improve Haywards and would love to achieve recognition from Michelin and the AA. We have also thought about opening a cookery school and outside catering company at some stage in the future.

DREAM DINNER PARTY GUESTS?

My grandmother as she would have been very proud of what I have achieved, Morgan Freeman as I just love his voice, the chef Michael Caines [Lympstone Manor, Exmouth] because I just love everything he does, and of course my wife Amanda.

MIDNIGHT FEAST?

I do like a sandwich, normally with lots of meat such as chicken, turkey and ham.

FAVOURITE KITCHEN GADGET?

My Thermomix and my plates! I love my display plates; I have a real collection and I am very protective of them.

PERFECT DAY OFF?

We always have a roast on our days off, and we also like to travel to Suffolk and Norfolk to stay in our favourite country house hotels such as Titchwell Manor in north Norfolk. We want to go to Rubino Kitchen in Maldon but it's closed on our days off! I also like to go to a spa, that's my guilty pleasure.

BIGGEST EXPENSE?

Going out to eat! We like to eat out with Amanda's parents and eat really good food. I also love to buy lots of food magazines and cookbooks.

COOKERY TIP?

Be organised, be prepared and be clean. When we first came back to the UK I cooked for our families for our first Christmas Day here. I got up at 9am and prepped and cooked dinner for 30. They couldn't believe I could cook that size dinner in such a short time but it was just because I had planned and organised everything in advance.

SIGNATURE DISHES

Starters

Roast artichoke & purée, comté dumplings, pickled onions

Roasted breast & confit leg of quail, fermented cabbage & pickled walnuts

Pan-roasted scallops, braised leeks, mussel cream, rye

Mains

Pea risotto, wild garlic pesto, goats' cheese foam

Braised short rib & roasted sirloin of beef, onion purée, kohlrabi

Roasted monkfish, prawn boudin, dashi & ginger broth, sea vegetables

Puddings

Banana soufflé, rhubarb sorbet, caramel

White chocolate & yuzu mousse, strawberry purée, strawberry sorbet

Chocolate & peanut bar, crystallised peanuts, malt ice cream

DISH OF MY CHILDHOOD?

Lamb. We'd have it every Sunday when I was growing up. As I am originally from Bermuda – I moved to the USA when I was 15 and studied culinary arts at college in Tampa, Florida – we would have fish every other day, and now I don't eat much fish because of that. Sunday was the best day for me as a child. Also loquat berries. Again, I used to eat them as a child and they were delicious.

Bowled over

You'd never guess that elegant Haywards was previously a skittle alley, coach house and stable that had been used as a storage area in recent years. Set right on the edge of Epping Forest in the grounds of the pretty, 17th century Forest Gate Inn free house, the restaurant was coaxed into its current form by Jahdre and his wife Amanda whose parents own the pub. Together, they designed and helped oversee the sympathetic restoration of the property, opening for business in May 2013.

With parts of the building dating back to the 1800s, it was full of original features many of which – such as the stained glass windows – the couple have carefully retained, but the look inside is essentially one of modern, clean lines, with a shine to the chic cherry wood tables, smart yet comfortable chairs and banquettes, plenty of fresh flowers, and lively art on the walls. Outside there's parking and tables at which to enjoy pre- and post-dinner drinks; and although it's not far from the main road, the restaurant is quietly composed and very much a space for grown-ups. A small bar on the left as you enter with the rectangular restaurant set out on one level.

The menu changes regularly and a set price à la carte is offered alongside a more compact lunch menu and an evening tasting menu (the latter with an optional wine flight), designed to showcase Jahdre's cooking to the full. The wine list is balanced between old and new world offerings, plus a smattering of English wines. "Our newest find is a white wine made from the Solaris grape – it's a crossing of Riesling, Pinot Gris, Muscat Ottonel, Zaraya Severa and Seyval Blanc – by Parvills Farm vineyard in Epping Upland, just 10 minutes away," Jahdre says. "Katherine Smith from Parvills arrived one day and asked us to try it; we were so surprised how good it was and we now sell it by the glass. It's a crisp white wine with a long length." Jahdre is also a fan of Martin's Lane Vineyard at Stow Maries near Maldon on the river Crouch. "Roy came with some friends one night and brought us his wine to try – we now sell their Pinot Grigio and Pinot Noir 'Blanc de Noirs'."

Haywards Restaurant
111 Bell Common, Epping CM16 4DZ
W: haywardsrestaurant.co.uk
T: 01992 577350
E: info@haywardsrestaurant.co.uk
/haywardsepping
@HaywardsRestaur
/haywardsrestaurant

Accolades: *Michelin*; Waitrose *Good Food Guide*; *Harden's*; semi-finalist Craft Guild of Chefs National Chef of the Year 2017 and 2018.

Winner, Chef of the Year, *Essex Life* Food & Drink Awards 2013; winner, Restaurant of the Year, *Essex Life* Food & Drink Awards 2014; winner, Fine Dining Restaurant, and Chef of the Year, Essex Tourism & Hospitality Awards 2014

Covers: 48 in main restaurant; 14 private dining

Cost: average carte £44.50; wine from £18; beer/lager from £4.75

Open: Thurs-Sat L 12-2.30; Wed, Thurs D 6-9.30; Fri, Sat D 6-10; Sun 12.30-3

Details: Private dining either in The Stable or exclusive hire of restaurant; diners welcome 10 years and over; accommodation available at the adjacent Gate House B&B; wheelchair access; walks in Epping Forest from the door; gift vouchers; parking

Sun, sun, sun, here it comes

The sun shone – appropriately – as Jack Levine chose day-boat fish to create a summery dish of sea bass with crab, clams, Jersey Royals and a golden saffron sauce

ZEEBRUGSE VISVEILING
EIGENDOM 2010
EIGEND. COOP. VISAFSLAG
DEN OEVER 2005
YM
CREVETTES
Cornouaille Port de Pêche
CCI de QUIMPER-CORNOUAILLE

Standing in the morning sunlight, taking in the watery vista of Wivenhoe Quay with its stylish riverside apartments overlooking moored fishing boats, we watch as fishermen hand over the day's catch to Phil Wright of The Little Fish Company.

Phil loads brimming crates of wild sea bass, kite-shaped skate, and distinctive dome-headed gurnard into the back of his refrigerated van. He used to be the one doing the fishing from his own boat, *Cathy Anne*, but these days he's too busy with trade deliveries and his wet fish shop in Kelvedon to have time to get out on the water. "Maria [Phil's partner] and I have just moved to Langham and we are going to concentrate on deliveries due to the number of restaurants we now have as customers," he explains. His brother Steven will continue to run the fresh fish shop with an apprentice, Daisy.

Jack Levine, head chef of the Sun Inn, Dedham, is eager to see what's in today's catch. He hops onto the brightly-painted fishing boat. "I use Phil's company because the fish is caught daily using small day boats, so it's fabulously fresh, and he consistently gives us top quality. Even the delivery drivers are friendly and helpful! I am forever having to call up with a last-minute order because we've sold out, and he turns up straight away – we'll always give him a beer at the bar for going that extra mile!"

Leaving the tranquil scene of bobbing fishing boats, we head just three miles inland to Dedham and into Jack's domain, a kitchen he shares with his sous chef, Emil Styczynski and four other members of the brigade. We watch while he deftly fillets the wild sea bass, then steams it in a bamboo steamer in keeping with his ethos of simple, fresh, local and seasonal food. Starting with his seafood sauce as a base, Jack carefully arranges the palourde clams, local samphire and courgette on the plate, adding a quenelle of potato before topping with the freshly steamed bass and crab.

"I really like to cook fish, and sea bass is so versatile. Sometimes I pan-roast it in butter and serve with Swiss chard, tomatoes, olives and 'nduja or slice it thinly and cure it in lemon, fennel, chilli. It's great with peppery wild rocket and radishes too. I like to cook using a few seasonal ingredients which are well balanced, giving the customer fresh flavours, and just letting the ingredients do the talking." At home, he will most often grill sea bass whole on the barbecue, adding nothing more than some lemon, fresh herbs and a drizzle of olive oil.

"I like to cook using a few seasonal ingredients which are well balanced, giving the customer fresh flavours, and just letting the ingredients do the talking."

Elsewhere on the Sun Inn menu, the tone is modern British with Italian influences. There's risotto primavera with mint, asparagus, pea, lemon and Parmesan alongside skirt steak with potato galette, sour cream, blue cheese, pickled shallot and more asparagus. Locally-grown baby carrots are on the menu served with cannellini beans, harissa yoghurt, coriander and served with flat bread, or you might be tempted by Dingley Dell pork saltimbocca with green bean, tomato and anchovy salad and lamb's lettuce. To finish you could try a chocolate pavé with vanilla ice cream, or hazelnut semifreddo with a salted caramel mousse and ginger meringue.

Jack's culinary inquisitiveness has taken him to other parts of the world too. "I'm particularly interested in the slow-cooked barbecue meats they do in Texas. It's really primal cooking, just great cuts of meat and fish cooked with a rub, over fire and smoke. It's very on-trend and a great way of cooking simply with plenty of flavours." It's a type of cooking he's looking forward more regularly to offering once his kitchen refurbishment is complete.

It was travel that first opened Jack's eyes to the possibility of becoming a chef too. "I went on holiday and stayed with my Nan who lived in China at the time. I remember lots of noodles and broths and also the people buying fresh ingredients each day from the local market. I just loved the freshness and immediacy of it all. From that moment on I knew I wanted to cook and I became curious about different styles of food."

On his return to the UK, he organised work experience in a local restaurant and worked in various Essex places before finding himself at The Sun Inn, initially as sous chef, and rising to head chef in 2015. For all his international culinary curiosity, though, he's happy in his home county where he enthusiastically supports local producers as well as The Little Fish Company. "We regularly use growers like Jane Marshall for raspberries and apples, Angela MacLauchlan for berries from Boxted and Alison Bond, Dedham and Lawford, for organic salad as well as apricots, aubergines and tomatoes in the summer months."

Wild seabass, saffron sauce, clams, crab, samphire and courgette

A real celebration of seafood and coastal vegetables, this elegant dish makes an impressive dinner party main course. Wild bass is well worth the extra expense but you can use farmed bass as a cheaper alternative. Ask your fishmonger to split your whole fish into the bones for stock and the fillets. (serves 4)

Stock

Sea bass bones (discard the head)
Half a fennel bulb
1 long shallot
1 celery stick
Few parsley stalks
Half a lemon
1 tbsp whole black peppercorns
125ml dry white wine
1700ml water

Add all the ingredients to a deep stock pot and bring to a gentle simmer, removing any froth or debris off the top as it heats up. Simmer for 30 minutes, skimming regularly. Drain through a fine sieve and return to a clean heavy saucepan. Boil hard to reduce to produce 1 litre of stock.

Saffron sauce

280ml white wine
1 shallot sliced thin
Half a garlic clove, thinly sliced
1 litre fish stock
200ml double cream
Pinch of saffron strands
150ml double cream
Juice of half a lemon
75g unsalted butter

Bring the wine, shallot, garlic, stock and 200ml cream to the boil in a large heavy saucepan and reduce over a medium heat by three-quarters' volume. Add the saffron, 150ml cream, lemon juice and butter before bringing back to the boil and reducing down to a light sauce consistency. Season to taste.

Potatoes

300g jersey royal potatoes
70g butter
Zest of half a lemon

In a large lidded saucepan, simmer the potatoes in salted water until tender for about 15 minutes. Drain and return to the pan. Add the butter, zest and seasoning to taste before crushing potatoes with a heavy serving spoon. Stir well and keep warm.

Crab salad

Good pinch of lemon zest
1 tbsp lemon juice
1 tbsp dill, finely chopped
1 tbsp crème fraîche
2 tbsp grated apple
100g white crab meat

Stir the first five ingredients well together before folding in the crab. Chill until needed.

To serve

2kg sea bass in boneless fillets
2 courgettes, cut into balls using a parisienne scoop, or diced
100g samphire, picked and washed
Knob of butter
20 palourde clams, cleaned and rinsed

Pre-heat your steamer with simmering water. Lightly season the bass fillets and lay flesh-side down in the basket before steaming until just cooked, about 8 minutes.

Meanwhile blanch the courgette and samphire in a saucepan of simmering salted water, draining well once back to the boil. Add to a hot sauté pan of melted butter and seasoning, tossing to glaze for a minute or two. Bring the pan of sauce to the boil, add the clams and simmer until they open, for about 90 seconds. Discard any shells still closed.

To assemble, place a good layer of sauce onto warm plates, scatter around the clams, samphire and courgette, place a neat spoonful of potatoes to one side, top with the bass, then the crab.

Set elderflower yoghurt with poached gooseberries

This summery dairy jelly sings of the hedgerow and we serve it with raspberries and honeyed oats for zing and texture. (serves 4)

2½ gelatine leaves
170g caster sugar
430ml double cream
80ml elderflower cordial
370ml natural yoghurt
80g sugar
50ml sweet dessert wine
25ml elderflower cordial
1 punnet of gooseberries, destalked

Soften the gelatine in cold water. Stir 170g sugar and cream in a heavy saucepan over a medium hob. When dissolved, remove from the heat and whisk in the gelatine. Decant into a glass bowl set over a bed of ice. Stir until it starts to thicken, then fold in the cordial and yoghurt, transfer to serving dishes and refrigerate to set for 4 hours or more.

Simmer 80ml of water, 80g sugar, wine and 25ml cordial until syrupy. Add the gooseberries and poach till tender. Serve cooled with the set yoghurt.

Brown shrimp tagliatelle with spring vegetables and lemon crème fraîche

We make our own fresh egg tagliatelle pasta and it is well worth the effort.

750g fresh tagliatelle
10 tbsp crème fraîche
Zest of 1 lemon
Juice of half a lemon
120g brown shrimps
2 large handfuls rocket leaves
100g broad beans
80g fresh peas
1 tbsp mint leaves, shredded
Good olive oil

Warm up pasta bowls for serving. Cook the pasta in a pan of salted boiling water until al dente, drain and return to the pan. Whisk up the crème fraîche, zest and juice before tossing through the pasta, then add the other ingredients. Mix thoroughly with tongs, season to taste, and serve drizzled with olive oil.

Skirt steak, sour cream, blue cheese, asparagus, pickled shallot, potato

Known as 'bavette' in French, this less-used but flavoursome, marbled cut needs to be lightly cooked. It is a delicious and inexpensive cut. I like maris piper potatoes for the rösti. We serve this with our own pickled shallot rings. (serves 4)

2 large potatoes, grated
2 tbsp chopped chives
75g unsalted butter, melted
Olive oil and butter for frying
4 skirt steak portions (about 200g each)
16 asparagus spears
250ml sour cream
100g blue cheese

Season the potatoes lightly, fold in the chives and melted butter. Press into 4 neat rounds, using rings if you wish. In a large hot frying pan over a low-medium heat, add a knob of butter and a little oil, then fry the rösti until browned, then turn over and cook until crisp. Remove to kitchen paper and keep warm. Heat up the oiled pan until smoking, season the steaks and cook on each side to your liking, then remove to rest somewhere warm.

Blanch the asparagus in a pan of boiling salted water for a few minutes, then drain well and toss in the hot pan with butter and seasoning. Carve the steak onto hot plates with the rösti and asparagus alongside, dotted with sour cream and cheese crumbled on top.

JACK ON HIS...

FAVOURITE COOKBOOKS?

The Pitt Cue Co cookbook by Tom Adams; *Bocca* Cookbook by Jacob Kenedy; *Spuntino* by Russell Norman, and *Grillstock: the BBQ Book* by Jon Finch.

COOKS CHEAT?

Salt is your best friend in your kitchen so don't be afraid to use it. Also, store truffles in jars filled with rice – the truffle infuses the rice so when you make a risotto it tastes amazing.

MIDNIGHT FEAST?

Cheese, Marmite and crisp sandwiches! Saying that, I'm partial to practically anything I can get hold of at that time of night so a scotch egg or cold sausages and mustard is great, and I've even been known to go for a Dairylea Dunker!

MUSICAL KITCHEN?

Yes, we like to listen to West Coast hip hop. It gets us geed up for service.

RECENT FOODIE DISCOVERIES?

I recently tried a goose egg for the first time and now I'm hooked!

FAVOURITE PART OF ESSEX?

Dedham of course! It's so picturesque. You have the river with the boats, some really nice pubs and lovely places to walk.

FOOD HEROES?

I take a lot of inspiration from Ben Tish who used to be at Salt Yard in London. Also Ruth Rogers and Rose Gray who set up the River Café, and Jacob Kenedy who is behind Bocca di Lupo.

BEST RESTAURANT I'VE EATEN IN?

I was in Jamaica with my girlfriend Kerry, the sun was shining and I had a beer in my hand as we sat together on the beach eating charcoal pit shark, jerk chicken and pork. Also, I once had a French dip sandwich [thinly sliced roast beef in a baguette] at Brennan & Carr in New York and that was pretty good.

FOODIE NOSTALGIA?

Pastrami – the taste of it always takes me back to Katz's Delicatessen in New York. They served fist-sized portions of pastrami which was hot and served in rye bread with spicy mustard and half-sour pickles on the side – just perfect!

UNFULFILLED DREAM?

To run my own barbecue shack.

SIGNATURE DISHES

Starters

Artichoke risotto, confit garlic, vermouth, lemon, thyme, parmesan, pangrattato

Nettle & chard ravioli, walnut sauce, pecorino

Beef carpaccio, pickled artichokes, taleggio, cobnuts

Mains

Veal saltimbocca, capers, sage, lemon, fine beans, tomato & anchovy salad

Whole grilled spring chicken, orzo, asparagus, buttermilk

Seared scallops, smashed cannellini, samphire, chilli, lemon

Puddings

Vanilla pannacotta, poached apricots, pistachio, lavender, honey

Salted caramel & chocolate tart, buttermilk sorbet

Pistachio cake, malt ice cream, praline

FAVOURITE TIME OF YEAR TO COOK?

It has to be the springtime. With all the new produce to pick from, the broad beans, peas, wild garlic, and of course asparagus – fantastic!

A shining example

This former coaching inn on the high street overlooking St Mary's church ticks all the boxes. Dedham is a picturesque Constable country village, and the Grade II*-listed Sun Inn fits in just perfectly with its open log fires in winter, parasolled areas in a leafy garden in summer, indoor tables set with pretty vintage china, and just enough luxury to feel spoilt but not under-dressed.

The magnificently glossy elm bar, created – allegedly – from one of the ancient Dedham elms that fell during a storm some 40 years ago greets you as you push open the traditional oak door. The exposed beams, oak floors, and dark panelled walls are softened by cherry red banquettes, cool olive green paintwork, and attractive work by local artists. There are different levels of dining, some parts welcoming dogs, several tucked-away nooks, squashy sofas in an adjacent bar, and tables for larger gatherings.

The award-winning wine list – the Sun Inn won the England and Overall AA Wine List of the Year 2015-16, as well as the Wine List of the Year award in the Waitrose *Good Food Guide* 2015 – leans towards Italy and France, but takes you way beyond the standard Pinot Grigio, Merlot and Sauvignon Blanc with wines supplied by natural wine specialists, Les Caves de Pyrene, and Alliance Wine, among others.

Anyone who wants to enjoy the list fully can stay over in one of the pub's seven individually-decorated en suite bedrooms.

The Sun Inn
High Street, Dedham C07 6DF
W: thesuninndedham.com
T: 01206 323351
E: office@thesuninndedham.com
/suninndedham
@SunInnDedham
/suninndedham

Accolades: Waitrose *Good Food Guide*-listed and Wine List of the Year award 2015; AA – Two rosettes, Wine List of the Year 2015, and Breakfast Award; *Michelin*; Editor's Choice, Best Gastropubs, *Good Hotel Guide* 2016; AA 5-star inn accommodation

Covers: 75

Cost: average carte £28.50; wine from £16; pint from £3.50

Open: All week L 12-2.30 (Sun 12-4); D 6-9.30

Details: Alfresco dining; afternoon tea; open fires; seven en suite bedrooms; wheelchair access; dogs welcome; parking

THE SQUARE AND COMPASSES, FULLER STREET

CRAIG LOVERIDGE

Tip top

Craig Loveridge buys first-rate asparagus from nearby Wash Farm for popular early summer dishes at The Square and Compasses

THE SQUARE AND COMPASSES CRAIG LOVERIDGE

A short drive from The Square and Compasses, in the village of Sible Hedingham, is Wash Farm. Run by Shirley and Peter Stevenson for the past 35 years, the 100-acre farm grows around three tonnes of asparagus each year in one five-acre field. Every spear is cut by hand, the pickers working painstakingly along the rows with the help of a small motorised buggy which the picker sits on, bent double, as they reach over to hand cut each of the green stalks in turn.

"It's a relatively small farm but we grow some niche produce," Shirley explains. "Peter moved here in the 80s and started with pick-your-own strawberries. We started growing asparagus in 2002 and with that crop we only dealt in direct sales to restaurants and local customers." Demand has grown, particularly over the past five years, and the Stevensons now grow not only strawberries, but raspberries, cherries, gooseberries, and blackcurrants too.

"The soil is ideal; it's heavy-ish and the river Colne is at the very end of the asparagus field. We can extract water from the river for irrigation purposes between October and March."

Craig Loveridge, head chef at The Square and Compasses, and his chefs are regular visitors to Wash Farm which supplies the pub not only with asparagus but also soft fruit and lamb reared by the Stevensons. "I arrived here eight years ago, the brigade has been working together for six years (that's unheard of in this industry!) and they are still very good at getting their heads down and doing the work. I find that if I teach them things, or we go out to visit a supplier, it keeps them motivated. We butcher the lambs here, and we also skin deer and forage for wild garlic and herbs in the local woods. It just keeps things interesting."

"It also means that we can support the farm throughout the year, not just for a few weeks during the asparagus season," adds Victor Roome who owns The Square and Compasses with his partner Susan Poole.

We return to the pub with freshly-cut asparagus and watch as Craig simply blanches the spears before drizzling them with olive oil and char-grilling them. He makes a sauce to go alongside with crème fraîche, mayonnaise, natural yoghurt, lemon and parsley, before

"Our menu is predominantly meat and fish. We do offer some vegetarian dishes though I try to avoid the V-word!"

bringing the whole lot to life with crumbles of blue cheese, and finishing the dish with peppery watercress leaves. Asparagus is a regular on the menu during the season when you might also find Craig cooking a creamy risotto of asparagus with fresh peas, broad beans and sage topped with Parmesan cheese shavings.

The menu includes plenty of pub classics including their most popular – homemade steak and ale shortcrust proper pastry pie which Craig makes with local beef, and locally handmade pork sausages served with spring onion mashed potato and Craig's onion gravy – or Craig's own favourite dish, pan-fried rib-eye steak with chips, mushroom and tomato. During the game season, you'll see dishes appearing including roast breast of very local pheasant wrapped in smoked bacon with celeriac purée, honey roasted carrots and parsnips, baby onion and red wine sauce, plus there's a sizeable blackboard of specials all year round. On top of that the pub hosts regular fish nights. Look out for pan-fried fillets of sea bass with provençal stuffed courgettes, sun-dried tomatoes, olives and basil, and also field to fork nights where the entire menu is vegetarian-friendly.

"Our menu is predominantly meat and fish. We do offer some vegetarian dishes though I try to avoid the V-word!" says Victor. "If you're looking for game, pheasant, pigeon, rabbit you'd come here, and I think meat-eaters will choose a dish without meat or fish in it but wouldn't class themselves a vegetarian so I don't like to label them or our dishes in that way."

Those with a sweet tooth are well-catered for too. Craig's homemade temptations include the likes of chocolate and almond praline torte with amaretto sauce and blueberry compote, or lighter options that use the abundance of seasonal strawberries, raspberries and gooseberries from Wash Farm.

If he's not buying from Wash Farm, you could well bump into Craig at a local market. "I love to get up close to food and ingredients – and also negotiate the price!" He may well also be tending his own produce, a small collection of thyme, chives and other herbs that he grows in butlers' sinks at the bottom of the pub garden.

Char-grilled asparagus with watercress and blue cheese cream

Our guests can't get enough of asparagus, and with it having such a short season – at most eight weeks – you've got to enjoy it while you can! A smart dinner party starter in late spring and early summer, this recipe is far more than the sum of its simple parts. It's really quick to serve as it's mostly part-prepared in advance, so you can be out enjoying your guests' company, rather than tied to the stove by your apron strings. It can be made into more of a light lunch with the addition of a poached egg or two and even some frazzled bacon rashers for contrast.

Which blue cheese you use to make this recipe is down to your personal taste. There are some lovely, creamy East Anglian varieties such as Binham Blue and Suffolk Blue, while further afield is the robust British classic Stilton or sharper continental delights of French Roquefort or Italian Dolcelatte.

Generally asparagus spears need to be trimmed before cooking as they have tough ends. If the spears are particularly narrow, called 'sprue', then it may still be tender throughout but most finger-sized spears need the woody bottoms removing. A quick chef's tip for the discarded hard parts (or a plea!), don't throw them away as they are too precious for the compost heap and make a wonderful soup. Just simmer them up in a pan of good home-made stock and white wine with a few root vegetables, season well and then push the whole lot through a sieve, making a thick velouté to serve either chilled or warm. Season well and scatter with some shelled seafood (crab, lobster, prawns etc) and more cooked asparagus. (serves 4)

Preparing the asparagus

600g asparagus spears

To prepare your asparagus, the first stage is to remove the tough ends by snapping them off. If you hold the top half with the bud end firmly in one hand and then grip just the bottom very close to the end with your thumb and forefinger and push it away, it will always snap where the woodiness finishes. Then just trim the jagged surface neatly and repeat until all are prepared.

Blanching the spears

Bring a saucepan of salted water to a boil and blanch the spears for 2-4 minutes depending on size. Meanwhile prepare a very large bowl with lots of ice and cold water to cover. Drain the asparagus carefully but quickly in a colander and swiftly decant into the iced water, stirring it around to cool. Remove and allow to dry on paper towel.

Dressing

50g sour cream
50g mayonnaise
1 tbsp lemon juice
75g blue cheese, crumbled

Whisk all together into a sauce texture, season to taste and set aside.

To serve

Olive oil
Small bunch of chives, snipped
1 large handful of watercress sprigs
4 tsp blue cheese, crumbled

Heat up the griddle over a medium heat. Toss the asparagus with a little oil and seasoning. Char-grill the spears and turn regularly until lightly coloured on all sides.

Lay the asparagus on to warm plates and garnish with the dressing, chives, watercress and the crumbled cheese.

Pan-fried skate wing with chilli and lime salsa

A popular flat fish, skate works well traditionally with brown butter, lemon and capers. This modern take on the classic has a similar freshness and zing. (serves 4)

2 medium tomatoes
1 small garlic clove, crushed to a paste
Half a red onion, finely diced
Half a lime
Handful of fresh coriander, roughly chopped
4 skate wings
50g seasoned plain flour
1 tbsp olive oil
25g butter

Peel, deseed and finely chop the tomatoes into a bowl, stir through the garlic and onion, squeeze in the lime juice and fold through the coriander. Season well to taste and chill until needed.

Heat up a large frying pan on a high heat and add the oil and butter. Coat the skate wings in the seasoned flour. Shake off excess flour before adding carefully to the pan. Fry on each side for 3-4 minutes until cooked through.

Serve on warm plates with the salsa on the side.

Slow-braised shin of beef and oxtail

A great winter stew, you can use featherblade rather than shin. (serves 6)

6 350g slices of beef shin
3 carrots, 1 celery stick and 10 shallots, sliced
1 whole garlic bulb, halved
2 tsp crushed black pepper
6 thyme sprigs & 4 bay leaves
Good rich red wine
4 thick portions of oxtail
3 tbsp butter & 3 tbsp plain flour

Mix the shin with the next 7 ingredients in a large bowl, then cover with red wine. Marinate and chill overnight. Pre-heat the oven to 150c. Reserving the marinade ingredients, remove the beef, drain well and dry thoroughly.

Heat up an oiled heavy ovenproof lidded casserole dish on a high heat and brown the beef all over and set aside. Repeat with the oxtail. Boil the marinade in the dish for 10 minutes, return the meats and bake, covered, for 3 hours. In a colander over a large saucepan, separate the oxtail from the vegetables and shin. Cool and debone the oxtail meat, adding it to the gravy pan.

In a heavy saucepan over a gentle heat, melt the butter and add the flour and stir for one minute. Add to the gravy and stir over a high heat whilst it thickens. Add more wine if the gravy is too thick. When it has simmered for a few minutes, return the shin and vegetables to the pan, removing herbs as you go. Bring back to a simmer and season to taste before serving.

Cherry and blackberry crumble

An indulgent nursery pud always goes down well, and crumble like your mother makes is always a firm favourite. I serve this with a rich simple vanilla ice cream for that hot and cold contrast. (serves 4+)

300g whole cherries
150g blackberries
Sweet white wine
2 tbsp caster sugar
120g plain flour
60g demerara sugar
60g unsalted butter, frozen overnight

Pre-heat the oven to 190c. Destone and halve the cherries, before placing with the blackberries, wine and sugar in a saucepan on a medium heat. Stir regularly until simmering, turn to low and cook for 15 minutes whilst starting the crumble.

In a large bowl, combine the flour and sugar before grating in the butter. Rub this in with your fingertips until it becomes a crumbly texture. Lay out in a shallow baking tray, lined with parchment and bake for 15 minutes until lightly-golden. Decant the fruit into a suitable gratin dish and spoon over the crumble. Bake for another 15 minutes until hot and golden.

CRAIG ON HIS...

BEST RESTAURANT I'VE EATEN IN?

Rules in London. The restaurant is the oldest in London and Victor took me there for a treat one afternoon. The wild boar pie was amazing.

FUTURE AMBITIONS?

To open a restaurant with my brothers in Spain or England.

DISH OF MY CHILDHOOD?

Kedgeree. Mum used to make it for my brothers and me when we were kids. It also went well with lots of ketchup!

'TAKE FIVE' RECIPE?

Smoked bacon carbonara. Cook some pasta in a large pan of water. Fry some chopped bacon in a little oil, add some broad beans and double cream. Reduce. Once cooked, add your pasta and toss with parmesan. Finally, while the pasta is moving add an egg yolk – a simple and delicious supper!

MIDNIGHT FEAST?

Macaroni cheese with too much tomato ketchup!

FAVOURITE TIME OF YEAR TO COOK?

Definitely spring. I love to grow food with my children, teaching them where food comes from and also how the seasons affect the growing.

UNFULFILLED DREAM JOB?

Head chef for the Arsenal first team. Victor would prefer I said Tottenham!

CHEF'S TIP?

Cook cauliflower with a piece of lemon to retain that crisp white colour. Always peel ginger with a teaspoon. Freeze butter and use it to grate over crumble toppings.

FAVOURITE PART OF ESSEX?

The village of Tollesbury near Maldon. I love boating and there is lovely wild samphire growing there which I forage. It's also a very picturesque and peaceful place.

SIGNATURE DISHES

Starters

Pan-fried local pigeon, crispy black pudding, swede purée, thyme sauce

Smoked mackerel & dill pâté, lightly-toasted brown bread, homemade beetroot & fresh horseradish relish

Terrine of local pheasant, partridge and rabbit wrapped in smoked streaky bacon, homemade beetroot relish

Mains

Pan-roasted local venison loin, braised sticky red cabbage, dauphinoise potatoes, port sauce

Wild mushroom charlotte wrapped in courgettes, sauté potatoes

Char-grilled sirloin steak, celeriac boulangère, wild mushrooms, baby onion & smoked bacon sauce

Puddings

Sticky toffee pudding

Chocolate & fresh orange cheesecake

Fresh berry summer pudding

FAVOURITE COOKBOOKS?

I love the River Cottage books by Hugh Fearnley-Whittingstall. I also have a signed copy of the River Cottage game handbook by Tim Maddams which I love.

FOOD HEROES?

Tim Maddams and Hugh Fearnley-Whittingstall. Clinton Arnold, my old head chef here, was a real influence – his knowledge and passion inspired me and still does.

Pointing in the right direction

It took Victor Roome and his partner Susan Poole four short months to bring the derelict Square and Compasses pub back to life ten years ago. "It was a non-trading business, everything was run-down and the garden was overgrown, the newly-appointed chef at the time and I moved in to do the renovation work, sleeping on blow-up beds!" Victor remembers. "We did it really quickly, we had to get trading because we had our first mortgage repayment due in December. We bought it in the August and reopened on December 8th 2007."

The collection of photographs now displayed on the pub walls are testament to just how far things have come since those derelict days. The free house is now a cosy, rural pub, packed with original features and bursting with memorabilia from days – and customers – gone by. A wall by the brass-topped bar is covered in old wooden tools which Victor inherited when he took over; glass and clay bottles, and sepia portraits fill spaces, and there are shelves full with previously-enjoyed wine bottles. A shiny copper pan was salvaged from a skip by Victor. "I'm a bit of a skip scrounger. I cleaned the pan up and hung it on the wall. People now bring me treasures from their own sheds or attics."

Local and regional cask ales are served from the stillage behind the Tap Room bar, and Victor takes personal interest in the wine list (it includes a generous 22 by the glass) supplied by Wine Fantastic in Great Tey, Nethergate Wines in Bury St Edmunds and London-based Liberty Wines.

The Square & Compasses
Fuller Street, near Fairstead CM3 2BB
W: thesquareandcompasses.co.uk
T: 01245 361477
E: info@thesquareandcompasses.co.uk
/fullerstreetpub
@SCfullerstreet

Accolades: *Michelin*; *AA Pub Guide*; *Good Pub Guide*; *Sawday's*; *Hardens*

Covers: 70

Cost: average carte £26; wine from £19.25; pint from £3.45

Open: Mon-Sat L 12-2 (2.30 Sat); D 6.30-9.30; Sun L 12-6

Details: private dining seats 16; wheelchair access; dogs welcome in the Tap Room and garden; walks from the pub including part of the Essex Way; cycling routes; near Chelmsford Racecourse; parking

ROB HORTON

The eel deal

Smoked eel is always well-received on the Rubino Kitchen menu – not surprising when the smokehouse is just a stone's throw away

Rob Horton, chef owner of Rubino Kitchen, knows he is a lucky chef, having one of the region's most respected smokehouses, Lambton & Jackson on his doorstep, in fact based at the same farm where coast meets countryside close to Maldon. Rob is a huge fan of the very local and high quality smoked fish produced by his neighbour, Sean Jackson just across the way from his restaurant kitchen at Chigborough Lodge. Such is their friendship and familiarity that Sean seamlessly deals with a restaurant booking from a couple who pop into Rob's restaurant door during our interview, a sign of how happily they work together in supporting each other's enterprises.

Sean and his business partner, Darcy Lambton, produce almost four tonnes of smoked fish a month at Lambton & Jackson. They sell their product throughout the UK and overseas to end users and chefs – "when Marcus Wareing put our Maldon Deep smoked salmon on his menu at The Berkeley it was a huge boost" he recalls – but one of their most loyal customers is right on the doorstep, literally steps away at Rubino Kitchen.

However cannily the question is posed and however frequently it is asked, Sean Jackson has a secret, which he won't divulge, namely exactly what does go into the Lambton & Jackson smoking process. It's an art that Sean learnt from a master smoker from Brightlingsea. "He's long-since retired, but he taught me everything," says Sean who has been smoking fish since he left school. "The art is having smoke not fire, and it's also down to the salting. Some people just shake a little salt on the top of the fish, but we literally bury our products in salt to draw the moisture out." We determine also that oak and beech chips are part of the mix, and that the traditional method used results in a full 40-day shelf life for the salmon and 21 days for the eel, the only products the company smokes. "We prefer to leave the duck and the chicken to others to smoke; we want to play to our strengths," Sean says.

Back at Rubino Kitchen, Rob enthuses "I find Sean's smoked eel is more flexible than just more familiar smoked salmon. It's also not used that much in other restaurants so it gives me the opportunity to put something a bit different on the menu, such as using it in a beetroot risotto, one of our very first dishes here. It almost has a baconesque flavour and its texture and smokiness just work brilliantly."

Today preparing a new dish, a smoked eel terrine, Rob describes it as 'a little work in progress'. "Getting the terrine to set is the hardest part," he admits as he cuts the skinned eel into even-sized pieces, then dicing freshly cubed apple to steep in an aromatic cider vinegar, sugar and water liquor. He fries wafer-thin sliced aubergine in olive oil and

"The smoked eel is more flexible than salmon and it gives me the opportunity to put something different on the menu."

letting them drain before lining the sides of the terrine mould. The steeped apple cubes are mixed with chopped parsley, the eel and seasoning, before being pressed into the mould and chilled in the fridge, weighted down, to set overnight.

Although he wouldn't normally, Sean is happy to open the doors of the smokehouse to us. Inside the smokey recesses are rack after rack, each holding silver trays of smoking salmon and eel. The smell is extraordinary but not hot as you might expect on being met with billowing smoke. The fish is cold smoked for between eight and 24 hours plus time for salting.

Rubino is Rob's first restaurant. Named after his five-year-old daughter, Ruby, it's what he calls a "patchwork quilt of a restaurant" pulled together with an eclectic mix of tables and chairs which rock a boho chic décor. Before moving to Essex, Rob worked in London with Gordon Ramsay's group of restaurants and at Angela Hartnett's Murano in Mayfair. Leaving the capital he moved to Essex and this former tearoom in Chigborough to transform it into Rubino Kitchen. "When I started back in 2015, I wanted this place to be a destination restaurant, but now I have regulars who come in every couple of weeks." A full night we can fit in 25 diners although ordinarily we say we are an 18-cover restaurant so the atmosphere is an intimate one.

It's a place to enjoy Rob's brand of relaxed, informal hospitality and a menu that can be as flexible as you wish – he'll happily create any starter as a main course and vice versa, and offers a six-course taster menu with optional wine flight. The one thing you won't find on the menu is chicken – "it's boring" – but come at lunchtime for fishcakes with chilli jam, beef carpaccio with green beans and hazelnuts, or a ham hock Caesar salad, or in the evening for haddock 'scotch egg', peas, raisin and curried puffed rice, or perhaps braised lamb tortelli with smoked aubergine purée, grilled gem lettuce and beans.

Where possible, Rob tries not to travel too far for ingredients: he'll go to Maldon Fruit Supplies or Sarah Green's Organics for produce, Wicks Manor for pork and he buys beef from Beatbush Farm in Latchingdon, and fish from day boats in Mersea. Wines are from local suppliers. "I use one place in Hertfordshire for a Romanian Pinot Noir which is our best-selling red, it fits our ethos of trying to do things a little bit differently."

Smoked eel, pickled apple and aubergine terrine

An interesting way to make delicious but expensive smoked eel go further. The fruit and savoury flavours in the terrine contrast with the smoky fish and give different textures. We serve this elegant starter with toasted brioche and watercress salsa verde to add further interest to the plate. It's well worth putting the extra effort into making this dish (it is a 3 day process). The terrine stores well in the refrigerator for an easy finish. (serves 6+)

Pickled apple

100g caster sugar
100ml cider vinegar
3 Braeburn apples, cored and cubed

Put the apple in a heatproof bowl. Dissolve the sugar in the vinegar and 100ml of water in a saucepan over a high heat, stirring continuously while bringing to the boil. Pour over the apple, cool and chill.

Terrine

3 large aubergines
1kg smoked eel as skinned, whole fillets
Large bunch flat leaf parsley
3g agar agar

The day before, thinly slice the aubergines, sprinkle lightly with salt before draining in a colander on a tray overnight in the fridge. The next day, wash off the salt and lay the aubergine slices on clean tea towels to dry. Generously line a terrine mould or loaf tin with clingfilm, avoiding air pockets and allowing sufficient overlap on all sides to cover the top. Heat a large oiled frying pan over a high hob and fry the slices to colour and soften them. Lay the slices along the bottom and sides of the mould, leaving a good overlap of aubergine hanging over the edges.

Cut the eel in half-centimetre cubes. Chop the parsley leaves. Sieve the liquor off the apples into a pan, reserving the fruit. Bring the liquor to the boil and whisk in the agar agar. When dissolved, allow to cool to blood warmth. Fold in the apples, eel and parsley.

Add a third of this mixture to the terrine, followed by a thin layer of aubergine, and repeat with another third of mixture, another thin aubergine layer and the remaining mixture before bringing over the overhanging aubergine to tightly cover it. Next layer over the overhanging clingfilm to wrap it tightly. Transfer to the fridge, press it down with heavy weights while it sets overnight.

To serve

Unwrap the terrine and slice carefully with a very sharp knife. Place on plates and leave to warm through at room temperature for 30 minutes before serving.

Pan-fried scallops and cauliflower 'cous cous'

A novel and tasty carb-free starter, this uses cauliflower in place of classic cous cous. (serves 4)

1 cauliflower, florets only
Small bunch of flat leaf parsley, shredded
1 red chilli, deseeded and finely chopped
12 large scallops, oven ready
1 tsp mild curry powder
Shredded radishes and baby capers

Reserving a couple of large florets, pulse the cauliflower down to a cous cous texture. Heat the cauliflower in a cold oiled frying pan over a medium heat with the shredded parsley and chilli but don't allow to cook. Transfer to a bowl and keep warm.

Mix 1 tsp of fine sea salt with the curry powder to make curried salt. Oil the scallops and toss with seasoning and the curried salt. Heat up an oiled frying pan until very hot and cook the scallops over a high heat, turning over once browned (try not to move them unnecessarily). Drain on kitchen paper.

Thinly slice the remaining cauliflower and use to garnish the edges of cold plates, along with radishes and capers. Place the cauliflower cous cous in the centre, topped with the scallops before serving.

Yoghurt cake

A Mediterranean classic, this makes a lovely simple dessert, especially if finished with colourful pomegranate seeds and pistachio nuts. (serves 6+)

5 eggs
150g caster sugar
100g plain flour
600g Greek natural yoghurt
1 orange and 1 lemon, zest only

Pre-heat the oven to 180c. Separate the eggs whites from the yolks. Whisk the yolks with half of the sugar in a large glass bowl over a pan of simmering water. Keep whisking until the sauce thickens to a glossy custard-like consistency. Cool, then refrigerate.

In another bowl, fold the flour and yoghurt together. Set aside.

Whisk the egg whites to soft peaks in a food mixer. Keeping the motor running, slowly add the remaining sugar and zests to make a meringue. Fold in the yoghurt mixture well. Transfer the mixture to a greased and lined springform cake tin. Bake for 20 minutes or until cooked through. Allow to cool and remove from tin.

Break the cake into rough pieces and fold with the custard sabayon.

Pan-fried sweetbreads and shallot purée

Much like a firm chicken mousse in texture, sweetbreads are mild in flavour and a luxurious treat. We serve this elegant dinner party starter with dressed fennel and spring onion. You need to first poach the sweetbreads for 2 minutes, before cooling and peeling off the outer casing. (serves 4)

300g shallots, chopped
Unsalted butter
Caster sugar
150g lamb's sweetbreads, cooked
Rapeseed oil

Heat up a deep lightly oiled frying pan on a medium-high heat. Sauté the shallots while stirring, adding a good knob of butter and a sprinkling of sugar to help them colour. Once fully-softened, remove the shallots and allow to cool. Process them in a food mixer into a smooth purée. Place in a small saucepan over a low heat to warm through.

Fry the sweetbreads in a hot oiled frying pan over a high heat. Cook them on one side till browned, then turn them over, add a good knob of butter, and baste them well for another minute or two.

Serve on warmed plates with the hot shallot purée.

FAVOURITE INGREDIENT?

Fennel. I use a lot of it and used correctly it can really add to a dish.

FAVOURITE KITCHEN GADGET?

My Thermomix or my Microplane grater.

FAVOURITE PART OF ESSEX?

Frinton. For me it's just lovely being by the sea. When Ruby's off school we go as often as we can and also to Little Monsters soft play centre in Dunmow – I'm a bigger kid than she is!

WHY I'M A CHEF?

I wanted to buy a car – so I worked in a kitchen to get some money. I bought a Vauxhall Nova, the biggest mistake I've ever made buying cars! I've owned 52 so far. I've already bought two this year alone. My favourite ever was an Audi TT.

BEST DISH I'VE EVER EATEN?

Texas breakfast potatoes - sauté potatoes, red peppers, parsley and loads of lemon juice. It's been on the menu here ever since I used to go to Texas. I went there many times when I was into cycling, usually every year. That was when I was very skinny – sadly not anymore.

SIGNATURE DISHES

Starters

Southminster asparagus, poached egg, hollandaise, hazelnuts

Parma ham, pickled peaches, watercress, chilli oil

Latchingdon organic broccoli, romesco, almonds

Mains

Duck breast, leg croquettes, peas à la française

Mersea-landed fish, scallop, cauliflower couscous, purée of caramelised cauliflower, salad

Nettle risotto, pecorino, shoots

Puddings

White chocolate fondant, raspberry sorbet

Yoghurt pannacotta, poached and grilled nectarines, hazelnuts

Strawberry ravioli, strawberry consommé, balsamic gel

ROB ON HIS...

FUNNY CULINARY MOMENT?

I was preparing for a private party and I put a load of sugar on top of 10 crèmes brûlées and they wouldn't flame, so I put more sugar on and they still wouldn't. It was then that I realised the sugar was actually salt! So it all had to be hurriedly scraped off. That was for one of my regular customers and he still doesn't know to this day!

MIDNIGHT FEAST?

Sweets and chocolate for me! I have a KitKat every day, or a Snickers and a Red Bull for breakfast.

FUTURE PLANS?

I'm just grateful for everything that I've got. I have aspirations but ultimately I just want to be happy and for my daughter to be happy too.

CHEF INFLUENCES?

Angela Hartnett has been a massive influence on me, and Brett Graham too – his restaurant The Ledbury in west London is amazing; I used to work for him.

TIME OFF?

I just like to go out and to eat different, interesting things. I recently ate at Frenchie in London and Grain in Colchester is on my list to try.

DISH OF MY CHILDHOOD?

My Nan used to make a German dessert which I loved, a really thick, stodgy cake with strawberry jam all the way through it. I just used to call it My Nan's Cake.

Perfectly formed

There may be just 18 covers in this tiny restaurant, but what Rubino lacks in square footage, it makes up for in quirkiness. Situated on the family-run Chigborough Farm site with its fishery, glamping, yoga studio, farm and craft shops, Rubino is at first glance little more than a black weather-boarded shack – it doesn't shout at you to come in. But step past the picnic tables, under the pergola covered in a tangle of vines and wisteria, and you'll find yourself in a quaint gem of an eatery that's been run by chef-owner Rob Horton since March 2013.

Flanked on two sides by picturesque fishing lakes, the interior of the 300-year-old building pays homage to its location with plenty of fish-related décor – fish glass-fronted cases, fishing rods and reels and fishing pictures hung between the building's exposed wooden frame beams. By day it's a popular spot for breakfast or a light lunch for visitors and guests at the Chigborough Farm complex; come evening though, Rubino takes on a softer look, crisp white cloths covering the daytime's bare tables, candles, and a kaleidoscope of colour from the teal, plum and lime wall lampshades which complement the scatter cushions along the banquettes. It's an intimate place for an evening meal – if you're lucky enough to get a table – with the restaurant and open-plan kitchen all on one level.

Just steps from the restaurant and you're at the Lambton & Jackson smokery with its array of smoked salmon and oak-smoked eel products many of which feature regularly on the Rubino menu.

Rubino Kitchen
Chigborough Lodge, Chigborough Farm, Chigborough Road,
Heybridge, Maldon CM9 4RE
W: rubinokitchen.co.uk
T: 01621 855579
E: bookings@rubinokitchen.co.uk
/Rubino-Kitchen
@Rubinokitchen
/rubinokitchen

Accolades: *Michelin*; finalist, Chef of the Year, *Essex Life* Food & Drink Awards 2016

Covers: 18; private parties up to 24

Cost: carte average £50; wine from £19; beers from £3.50

Open: Wed-Sat B 9-11:30; L 12-3; D 6-9; Sun L 12-3

Details: Occasional theme nights; alfresco picnic tables; private dining available; surrounded by fishing lakes; wheelchair access; parking.

LUCCA ENOTECA, MANNINGTREE
MICHAEL BONACCORSI

Pinch perfect

Maldon Salt brings out the best in the powerful Italian flavours of Michael Bonaccorsi's wood-fired wizardry

Michael Bonaccorsi cannot remember a time when his life did not revolve around food. Back in his native Tuscany, he was plucking chickens by the age of five – there are family snaps to prove it – and from the age of seven he was helping his chef father, Mario, mix pizza dough in Montecatini, a small town between Florence and Pisa. "Dad's nickname was 'Il Direttore' [the director] and that was also the name of our family restaurant where I loved helping out," Michael says. "If I wasn't at school, I was in the kitchen!"

Now head pizzaiolo at Lucca Enoteca in Manningtree (he manages the wood-fired oven while head chef Jonathan 'Wiggy' Whitfield leads the brigade of nine in the conventional kitchen), Michael moved from Italy to the UK at the age of 14. "My father took a job, when we first moved here, at Giorgio Locatelli's famous restaurant in Belgravia, Zafferano. Over the years Giorgio became a firm family friend and I also worked for him alongside my dad. After Dad died, it was hard to go back there, seeing his old chopping board without him, so I left there and the industry altogether. It took a family occasion here in Essex and meeting my partner, Lauren, to bring me back to restaurant life, that was seven years ago, and I'm still here, happy to be cooking again!"

Michael swells with pride at the mention of his family both past and present – he even has a pizza named after his father on the menu, called Il Direttore, a classic margherita base topped with piccante and milano salami, fennel sausage and speck ham.

It seems fitting that the producer he wants to take us to has similarly deep family roots. Further around the Essex coast, Maldon Salt has been owned by the Osborne family for four generations, its history tracking back a full 135 years. It's here on the Blackwater estuary, that salt makers have been hand-harvesting the naturally formed pyramid crystals using a process that remains unchanged since 1882.

Sea water is taken directly from the estuary, pumped into stainless steel pans, then gently boiled and left to evaporate for 24 hours. The following day, a rake is used to 'draw the pan' and lift the snow-white salt into large tubs to drain. That's not to say the process is simple. "The art is in the temperature and timing," says Gary. "Getting that right is vital if we are going to create those distinctive soft crunchy flakes." Despite this heritage and traditional production, their workforce is relatively small, some thirty-strong, even more surprising in light of their global impact supplying some 60 countries around the world. Of course their biggest market is here, creating that essential kitchen staple for chefs and home cooks throughout the UK. "We're proud to have had such a profound and positive effect on people's taste buds for so long," says salt maker Gary Bentley.

Boxes of Maldon's glittering finest in hand, we head back to Lucca to watch Michael get hands-on with the white stuff – combining special tipo 00 Caputo flour from Naples (of course), the frothing ferment of fresh yeast and warm water, and of course a generous seasoning of Maldon's jewelled sea salt crystals. He shows us how his authentic pizza dough is made from scratch but soon sets aside the freshly kneaded batch for a puffed-up, plump one from the fridge, explaining "long and slow proving gives that unique, authentic taste and texture, working it naturally for 36 hours lets the gluten relax and the flavour develop during its gentle rise".

Michael next makes an interesting alternative to the classic margherita tomato base for his pizza, blending unusual seasonal foraged greens of nettles and wild garlic into a reduced creamy green sauce, cooled and spread on to the shaped and flattened dough. Topped with luscious burrata mozzarella, parmesan shavings, olive oil and walnuts, the impressive pizza slides on Michael's peel into the heart of Lucca's glowing centrepiece, the enormous, furnace-like oven, fired by seasoned local logs blazing at some 400c. Just two minutes later, Michael skilfully retrieves it, baked to perfection.

The culinary heartbeat of the Lucca Enoteca menu unsurprisingly is the wood-fired pizza and pasta specialities, the domain of Michael and his pizzaioli colleagues, but the Lucca menu offers much more besides. Their cuisine may be largely inspired by traditional southern Italian dishes – the likes of 'verdura e formaggi' (a starter of grilled seasonal vegetables, olives, three cheeses – buffalo mozzarella, pecorino, fontina – and oven-roasted tomatoes), or 'tagliatelle con funghi' (homemade pasta, mushrooms, double cream, Parmesan and truffle oil) – but Wiggy and his team of chefs emphasise locally sourced ingredients whenever they can. Green-fingered Alison Bond of Alison's Organics grows much of the restaurant's salad produce such as unusual leaves and herbs – "We use her purple basil to make a colourful, zingy pesto which always impresses customers" and, when not foraged in the wild, tamer fungi come from the Hearne family's Capel Organic Mushrooms. Shaws Farm Meats at Parsons Heath near Colchester and Direct Meats in Chappel supply most of Lucca's salami, hams and meat.

Michael is a qualified deerstalker and furnishes Lucca with venison whenever he can, helping on his days off to organise shoots for Lauren's gamekeeper father. "I have a real interest in game, I suppose that's why autumn is my favourite time of year to cook, but really I'm happy to be at the stove any time because you can always create a delicious meal if you have good local meat, fruit and vegetables."

Wild garlic and nettle pizza

This is a quick yet interesting and very seasonal dish, adaptable to whichever greens you can forage or have growing in the veg patch. Naturally the dough recipe works well whatever your favourite pizza combination. Less is more, though, so a smearing of classic tomato ragù and a couple of toppings is great – just no pineapple please! And if you don't have an oven stone, pre-heating a sturdy metal pizza tray until very hot can work but you will not achieve the same stone-baked finish. (serves 4)

Pizza dough

Like all breadmaking, fresh yeast makes for a far superior texture and flavour, but for speed you could use quick-acting or dried yeast, adjusting the amounts and method to the instructions on the packet.

10g fresh yeast
400g unbleached strong plain flour

Dissolve the yeast in 25ml (1½ tbsp) of lukewarm water. Add 2 tbsp of the measured flour. Mix together into a smooth paste and leave to prove under a tea towel somewhere warm for about 30 minutes.

Pour the flour and 1 tsp of finely ground sea salt into a large bowl, stir well and create a deep well in the middle. Pour the yeast liquid and another 225ml of lukewarm water into the centre of the hole. Bring the ingredients together with well-floured hands into a rough mass. Turn out onto a clean surface and knead continuously for 8-10 minutes or until smooth and elastic. After kneading, cut the dough into 4 equal-sized pieces, separate, dust with flour and leave to rise under a tea towel for about one hour or until they have doubled in size.

Pizza

Unless you are brave or foolhardy, please use rubber gloves when handling the nettles. You do need to bake the pizza in turn so it really is best for a casual supper with generous helpings of wine, gluggable Italian vino if you don't have an excellent East Anglian Bacchus chilling in the fridge.

4 tbsp unsalted butter
1 handful wild garlic leaves, washed and thinly sliced
2 tbsp dry white wine
250ml double cream
Semolina flour for dusting
Four pizza dough balls, as above
350g buffalo mozzarella or burrata, sliced
225g small nettle leaves, washed and dried
2 tbsp extra-virgin olive oil

Melt the butter in a saucepan over a low-medium heat and add the garlic leaves. Toss with tongs until just wilted, for about one minute. Pour in the white wine and simmer for 2 minutes. Next add the cream and cook over a low heat until the mixture is reduced by half, for about 5 minutes. Set aside to cool.

Dust your work surface lightly with semolina. Using one ball for one pizza, slightly flatten out the dough into a thick round. Using your fingertips, press an indentation about 2cm inside the edge to make a raised ridge. Next push out the centre of the dough with the palm of your hand into a thin, round circle, avoiding the ridge. The pizza is now ready to be topped.

Spread one quarter of the wild garlic mixture inside the raised ridge. Top with a quarter of the mozzarella or burrata and season with salt and black pepper. In a bowl with a pair of tongs, toss the nettles with the olive oil and season to taste with salt and pepper. Mound a quarter of the nettles onto the top of the pizza.

To serve

Parmesan cheese, shaved with a potato peeler

Remove the racks from your oven and place a pizza stone on the floor of the oven and heat to 250c (or as hot as the temperature will go) for 30 minutes.

Using a wide fish slice or pizza peel, carefully slide the pizza onto the hot stone and cook for about five minutes, depending on your oven temperature.

Once it is hot, golden and bubbling, carefully remove the pizza from the stone and transfer to a wooden chopping board. Scatter with some parmesan shavings. Cut the pizza into four wedges and serve immediately.

Repeat to make the rest of the pizzas.

Ciabatta

To make great bread, you need good flour – we use Italian tipo 00. For warm water, best to use 2 parts cold tap to 1 part boiling water. This dough can obviously be baked as a simple white tin loaf.

50g Maldon sea salt
1.6kg strong bread flour
5g fresh yeast

Dissolve the sea salt into 850ml warm water in a very large bowl or food mixer with a dough hook. Sieve in the flour and the crumbled yeast. Mix until it starts to come together, then add 150ml warm water and continue until the bowl becomes clean. Knead until it is elastic and smooth. Cover loosely with clingfilm (with enough room to double in volume) and prove overnight at room temperature.

Split the dough in two. Press each half into a rectangle and roll up into a 'swiss roll' shape (press the end into the underside of the dough to seal). Shape each into a flattened log on a floured tray and leave to rest, laying over, but not tucking in, a sheet of oiled clingfilm. After 4-5 hours, it should have doubled in size. Preheat the oven to 220c.

Score the top of the bread with shallow cuts of a sharp knife diagonally.

When you put the tray in the oven, lower the temperature to 200c. Bake for 25-30 minutes until golden brown. Carefully turn the loaf over and tap the bottom to check it sounds hollow, or cook for a few more minutes if not.

Focaccia

This classic Italian herb bread is great on its own dipped in a ramekin of olive oil and balsamic vinegar or to accompany simple antipasti.

Proved ciabatta dough recipe
Extra virgin olive oil
Dried oregano

After the dough has proved overnight, halve the dough and roll each into a ball shape, leaving to rest for 20 minutes. Next roll them out on an oiled worktop to an approx. 20mm thick rectangle. Make dimples all over deeply with fingertips. Sprinkle with oregano to taste. With the dough placed lengthways in front of you, fold the left third into the middle and then repeat with the right. Dimple again, turn lengthways again and repeat folding in each side to become a square before dimpling once more.

Oil a large deep baking tray, place focaccia on and brush with oil. Cover with clingfilm and leave to rest for 2 hours. Stretch to fit the tray. Dimple the top again, cover and rest for 2 hours. Preheat the oven to 220c. Uncover the bread and sprinkle with sea salt and olive oil to taste. Bake for 25 minutes.

Grilled apricots with mascarpone cream and salted caramel sauce

A lovely late summer treat, sweet ripe apricots and luscious cheese combine deliciously with a nutty crumble top and a rich salty caramel.

200g caster sugar
120ml double cream
25ml bourbon whiskey
½ teaspoon Maldon sea salt
1 tsp vanilla bean paste
250g mascarpone
Rapeseed oil
8 ripe apricots, halved
8 amaretti biscuits, crushed
Maldon sea salt to taste

Pre-heat the oven to 180c. Simmer the sugar and 60ml water in a small saucepan over a medium heat, swirling the pan carefully as it bubbles to dissolve (do not stir). Cook until it changes to a light brown colour, approx. 5 minutes, then turn off the heat.

Stir in the cream, followed by the bourbon and sea salt until well combined. Put to one side.

Combine the vanilla and mascarpone in a bowl and refrigerate.

Lightly oil the apricots. Place them cut-side down on a hot char-grill for a few minutes until warmed and lightly scorched. Fill the apricot halves with the mascarpone and place on a serving platter or in bowls.

Spoon the warm caramel over the apricots. Sprinkle the crushed amaretti over the top, along with a bit more Maldon sea salt and serve.

MICHAEL ON HIS...

FUNNY CULINARY MOMENT?

I'm not sure it was funny at the time but one bank holiday our Orbital mixer broke down on the Thursday night and we had to mix 54 kilos of dough by hand, each day of the bank holiday from the Friday through to the Monday!

SOMEWHERE STILL TO DINE?

Most of my favourite memories have been with my dad, so I couldn't imagine eating out anywhere in Italy without thinking of him and remembering my time with him. I think if there's one place I'd still like to eat it would be Giorgio's current restaurant, Locanda Locatelli.

FAVOURITE INGREDIENT?

I am happy to cook with any ingredient. I have been making use of local beetroot recently, it's especially good to make pasta, turns it bright pink of course! I also love to cook with game.

WHERE I'M HAPPIEST?

Here in front of the wood-fired oven, and also at home with my boys and Lauren.

FAVOURITE COOKBOOKS?

The Silver Spoon by Clelia D'Onofrio – I have the original hand-bound version from 1962 which was my father's. I also like *Made in Italy: Food & Stories* by Giorgio Locatelli. These two are my bibles.

FUTURE DREAMS?

I think I'm already there. I'm in a very good place but I would like to be able to see my oldest son Vinnie (11) a bit more. He lives in Norwich and with my unsociable hours it makes it difficult to see him as much as I'd like. I also enjoy teaching so perhaps more of that. I teach at the Mistley Kitchen [butchery and game cookery, barbecue cooking and pizza classes] and I also teach for fun at the nursery my youngest son Mario (2) attends. I cook them lunch and the kids get to play around with the dough.

FAVOURITE PART OF ESSEX?

We like to go to Frinton-on-Sea. Lauren's cousin has an ice cream parlour there, Pop-Pins, and she does overloaded milkshakes with whole bits of doughnut and spoonfuls of Nutella.

SIGNATURE DISHES

Starters

Funghi ripieni: baked chestnut mushrooms stuffed with fresh ricotta, gorgonzola, herbs

Zucchini fries: deep-fried lightly battered courgette batons, shaved pecorino, lemon oil

Mussels in Trebbiano wine with fennel, garlic, roasted red peppers, garlic olive oil crostini

Mains

Rigatoni with game ragù

Pizza romana: tomato, fior di latte mozzarella, cooked ham, Capel portobello mushrooms

Calzone contadino: roasted peppers & aubergine, spinach, caramelised onions, fior di latte mozzarella, goats' cheese, pesto, tomato, rocket

Puddings

Pizza Nutella: pizza dough with Nutella, icing sugar, ice cream

Vanilla pannacotta

Traditionally made tiramisù

BIGGEST EXTRAVAGANCE?

Probably my collection of professional Henckels knives which are insured for around £2k. I also love kitchen gadgets at home so I have a sausage maker and a pasta maker.

All fired up

You can't help but notice the impressive wood-fired oven as soon as you step through the front door of Lucca Enoteca; it is truly at the heart of this family-friendly, town-centre Italian restaurant. Previously home to the Stour Bay Café which owners Sherri Singleton and David McKay ran until 1997, the Tudor grade II-listed building is packed with interesting architectural features: the wood plank floors are from old sailing barges, and while some of the beams are original, those which have been added are from a nearby deconsecrated church before it was demolished. There are views of the quayside from the upstairs dining room, while to the back of the restaurant, down a couple of steps, is an intimate terrace with a large fig tree and ruby-red parasols.

Lucca was to be the name of Sherri's first son – it's also the name of a Tuscan town and a favourite holiday destination of Sherri and David – but when the couple were blessed with a daughter, they decided that the name should be given to their reincarnated restaurant. Sherri explains the efforts they went to in creating Lucca: "our pizza mentor Enzo Coccia, the maestro pizzaiolo from Naples, taught us everything we know. Quite a celebrity in Naples, Enzo even demonstrated how to create the perfect pizza to Heston Blumenthal. David secretly arranged for Jamie, my stepson, and me to head out to Naples and learn alongside Enzo. It was an absolute joy but he did work us like dogs!"

A modest all-Italian wine selection mainly sourced by Liberty Wines complements the Italian food: choose a crisp vino bianco such as Gran Sasso made from the Trebbiano d'Abruzzo grape, or traditional Veneto Soave from Leonildo Pieropan, to cut through all that melting cheese.

Lucca Enoteca
39-43 High Street, Manningtree CO11 1AH
W: luccafoods.co.uk
T: 01206 390044
E: luccafoods@gmail.com
/luccamanningtree
@LuccaEnoteca
/luccaenoteca

Accolades: runner-up, Best Cheap Eats, *Observer Food Monthly* awards 2016, 2015; *Hardens*

Covers: 100 inside; 40 outside

Cost: carte average £17; wine from £16.50; draft Peroni from £5

Open: all week 12-9.30 (10 Fri-Sat)

Details: alfresco dining in private courtyard; takeaway available; village location close to quayside; wheelchair access; parking on the High Street

Well spotted

Why mess with what works? Simon Edwards champions resolutely classic dishes on his appealing menu – with local pork taking centre stage

One of the Spotted Dog's most popular dishes might never have come about if it wasn't for a chance meeting some seven years ago between local farmer, Jonathan Smith, and Simon Edwards soon after he took over this free house pub-restaurant in the hamlet of Bishop's Green, near Dunmow. "I'm the bossy one," says Jonathan's wife, Julie, "so it's always me who goes in to see potential new customers. We'd heard really good things about Simon – he used to be at The Duck Inn at Writtle – so one day I just popped in to have a chat and see if he'd like to buy our pork."

It was a no-brainer for Simon. "Julie introduced herself, said she was from Great Garnetts, the farm down the road, and left me some pork fillet to try. I remember I pan-fried the pork as medallions, with sautéed spinach and a Dijon mustard sauce. The first thing that struck me was the freshness. I get my pork from them the day after slaughter and it really shows in the look, texture and taste. We were still refurbishing so we had the Saturday off that week, and Anita my wife and I went along to the Great Garnetts farmers' market and they gave us a leg of pork, and we cooked that up too to try before we opened. It tasted fantastic, and we've used them ever since."

That was back in April 2010. Simon orders pork fillet pretty much every week to make his enduringly popular rolled pork stuffed with spicy mushroom duxelles, spinach and mozzarella. Occasionally he'll buy a loin of pork. "Rolled and stuffed once boned, I serve the loin with a fat chop as a duo of pork dish." There's a secret ingredient beyond the wild mushrooms, medium-hot chilli and tarragon, that he won't reveal, but he spreads the mixture, along with mozzarella cheese and spinach on the tenderised meat before skilfully rolling it up and wrapping it in Parma ham, then leaving the whole joint to rest twisted tightly in clingfilm. Removing the clingfilm he then re-rolls the meat, this time in foil, and roasts it for 20 minutes or so. He then lifts it out of the oven, glistening with pork juices and rich with the aroma of all those marvellous ingredients now fabulously fused together. "If it wasn't for Great Garnetts, this dish might not ever have come up, so I'm very glad Julie came in that day."

Julie and her husband care for 160 breeding sows on their farm – along with several thousand turkeys for the Christmas market – meaning that at any one time there can be up to 4,000 pigs at various stages of development, enough to have around 2,000 pigs to take to market every year.

The females are Large White crossed with Landrace, the males 50% Large White and 50% Duroc Hampshire Landrace. It's a cross that appears to work, Jonathan explains, the sows having tremendous mothering ability, while Duroc in the male line gives fantastic tasting pork. "To produce quality pork you need the right breed to give the shape and vigour," he says, "then it's about what you feed

"If it wasn't for Great Garnetts, this (stuffed pork) dish might not ever have come up, so I'm very glad Julie came in that day."

the animals. We buy our food from local feed millers, sometimes Marriages in Chelmsford, who make a mixed cereal of wheat, barley, peas, beans and soya – it's high energy and a balanced diet which is vital if you're going to get that right balance of fat and meat."

The heavy Essex clay makes the soil too claggy for the pigs to be outside year-round. Sows farrow outside during the summer, but at other times are housed in large deep-strawed pens. "Our methods are traditional, so our pigs always have something to forage in which means they're content and stress-free. There's a direct link between that and the taste of the meat of course," says Jonathan.

The pork fits on Simon's reassuringly classical menu. You might start a meal at The Spotted Dog with a veal, pork and black pudding terrine, or a pigeon and Stilton salad with croûtons and a balsamic dressing, the pigeon brought in by a trusted local retired man who shoots pigeons on a local farm. You could follow it with salmon en croûte with chive sauce, rack of lamb with roast potatoes and a mint gravy, or pan-fried medallions of Great Garnetts pork which Simon tops with sliced tomato and Stilton and serves with a red wine sauce. Favourite puddings include sticky toffee, a homely syrup sponge or classic crème brûlée.

It's a style of cooking that Simon has developed over many years in the trade. "I didn't start with catering, though. My first job was as an office junior messenger in Thurrock. I lasted just two months as I hated it and so I quickly moved into the catering trade and became a commis chef in Basildon." It was a move to Jersey aged 21 that ignited his love for all things culinary, however. "There's so much wonderful fresh fish, seafood and produce out there; it was a completely new ball game." Working his way up through the kitchen ranks and gaining experience at every stage, he finally became landlord at The Duck at Writtle, near Chelmsford. When he and Anita found The Spotted Dog, they knew they'd found the place to really make their mark; it doesn't look like they'll be moving anywhere soon.

Ham-wrapped pork fillet, stuffed with wild mushrooms, spinach and mozzarella

Full of rich, contrasting ingredients, this dish adds texture and taste to the naturally sweet and succulent pork. Much like an lighter alternative to pastry in a wellington, the covering of salty thin ham adds a savoury edge once baked and crisp. A good local butcher will butterfly and flatten out the tenderloins for you but a careful cook can easily manage it with a sharp knife. This dish eats well with a light potato dish on the side, plus some simple buttered seasonal vegetables. (serves 4)

Port gravy

500ml home-made beef stock
125ml good port

Boil the stock until reduced by two-thirds. Add the port and reduce again to a syrupy gravy texture. Set aside.

Mushroom duxelles

2 long shallots, peeled and diced
4 red and green chillies, seeded and diced
4 garlic cloves, peeled and diced
500g fresh wild mushrooms, shredded
1 tbsp fresh tarragon, chopped

Heat a large sauté pan over a high heat until smoking and stir-fry the first four ingredients for 5 minutes. Remove, season lightly and stir through the tarragon. Transfer contents to a processor and purée well. Return the mixture to the pan and cook for 20 minutes over a low heat, stirring occasionally, until it becomes a dry mixture. Decant and cool.

Pork fillets

2 handfuls baby spinach
2 pork tenderloins, trimmed
8 slices of parma ham
125g mozzarella, sliced

In a hot, oiled sauté pan, quickly toss the seasoned spinach over a high heat, until just wilting. Set aside to cool.

Cut each loin into two portions. Slice lengthways through the pork to three-quarters depth.
Open each loin out and lay between two sheets of clingfilm. Using a rolling pin or meat hammer, gently flatten out the meat until about 1cm thick. Repeat with all four pieces and place separately on large pieces of clingfilm. Leaving a good margin on the edges, spread the duxelles over the pork, followed by the spinach and then the cheese. Roll up into firm parcels and wrap round with the ham. Clingfilm each tightly and refrigerate for 2 hours. When ready to cook, pre-heat the oven to 200c. Remove clingfilm and rewrap the meat with foil, securing the ends. Bake until cooked through, about 20 minutes. Remove and rest somewhere warm.

To serve

1 small savoy cabbage
Good olive oil
Unsalted butter
1 tbsp wholegrain mustard

Put the gravy on a low hob to reheat. Remove coarse cabbage leaves and stalk. Finely shred the tender leaves. Heat a large sauté pan over a high heat, then add a glug of oil and the cabbage. Stir-fry till heated through and wilting. Finish by stirring in a good knob of butter, the mustard and generous seasoning to taste.

Carve the pork into thick slices and place on top of a bed of cabbage on warm plates. Drizzle with gravy.

Coconut and herb-crusted lamb loin

A fragrant, interesting foil to the sweetness of the meat, the crumb crust can be made with your favourite fresh green herbs instead of dried ones, but the other proportions then need to be adjusted for the extra moisture. This dish holds together well if wrapped in pig's caul fat, which is available from your butcher. I like to eat this with creamed leeks and a vanilla-scented red wine gravy. (serves 4)

4 lamb loin portions
125g desiccated coconut
1 tbsp dried herbs
125g breadcrumbs, oven-dried
125g melted butter
1 egg yolk
Pig's caul

In a pre-heated frying pan over a high heat, brown the lamb all over. Place the remaining ingredients (except caul) in a processor and blend to a paste. Top the lamb loins equally with the mixture (and wrap in caul if using). Chill for 30 minutes to firm up. Pre-heat the oven to 200c. Bake on a roasting tray for 7-12 minutes until cooked to your liking.

Gingerbread and pear pudding with butterscotch

A classic nursery favourite, this steamed pud combines sticky toffee, fruit and ginger flavours, complemented by the pear jam and star anise ice cream we serve with it. (serves 4)

100g light brown sugar
100g salted butter
100g golden syrup
200ml double cream
110g plain flour
¼ tsp bicarbonate of soda
½ tsp ground cinnamon
¼ tsp ground ginger
¼ tsp nutmeg
50g salted butter
110g golden syrup
2 eggs, beaten
50g peeled pear, grated

Dissolve the first three ingredients in a large heavy saucepan, mix well and stir in the cream. Carefully simmer to a thick sauce consistency. Decant and set aside.

Pre-heat the oven to 200c. Sieve together the dry ingredients. In a large heavy saucepan over a medium heat, warm the butter and syrup together until melted. Take off the heat, slowly add the eggs whilst beating and fold in the dry ingredients. Finally stir through the pear. Pour into four greased individual ovenproof moulds and sit in a roasting tray of shallow hot water. Bake for 40 minutes. Unmould and serve with the butterscotch.

Monkfish and king prawn brochette

These light zesty skewers are popular at The Spotted Dog, eating well with our saffron basmati rice and a dill herb sauce. Moderate the chillies and tabasco for a lighter heat. Local dogfish and cod also work well. (serves 4)

500g monkfish
16 king prawns, peeled
8 red and green chillies
6 garlic cloves, peeled
1 inch ginger root, peeled
Small bunch of dill
Tabasco sauce to taste
275ml good olive oil

Cut the fish into 16 chunks and place in a large bowl with the prawns. Liquidise the remaining ingredients and pour over the seafood. Stir well, cover and refrigerate for 24 hours.

To cook, thread the seafood alternately onto soaked wooden skewers and then char-grill on a pre-heated griddle over a medium-high heat until cooked through.

FAVOURITE PLACES TO EAT IN ESSEX?

We like the Square and Compasses in Fuller Street – there's a really good atmosphere there. We're still hoping to try Haywards. Anita's son, Michael, works at The Bell Inn at Horndon-on-the-Hill, and I trained both him and their head chef, Steve Treadwell, so we go there too. I worked at the Bell when I was 16 and then returned when I was 32.

FOODIE FAD?

Samphire. I don't usually use it, but I've started to use it in stir-fries and it gives another dimension, and of course it works brilliantly with fish.

COOKERY TIP?

Make sure your food is seasoned before it's cooked!

FAVOURITE KITCHEN GADGET?

My whizzy woo! It's a stick hand blender and I use it every day.

WHY I'M A CHEF?

I would have liked to have been a professional golfer, and when I was growing up I was very into horse jumping; I'd travel all over the country competing. Unfortunately, it was expensive and when one of my sponsors had to pull out at the last minute I realised I'd have to get a proper job. That's when I looked to become a chef.

SIGNATURE DISHES

Starters

Beef fillet strips and stir-fry vegetables baked in filo pastry, hoisin sauce

Spicy salmon & cod fishcakes, light curry sauce

Baked goats' cheese & figs on olive crostini, beetroot & apple chutney, honey & wholegrain mustard dressing

Mains

Grilled salmon fillet, spinach, king prawns, saffron sauce

Pan-fried calf's liver & bacon, horseradish mash, balsamic gravy

Beef wellington, shallot & port sauce

Puddings

White chocolate pannacotta, raspberry compote, crème anglaise, coconut sorbet

Summer fruits terrine, chantilly cream, fruit coulis, blackberry ice cream

Bread & butter pudding, clotted cream ice cream, crème anglaise

SIMON ON HIS...

DISH OF MY CHILDHOOD?

Mum used to do a mean Bakewell tart. Now I'm a chef I realise it wasn't a proper Bakewell tart but it was her take on it and it was delicious.

FAVOURITE PART OF ESSEX?

We are lucky to have Stansted airport just 10 minutes away so we use that local connection to fly off to many European destinations.

FUNNIEST FOOD MOMENT?

When Phil Warren, who has been with me now for 20 years, was training I left him to finish the crème brûlées. I told him they'd be ready in 20 minutes, to open the oven and give them a shake and see if they wobble. If they do they are ready. When I got home he phoned me to say he couldn't tell if they wobbled. I had to drive back to the restaurant to take them out of the oven.

FAVOURITE TIME OF YEAR TO COOK?

The game season. I love it to start with because you've suddenly got venison, pheasant and partridge and it's great to have something different on the menu. However, by the end of the season I'm thinking "oh no I'm not cooking game again today"!

STYLE OF COOKING?

Old school. I don't have any modern equipment like water baths or the like. We cook with a traditional oven, and I use the old methods for preparing my stocks. Our food isn't minimalist or as pretty on the plate as some, but flavour is the most important thing to me.

ANY CELEBRITY MOMENTS?

Yes, Tommy Cooper! I served him when I was working on a carvery in a hotel in Purfleet. I asked him "how do you like your beef sir" and he said "just like that!" in his comical voice!

A dog's life

Behind a picket fence on the side of the road in the hamlet of Bishop's Green, stands this pretty, thatched pub-restaurant. The 18th century building with its sign painted boldly on the outside is both workplace and home to Simon Edwards and his wife Anita, and is every bit your charming country pub.

The couple bought the free house back in 2010, re-opening the pub in the April after ploughing over £200,000 into refurbishing the property, and adding their own style to the interior with high-backed leather chairs around contemporary, chunky, bare tables that are well-spaced beneath the original beams. Shades of sage green inside and out, some exposed brickwork, and an open fire in the winter complete the look.

The small bar is well-stocked with the beers you'd expect, and a range of wines curated by Peter Watts Wines of Coggeshall. "He only uses individual vineyards and he's very knowledgeable about them," says Simon. "We particularly like Peter because when he comes to change the wine list he will always bring us a few samples!"

Outside, an attractive gravelled area at the front of the pub provides summer alfresco dining under vast parasols.

Don't expect pomp and circumstance on a plate here: Simon is a chef who likes to give generous portions, put flavour first and live up to the awards he's collected over the years for his food and customer service.

The Spotted Dog
Bishop's Green, Barnston, Dunmow CM6 1NF
W: the-spotted-dog-bishopsgreen.co.uk
T: 01245 231598
E: spotteddogdunmow@aol.com
/Spotted-dog
@SpottedDog_PH

Accolades: Essex Tourism and Hospitality Awards Best Gastro Pub 2013 and 2014; Best Restaurant Service 2013 and 2014; Best Customer Service 2013; *Essex Life* Food & Drinks Awards winner, Top Chef, 2014; finalist 2013, 2015, 2016; winner Customer Service Award 2014, 2015

Covers: 50

Cost: average carte £30; set menu Mon-Sat L and Mon-Thurs D £16.95 for 2 courses, £18.95 for 3; wine from £19.50; pint from £3.80

Open: Mon-Sat L 12-2; D 6-9; Sun 10-3 (last food orders 1.30)

Details: vegetarian menu; al fresco dining; children welcome; wheelchair access; free wifi; parking

What's your beef?

Darren Bennett argues the case for choosing top-quality organic beef from a farm close to his Billericay restaurant – and his customers love it

Most days, Darren Bennett wears two chef's jackets at once, one on top of the other. There's a logic to his actions, and it's not that he feels the cold. "I often get called mid-service to meet a regular customer in the dining room. By wearing two jackets I can just remove the top one and – voilà! – I have a fresh, clean one underneath, ready for meeting and greeting."

It fits with the immaculate setting of The Magic Mushroom, where trademark circular and square tables are covered with pristine white cloths, glittering glassware, gleaming crockery, and a single stem rose. Cream leather seats and gentle lighting add to the glamour. A spattered jacket would look right out of place.

Chef-owner Darren and his team have been working hard recently on the restaurant's image as part of its 20th birthday celebrations, extending it to add another 40 covers and doubling the size of the kitchen to accommodate a host of new kitchen gadgets, including an eagerly awaited Rational combi-oven which will help the team with serving larger numbers.

Exciting though material improvements might be, it's what comes out of the kitchen and is put in front of customers that is most important to Darren. He is as meticulous about ingredients as he is convivial with his customers, and is particularly careful with ever-popular steak, so it's not surprising that he wants to take us to French's Farm on the edge of nearby Brentwood. "French's is not only a really good local supplier," he explains, "it's also completely organic, and that's what interests me the most."

Malcolm Knox, master butcher and owner of the 80-acre farm is in charge. He established French's Farm initially as a way of providing his own family with organic meat, but the business has expanded since its 1980s beginnings and now sells beef from the resident Limousin-cross suckler herd, as well as poultry, salt marsh lamb, pork and fish from local farmers and fishermen, to the public and chefs.

French's Farm is only a short drive from the restaurant – and moments from the busy A12 and M25 – but rolling Essex pasture gives the impression that you are actually in the deepest countryside. At the end of the track the farm shop brims with meats, poultry and homemade pies. After a warm welcome from Malcolm's terrier we make our way around the traditional weatherboard barns and into the pasture to meet the cattle happily munching in their grassy paddock. Of course, this being an organic farm, no chemicals are used at all. "Yes, it is more labour intensive, and our calves are slow-growing," says Malcolm, "but the meat we produce is the crème de la crème. Everyone says how wonderful it tastes."

Malcolm's cattle are Limousin crossed with Hereford and Aberdeen Angus. "They are a good-sized animal, he says. "All the calves are born outdoors to good mothers, and stay with them for up to nine months." During winter, the animals are fed indoors on home-grown silage, hay

and organic feed before returning to their outdoor environment in the spring, rotating through different pasture to enable grass to rest. Slaughter happens at 18-24 months of age. "The animal has to look right, so if it hasn't made the weight it gets to have a longer holiday with us!"

Back at the restaurant, Darren trims and seasons the sirloin – it's beautifully marbled, the layer of fat a rich creamy yellow – before pan-frying it with oil, a couple of cloves of garlic and sprig of thyme. He cooks it for two minutes on each side then two minutes under the grill each side. "The key is to rest the meat for at least five minutes before serving. The meat doesn't shrink, you notice," Darren observes. "That's the sign of a good steak." He slices the butter-soft, pink-centred meat, its fat perfectly rendered, plating it up attractively with honeyed carrots and deep-fried shallot rings. He makes crispy bon bons using meat from a slow-cooked rib of beef that he works into a ball, rolls in breadcrumbs and fries quickly in garlicky butter.

The dish fits with Darren's preference for cooking traditional favourites with a modern slant. Beef will turn up in various guises: the kitchen will roast a whole sirloin for Sunday lunch, but midweek you might find fillet with fondant potatoes, featherblade with all the trimmings, or a rich stroganoff. Other meat comes from local sources: the Philpot family who farm the land around The Magic Mushroom, supply pheasants during the season, while pork (and asparagus) is from Canewdon just north of Southend. "As a family we go to Norsey Wood to find puffball mushrooms, but I use a certified forager to pick for the restaurant."

Darren's is a style honed over many years at the stove where he has nurtured a passion that tracks back to his early teens when he decided, aged 14, that he wanted to have his own restaurant one day. Inspired by his college lecturer, Chris Galvin (now Michelin-star chef and renowned restaurateur), Darren took the leap at the age of 25 when the tearooms at Barleylands became available. Many told him that it would not work, that the location was too remote, but 20 years down the line, the naysayers have been proved wrong and it all seems to work perfectly.

"Our customers love traditional favourites, so we will always do steak and chips and a blackberry and apple pie. My younger chefs like to be creative, and we put their ideas onto our specials menu, then if they sell well, they might go onto our main menu. I also watch *Saturday Kitchen* – if you put the dish they've cooked in the morning on the menu you'll sell 40 that night, no problem!"

Rare seared sirloin with crispy beef bonbons and dauphinoise potatoes

Try and source the best quality, well-matured beef for this hearty yet elegant autumnal main course. We serve this dish with crispy peppered shallot rings, roasted baby carrots and leeks for colour and contrast. You may need a 'sous chef' to help juggle the final simultaneous stages. (serves 4)

Short rib bonbons

Approx. 1.5kg short rib of beef
Olive oil
1 garlic bulb, halved horizontally
1 large onion, sliced
4 celery sticks, sliced
1 leek, sliced
1 tbsp tomato purée
200ml good drinkable red wine
Approx. 1 litre good beef stock, simmering
Plain flour, seasoned
3 eggs, beaten
Fresh white breadcrumbs

Preheat the oven to its hottest setting. Oil the ribs and season well. Place in a hobproof deep roasting tray in a single layer and then roast until well-browned all over. Remove the tray and reduce the oven to 170c.

Place the tray on a high heat, then add the garlic halves cut-side down and the vegetables, before stirring in the tomato purée. Cook for 5 minutes, stirring often, then add the wine to deglaze, scraping the bottom of the tray well. Simmer for 10-15 minutes until reduced by half in volume, then add stock to just cover the ribs. Bring to a simmer, cover with foil and bake in the oven for 3-4 hours, basting occasionally.

Remove from the oven and allow to cool in the tray. Sieve the liquor and reserve before shredding the meat off the ribs into a bowl. Fold in enough liquor to just bind the meat (reserving the remainder for the jus). Refrigerate the mixture and when cold, roll into golf ball-size bonbons.

Prepare three soup plates with the flour, egg and crumbs. Roll the bonbons alternately in all three to coat, before chilling on a clingfilmed tray until required.

Dauphinoise potatoes

8 large maris piper potatoes, finely sliced
3 cloves garlic, crushed
1 litre whipping cream
100g parmesan cheese, grated
200g cheddar cheese, grated

Pre-heat the oven to 160c. In a large bowl, combine the garlic, seasoning and cream before folding in the parmesan and half the cheddar. Mix with the potatoes, then layer them to a depth of three fingers in a deep baking tray. Pour any left-over cream mixture on top and scatter with remaining cheese. Cover with foil and bake for 45 minutes until the centre is tender to the point of a sharp knife. Set aside for 30 minutes. Cover with a clingfilmed baking tray and weights before chilling. Cut into portions before reheating.

To serve

4 200g portions of sirloin steak, boneless
Rapeseed oil
Unsalted butter

Pre-heat the oven to 180c and the deep fat fryer to 170c with vegetable oil. Reheat the dauphinoise portions on a tray for approx. 20 minutes or until piping hot. Remove the steak from the refrigerator 10 minutes before the potatoes are ready. Season the steaks well all over. Oil a hot frying pan on a high heat, lay in the steaks, reduce heat to medium, add a good knob of butter and cook for two minutes on each side, basting regularly. If you wish it to be cooked more than rare, continue until done to your liking. Rest the meat on a board somewhere warm for 5 minutes. Meanwhile, bring the rib liquor to a simmer in a small saucepan over a medium heat. Deep fry the bonbons until golden and crispy, then drain on kitchen paper. Carve the steak onto warm plates and serve the potatoes, bonbons and jus alongside.

Smoked wood pigeon risotto

Our local smokehouse provides us with lovely smoked pigeon but if you are unable to source this, you could substitute it with smoked chicken or even smoked salmon or mackerel. (serves 4)

2 tbsp rapeseed oil
Unsalted butter
2 long shallots, diced
250ml volume of risotto rice
150ml good dry white wine
750ml vegetable or chicken stock, simmering
Handful grated parmesan
Small bunch of chives, snipped
4 smoked wood pigeon breasts, warmed
Parmesan shavings

Heat the oil and a knob of butter in a deep frying pan on a medium heat until sizzling. Add the shallots and stir until softening. Pour in the rice and stir until crackling and translucent. Add the wine, season lightly and stir until evaporated. Pour in a ladle of hot stock, and stir until drying out. Repeat until the stock is used up and the rice is just cooked al dente.

Remove from heat, fold in a knob of butter, parmesan, chives and more black pepper to taste.

Slice the pigeon and serve on top of the risotto in warm soup plates, garnished with parmesan shavings.

Wild mushroom pithivier with goats' cheese and red onion marmalade

This classic savoury is a popular starter with vegetarians and carnivores alike. It's not surprising as it has all the best things – crisp pastry, oozy cheese, sweet chutney and earthy mushrooms. (serves 4)

2 tbsp rapeseed oil
Large slice unsalted butter
500g mixed wild mushrooms
500g puff pastry
3 heaped tbsp red onion marmalade
100g goats' cheese
1 egg, beaten

Heat the oil in a deep frying pan on a high hob, add the butter and when foaming, cook the mushrooms, seasoning to taste, stirring regularly until browning and just tender. Tip into a colander to cool and drain.

Pre-heat the oven to 190c. Roll out the pastry between cling-film to approx. 2mm deep, then cut two large discs, side-plate diameter. Place the marmalade over one disc, leaving a one-inch border clear and top with the mushrooms and crumbled cheese. Egg-wash the border and top with the other disc, pressing firmly to seal. Egg-wash the top and bake for 20-25 minutes or until golden-brown and hot.

Apple tarte tatin

This classic French dessert is best enjoyed warm, not piping hot. We like it served with berries and vanilla ice cream. (serves 4)

300g puff pastry
60g caster sugar
60g unsalted butter, diced
6 medium cox apples, peeled, quartered and cored
Melted butter

Pre-heat the oven to 180c. Roll out the pastry to around 3mm thickness and at least 23cm wide. Lay the pastry on a baking sheet, cover with clingfilm and place in the freezer. Heat up the sugar over a medium hob in a 20cm ovenproof frying pan and cook without stirring until it becomes an amber-brown caramel and slightly smoking. Remove from the heat and stir in the butter.

When cool, arrange the apples tightly packed in a circle in the pan. Brush with melted butter and then bake for approx. 20 minutes until tender. Remove and very carefully lay the pastry over the apples but not the pan, tucking in the edges with two spoons. Prick through the pastry in several places. Bake for 25-35 minutes until the pastry is golden and crisp.

Allow to cool for 45 minutes before running a knife around the edge and carefully turning out the pastry, flipping it the right way up with the use of an inverted serving plate.

CHILDHOOD DISH?

Chicken livers. When I cook them now it reminds of me of when mum used to make a big steak and kidney pie. Also bacon which reminds me of Sunday mornings at home.

FAVOURITE COOKBOOKS?

We've got quite a few. I like *Larousse Gastronomique*; I like the way it's written more than anything else.

BEST MEAL EVER EATEN?

Chilli crab, a whole crab in a chilli soup. I was sitting by a river in Singapore and it was just unreal; it inspired my chilli fish chowder. Another was a dish cooked by Wayne Hawkins who used to own a restaurant in Southend called Paris. It was braised shin of beef with baby honey-roast vegetables – I came back and thought 'that has to go on the menu here'.

PERFECT DAY OFF?

My wife Catherine and I try to eat out in Essex or London as much as we can, taking the children with us – Liam is 11, Kiera 8 (or it might be 9 – I've not been home much since this renovation!). Another favourite is going racing with the family and watching my son compete in motorcross events or just a precious day relaxing at home!

TV CHEF MOMENT?

I was invited by Brian Turner to go on BBC1's *A Taste of Britain* with Janet Street Porter. They filmed us cooking trout with them on the beach at Mersea.

DARREN ON HIS...

KITCHEN GADGET?

I've just bought a Rational oven to go in our newly extended kitchen. We've not had one before, it cooks faster, saves energy, and you can get really accurate cooking.

FAVOURITE TIME OF YEAR TO COOK?

The summer when you can cook outside. I have a hotplate which I can cook everything from fresh fish to marinated meats along with fresh roasted vegetables.

CELEBRITY GUESTS?

Chris Galvin is always sending people down here. David Moore, the owner of Pied à Terre, has visited. The comedian Lee Evans, and retired snooker player Steve Davis, have also dined here on numerous occasions.

MIDNIGHT FEAST?

Vodka and tonic!

SIGNATURE DISHES

Starters

Mushroom & truffle soup

Oak-smoked salmon & orange pâté, peppered rocket & caper salad, melba toast

Cod & crab thai-spiced fishcake, wasabi mayonnaise, cucumber, chilli & ginger salsa, micro coriander

Mains

Confit shredded lamb bonbons, cucumber salad, plum dressing

Spiced pork belly, creamed potatoes, baby winter vegetables, apricot gel, maple & mustard velouté

Chilli fish chowder, coriander, coconut, lemongrass

Puddings

Apple tarte tatin, vanilla bean ice cream, caramel sauce

Chocolate & orange mousse, blackcurrant sorbet, pistachio crumb, vanilla brioche

Strawberry & clotted cream baked alaska

CHEF MENTORS?

I was lectured at college by Chris Galvin. I also worked for a couple of days with Marco Pierre White at his restaurant Harveys in Wandsworth. I was only 16 and he was about 22. He was immense. The restaurant was beautiful. But every four hours he'd need chefs to skim the stock, so he made them sleep on the floor overnight! I also admire Richard Neat at Pied à Terre and Tom Aikens.

Magic moments

The Magic Mushroom has been owned by Darren Bennett since 1996. It was originally a tearoom, but Darren, aged just 25 and with no business partners or investors, had ambitions to open a smart à la carte restaurant on the premises. The early days were a struggle, he admits, but he was lucky that loyal clientèle followed him, supporting his vision. "Creating this place is definitely one of my biggest achievements," he says, proudly.

Set at the front of the Barleylands Craft Centre, the restaurant is like a Tardis, the small outside appearance, belying the generous space inside. Extension work completed in May 2017 has increased the inside covers by 40 and provided a stunning new Mediterranean-style stone terrace with rattan seating and fire pits.

There's a natural flow between this exterior space with its sail canopy and glass balustrade for privacy, and the vaulted-ceiling dining room inside with its collection of elegantly-dressed square and round tables. The walls are glazed on one side, the other covered with silver-feather flock wallpaper, and hanging from the ceiling is a dramatic cascade of twinkling lights which spread sparkle through the room, bouncing off the vivid colours of oil paintings.

Fold-back doors allow for flexibility when it comes to accommodating private functions, from small gatherings to full-blown wedding breakfasts (the restaurant has a licence too), parties and corporate events.

Wine has been supplied by Braintree-based Brian Wilks & Co, for the past 15 years. "Brian travels to vineyards throughout world and has close relationships with wine and Champagne producers," Darren says. Bestsellers include Chakana Malbec from Argentina, and New Zealand Marlborough Sauvignon Blanc 'The Crossings'.

The Magic Mushroom Restaurant
Barleylands Road, Billericay CM11 2UD
W: magicmushroomrestaurant.co.uk
T: 01268 289963
E: info@magicmushroomrestaurant.co.uk
/themagicmushroomrestaurant
@MMRestaurant
/magic-mushroom-restaurant

Covers: 160 inside; 30 outside

Cost: average carte £40; wine from £16.95; beer from £3.50

Open: Tues-Sat L 12-3; D 6-9.30; Sun L 12-4

Details: private dining for 26; alfresco dining; wedding licence; wheelchair access; parking

Birds in the hand

Wood pigeon is a popular and sustainable staple on Sam Baxter's menu at this delightful village pub

Whether braised slowly to make a terrine, stuffed whole, or simply charred and served with pickled mushrooms, lentils and sweetcorn, wild wood pigeon is a regular on the menu of The Bull at Great Totham.

Head Chef Sam Baxter first met his pigeon supplier Robert Ashcroft when the latter popped into the pub one day last year. "He brought some wild duck breasts and we tried them and they were lovely, so we went from there. That was autumn 2016 and we've worked together ever since."

It's the sort of relationship Sam likes. With many of the ingredients for his pub menu sourced locally, he enjoys working with local producers such as Robert, or the likes of the Thorogoods who have been growing asparagus on their farm near Southminster for the past 25 years, or Lambton & Jackson smokehouse which supplies the hot smoked salmon to make a popular salad with picked fennel and caviar.

"We use quite a lot of pigeon and as much game as we can get during the season," says Sam. 'A dish of wild duck breasts with sweet potato purée, roasted cauliflower and a blackberry jus is really popular, as is pheasant breast with lentils and roasted parsnips. I love that it's sustainably sourced and delicious, and also that by shooting the birds we're helping keep the population in check – pigeon are a real menace for arable farmers. At this time of year, asparagus is one of my favourite ingredients though: you can't beat it cooked simply with butter and served with Parma ham, a crispy duck egg and mustard dressing."

We head out to Robert's farm at Tolleshunt d'Arcy. High Hall Farm – aptly named as it's perched on top of a hill with some far-reaching views of gently rolling Essex farmland – has been the Ashcroft family's home for over 100 years having been bought originally by Robert's grandfather. "The family used to work in the mills in Lancashire but moved to Essex – I think there was a fire and they had to relocate – and they first settled in Maldon to run a stud farm before moving here." The Ashcroft name is associated with the arable farm, D A Ashcroft & Son, and Robert's own business, Robert Ashcroft Game, which he has built over the past 25 years as a supplier of high quality game to many of the region's chefs.

Robert shoots the birds on the farm where a large pond and woodland provide an ideal habitat and the perfect spot to roost-shoot as the birds return to the trees towards the end of the day. The birds are not all shot by Robert, at busy times he buys them in from other Essex- or even Suffolk-based gamekeepers. February is his busiest time of the year for roost shooting, and then from March until May he shoots on freshly drilled crops with decoys.

Once he shoots his birds they are retrieved unharmed by Robert's faithful black labrador, Ben, before being prepped for sale in the large warehouse next to the house. In a typical year, he will process some 1,000 birds, selling them to his core of 50 or so regular chef customers plus a very small amount to retail customers.

Sam is eager to get back to the kitchen and turn the plump pigeon into something delicious. He works quickly, stuffing the bird simply

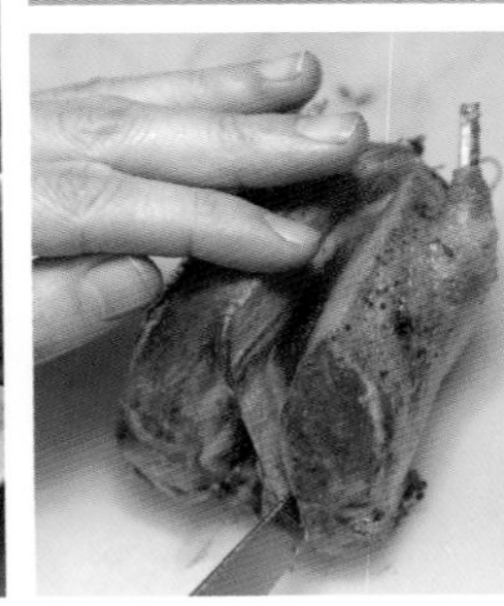

with wild garlic and thyme and tying it securely before searing it in sizzling herb butter. Browned, the pigeon is finished in the oven for five to six minutes. He slices it up carefully, allowing the succulent slivers to topple onto the waiting plate before garnishing it with pearl barley, beetroot and wild garlic leaves. In the autumn he might use butternut squash and some micro watercress.

Sam fell into cheffing, he says, starting as a part-time kitchen porter to earn pocket money. "One Saturday they asked me to go onto sandwiches as the chef was off sick. I got some nice compliments about the food and it gave me confidence. I suppose I couldn't believe that people were trusting me to send out food to diners when I was just 15 or 16. It made me feel like an adult, I loved it, and never looked back." After three years at Colchester Institute, he spent some time working in London for the ETM Group, John Torode at Smiths of Smithfield, Claridge's under Gordon Ramsay before returning to his home county in 2014. Sam worked at Le Bouchon Brasserie and Hotel in Heybridge and Greenwoods Hotel and Spa in Stock prior to working at The Bull and Willow Room.

"The food I cook here is a balance between classic pub dishes and finer dining. We do some dainty dishes but we also have our locals who just want some really good fish and chips." And while Sam says his real culinary influences are modern European food, his chef idol is Thomas Keller from the legendary French Laundry restaurant in Yountville, California. "His style is so simple but it's clean, maybe just three flavours on a plate but they'll be the most incredible three you'll ever taste."

Sam works in the business with his fiancée, Harriett. "We met three years ago when we were working at another restaurant in Essex, and we're getting married next April at the White Hart in Great Yeldham, a pub I used to work in," says Sam. "It's a beautiful location." The couple plan to honeymoon in South America on a road trip that will take in some of the best restaurants in the region, though for now their energies are focused on settling into their new home in nearby Tiptree. "I've been allowed half the garden for vegetables," Sam says. "Last year, the Swiss chard I grew in my father's garden found its way onto the menu here which was wonderful."

The couple clearly live and breathe a food-centred world and appear to be planning plenty of home entertaining, as Harriett jokes: "He's already bought a six-foot table and we've only just exchanged contracts on the house!"

Butter-roasted pigeon, pearl barley, beetroot and wild garlic

For this lovely seasonal game main course, I ask my butcher to clean the wing bones back on the birds for presentation later. For the beets, I use both classic purple and candy cane-striped varieties for interest and flavour. Start infusing the beetroot the day before. When ready to finish the dish, start the birds once the barley is simmering. (serves 4)

Striped beet rings

1 raw striped beetroot, peeled
75g caster sugar
150ml white wine vinegar
1 pinch fennel seed
1 pinch coriander seed
1 star anise

Very finely slice the striped beetroot on a mandolin and cut into rings with a circle cutter. Simmer the sugar, vinegar, fennel, coriander and star anise with 100ml of water to dissolve. Take off the heat and add the beetroot rings. Cool and chill to infuse.

Purple beet purée

1 raw purple beetroot, peeled

Cut the purple beet into chunks, bring to a simmer in a large saucepan of water and cook until soft. Drain, reserving the cooking water. Purée the beet in a processor, loosening with some of the water if needed. Season to taste. Sieve and reserve.

Pearl barley

Rapeseed oil
1 banana shallot, finely diced
2 garlic cloves, finely diced
75ml white wine
200g pearl barley
300ml chicken stock

Heat 2 tablespoons of oil in a hot, lidded, deep sauté pan over a low-medium heat. Add the shallot and garlic, and cook while stirring until softened but uncoloured. Pour in the wine and boil to reduce by half. Add the barley and stock and bring to the boil. Simmer for about half an hour until the grain is cooked but still al dente.

Pigeons

4 pigeons, oven-ready
4 garlic cloves
4 sprigs of thyme
60g butter

Pre-heat the oven to 180c. Stuff each pigeon with a garlic clove and a sprig of thyme, and if you wish, tie the legs together with butcher's string. Oil and season the birds. Heat a large ovenproof frying pan until smoking over a high hob. Brown the birds on all sides quickly. Add the butter, and when it is foaming baste the pigeons all over for a minute or two. Bake for 5-6 minutes. Remove the pan from the heat, baste again and leave to rest somewhere warm.

To serve

1 handful wild garlic leaves
Watercress sprigs

Quickly blanch the wild garlic in a pan of boiling water and drain well. Dry on a clean tea towel. Place the hot purée and barley onto warm plates. Carve off the breasts and legs of the pigeons and plate up, finishing the dish with the wild garlic, pickled beet rings and the watercress.

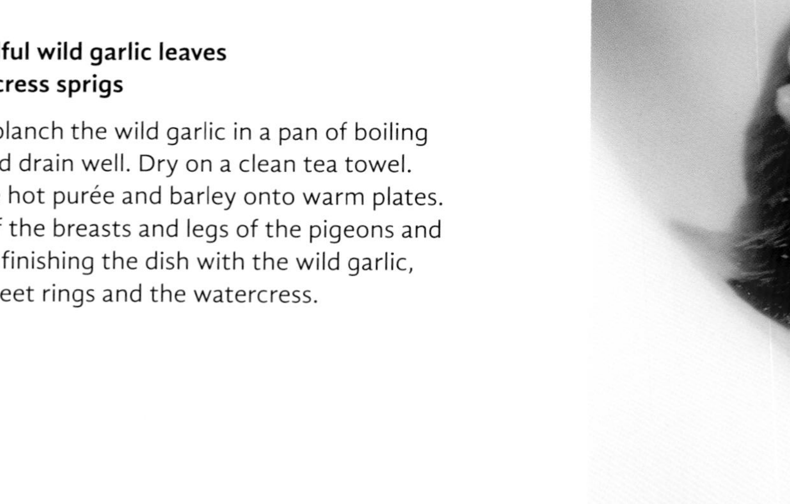

Oxtail ravioli

At The Bull and Willow Room, we garnish this rich, savoury pasta with a silky shallot purée, wild mushrooms and zingy leaves. (serves 4)

1 carrot, leek, onion and celery stick
Rapeseed oil
800g oxtail on the bone
100ml red wine
2 sprigs thyme
1 litre beef stock
500g fresh lasagne sheets
2 egg yolks
2 tbsp milk
Unsalted butter or more oil

Roughly dice the vegetables. Brown the meat and vegetables separately in a hot oiled heavy casserole. Add the wine, thyme and stock, cover and simmer for 3-4 hours.

Carefully empty into a colander over a large pan. Discard the vegetables and remove the oxtail.

Bring the liquor pan to the boil and reduce to a syrupy glaze before cooling. Pick the oxtail from the bones and fold with enough glaze to hold it together. Make into 100g balls. Cut the unrolled pasta in two lengthways. On one piece, space out the balls 5cm apart with a 2cm margin on the edge. Whisk the yolks and milk together. Brush over the pasta around the meat and lay over the other sheet. Press around each ball, cut with a ring cutter, giving a 2cm margin and then firm together.

Simmer ravioli in boiling water for 4 minutes until al dente. Drain and glaze with butter or oil plus seasoning to taste.

Vanilla pannacotta, treacle and poached strawberries

This simple set cream dessert is delightful against the texture and fruitiness of the berries. We also add honeycomb for crunch; it's easy to make with a little caution or you could just break up a shop-bought variety. (serves 4)

1 vanilla pod
400ml milk
400ml cream
60g sugar
3 gelatine leaves, softened in cold water
100g caster sugar
10 strawberries, hulled and quartered
50g treacle

Split and scrape the seeds from the vanilla pod. Place in a heavy saucepan with the milk, cream and sugar and heat, stirring continuously to dissolve the sugar. Turn off and infuse for 15 minutes. Stir in the gelatine to melt, heating if needs be. Sieve into a wide jug and allow to cool. Pour into prepared moulds and refrigerate to set for a few hours.

Line a roasting tray with baking parchment. Simmer 100g sugar with 100ml of water in a saucepan and remove from the heat when dissolved. Fold the strawberries into the sugar syrup and leave to cool. To plate up, smear the treacle on cold plates. Dip the sides of the moulds into hot water and tip out the pannacotta onto the plates before dotting with the berries.

Asparagus, sorrel purée, crispy chicken skin and broad beans

This calls for crisping and crumbling the raw skin from a very large chicken. The flavour and texture is well worth the effort! I use peppery nasturtium leaves for garnish, but any bitter leaf such as watercress or rocket will suffice. (serves 4)

Chicken skin
60g shelled broad beans
1 tbsp extra virgin olive oil
Flat leaf parsley, finely chopped
1 large handful sorrel leaves
20 asparagus spears, woody ends snapped off
Nasturtium leaves (optional)

Pre-heat the oven to 180c. Flatten the chicken skin between two baking sheets and bake for 20 minutes. Remove and cool.

Crush the skin in a large pestle and mortar. Boil the broad beans for a few minutes, drain and when cool enough to handle, remove the skins. Fold through with the olive oil, parsley and seasoning to taste.

Cook the asparagus in a large pan of boiling salted water for 3 minutes. Meanwhile blanch the sorrel in boiling water for 30 seconds, drain well, reserving some of the water to loosen the leaves if needed while puréeing in a processor.

Drain the asparagus and place onto warm plates, dot the purée around, sprinkle the skin over the top and spoon around the beans.

SAM ON HIS...

NEW INGREDIENT?

Fermented cabbage. Fermenting is another way of preventing waste, the next step up from pickling and smoking. We have Kilner jars everywhere!

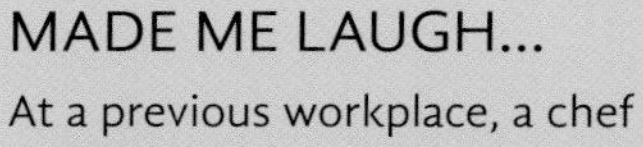

MADE ME LAUGH...

At a previous workplace, a chef forgot to take the insides out of a pigeon and cooked the whole lot. When he took it out of the oven and began to carve it stank the entire kitchen out! Mid-service we all had to untie his pigeons while opening all the kitchen windows!

MIDNIGHT FEAST?

Normally its hummus and pitta bread and a couple of glasses of wine

FAVOURITE KITCHEN GADGET?

Mine must be the dehydrator, almost like an easy bake oven which goes up to 65C. A big thing for me is to minimise waste; so for example, when I make baba ganoush, I burn the whole aubergine on a fire and take the insides out and blend them with tahini, cumin, coriander, olive oil and salt and pepper. Then, instead of throwing away the burnt aubergine skins I can dry them out even more and grind them into a powder and add them to mayonnaise.

WELL-THUMBED COOKBOOKS?

I have a lot of cookbooks at home. I always go back to *Larousse Gastronomique* and I also like *Coco* by Mario Batali where 10 of the best chefs in the world each choose 10 of their favourite chefs so it literally has hundreds of recipes.

DREAM JOB?

To have my own 40-cover restaurant with a little garden to grow my own vegetables.

FAVOURITE PART OF ESSEX?

Has to be Burnham-on-Crouch for me, walking down by the sea front there is perfect. We love the Ship restaurant and if I wasn't working here I'd quite like to work there.

COOKERY TIP OR CHEF'S CHEAT?

If you are cutting a pastry tart case, peel it with a potato peeler once cooked rather then cut with a knife and then you'll get much better edges.

IF I HADN'T BEEN A CHEF?

For a few years I wanted to join the RAF and to be a pilot. I was in the Air Cadets for a few years – then I found out that pilots weren't allowed to drink so I changed my mind! Maybe I would have been something else using my hands, perhaps a plumber or an electrician.

MUSICAL KITCHEN?

Oh yes it's Bob Marley, especially when everything gets a bit stressful. I turn some Marley on and everything calms down.

SIGNATURE DISHES

Starters

Chicken liver parfait, spiced apple compote, watercress and bread crisp

Salt baked ricotta, roasted and pickled beetroot, thyme granola

Pan fried scallops, brown shrimp, purple sprouting broccoli, almond butter

Mains

Chargrilled 10oz ribeye steak, peppercorn sauce, chips, grilled mushrooms and tomato, watercress

Pan-fried hake, sea food tagliatelle, sea vegetables

Grilled violetta artichoke, tenderstem broccoli, asparagus, new potatoes, smoked cheddar

Puddings

Sticky toffee pudding, toffee sauce, vanilla ice cream, brandy snap

Passion fruit tart, raspberry gel, vanilla mascarpone

Creamy rice pudding, biscotti, berry compote

FAVOURITE TIME OF YEAR TO COOK?

Springtime for me as there's asparagus, wild garlic and all the different fresh green vegetables. I'll often walk out with my dog to see if I can forage some wild garlic and my fiancée's god-parents have some that grows at the end of their garden which is handy.

The shape of you

If the painted sign on the pub wall wasn't enough of an indication, the life-size 2D shape of a bull cut from rusty metal to the side of the pub confirms that we have arrived at The Bull.

The pretty, whitewashed, pub-restaurant (it has two AA Rosettes and is recommended in the Michelin Guide 2016) is in a renovated 16th century former coaching inn at the heart of the attractive Essex village of Great Totham, just a few miles from Tiptree.

Inside, flag stone floors lead past wooden tables with crisp white linen napkins through to more intimate banquette seating. There are fresh flowers on the tables and the walls are painted a soothing sage green with an interesting feature wall filled with pewter tankards.

Owned by Satin Singh, who has a corporate finance background, since December 2016, and with a kitchen led by head chef Sam Baxter, The Bull offers a mix of robust, seasonal pub staples and a separate menu of more refined dishes. Adjacent to the pub is the Willow Room, a purpose-built space at the back of the pub able to seat up to 120 for private parties, musical nights, and a monthly supper club hosted by Sam and his team. Sam works closely with operations director Umesh Sewnundun, whose wealth of experience in front-of-house management includes 17 years with Le Talbooth Milsom Hotels.

A cottage in the grounds has been renovated to provide four double en suite bedrooms, each one decorated in a contemporary style with luxurious bedding, carefully chosen accessories, and all the other trimmings you'd expect.

The Bull and Willow Room
2 Maldon Road, Great Totham CM9 8NH
W: thebullatgreattotham.co.uk
T: 01621 893385
E: reservations@thebullatgreattotham.co.uk
/thebullatgreattotham
/Thebullandwillowroom /chefsambaxter

Accolades: AA two rosettes; AA highly commended 2013; *Michelin* 2013

Covers: 120

Cost: average carte £25; wine from £16; pint from £3.50

Open: Mon-Sat L 12-3; D 6-9; Sun 12-6 (closed Sunday eve)

Details: 4 en suite rooms; wheelchair access; dogs welcome in the bar

THE WHITE HART INN, MARGARETTING TYE
KAREN STEELE

Seasoned to taste

Lamb reared on the salt marshes of coastal Essex takes on a particularly delicious natural flavour. Karen Steele loves to bring its nuances to her popular pub menu

Tigers Island is an incongruous-sounding name for somewhere so peaceful. This green in the hamlet of Margaretting Tye – a place that could not roar 'rural England' more loudly if it tried – is a million miles from anything remotely fierce. It is peace personified. It perhaps wasn't the same in the 19th century when railway workers building the main line from London brought apparently untameable behaviour to the village – hence the 'tigers' part of the name – the 'island' referring to the fact that the nearby river Wid would often flood and cut the pub off. It goes without saying that the workmen frequented the pub on the green, The White Hart Inn.

Tigers long gone, the 250-year-old free house, owned by Liz Haines and Arthur Gilchrist since 2002, is now a favourite with walkers – the long-distance St Peter's Way that winds through pretty Essex countryside from Chipping Ongar to Bradwell on Sea passes right past the door – and for visitors wanting a tasty bite to eat.

That part lies in the hands of executive chef Karen Steele who is also in charge of the food at sister pub, The Star at Ingatestone, and works closely with head chef Rachel Diwell. We meet at Blue House Farm at North Fambridge, home to farmer Edward Hull's flock of Poll Dorset sheep and the source of the salt marsh lamb that Karen loves to put on the White Hart menu. "It's always on our menu due to its popularity with our customers. The salt marsh lamb when available has an even sweeter yet slightly saline flavour and customers like to know that it's local Essex lamb too."

She's familiar with the lamb, but it's her first visit to the farm and she's glad to see the way the animals are reared, living a seemingly idyllic outdoor life – as do Edward's cattle – on the marshes that run along the north bank of the river Crouch. The lambs are skittish, camera-shy at first, then curious about the visitors to their pasture. The tips of yacht masts peeking over the headland nearby are a reminder that the shoreline is close by.

"We are very careful how and when they graze so that we allow the meadows to flower," Edward explains. "The sheep just feed on grass apart from in the middle of the winter when we give our own cereal mix of home-grown lupins, barley and wheat to the animals that need it." Animals are slaughtered just five miles away and the meat distributed by Howard Blackwell who runs Blackwells Farm Shop, and supplies meat from his network of local farmers to restaurants and butchers through his Coggeshall-based Rare Breed Meat Company.

"It began really because we couldn't produce the amount of meat needed for our customers," Howard explains, "so I contacted farmer friends along the Colne Valley in north Essex. They are all smaller farms that can't do the whole job; it's not just raising the animals, there's the butchery and getting meat to market which is where we come in. I contacted Edward because we wanted to expand into niche traditional products such as his salt marsh lamb." It's clearly a happy two-way relationship. "Our link with Howard goes back over 10 years," says Edward. "It's nice to know you are producing something that is wanted and having a secure outlet for your products is reassuring."

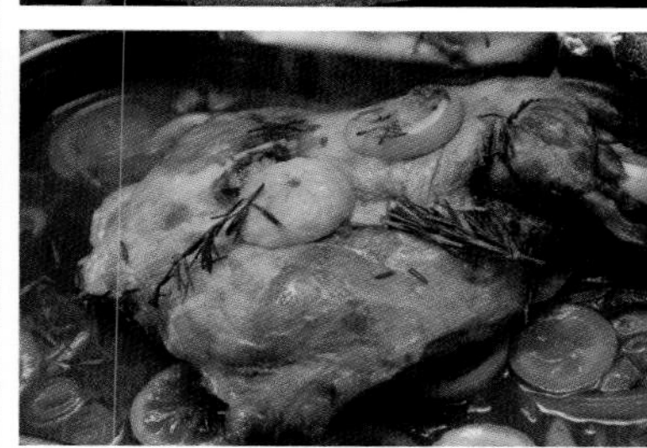

Karen is comfortable among the animals, having started her career with part-time work at an open farm and farm shop. "They reared pigs, cows and sheep, so I learned all my butchery as a teenager," she says. A subsequent job in a local hotel, despite making a success of it, made her recognise that she preferred the gastro pub scene. "Although I was due to be promoted, I realised I didn't like cooking 70 of one thing! I enjoy plating a different dish every few minutes, it broadens your skill base." So she moved to a local pub where she built the food offer from virtually nothing, becoming head chef at the age of just 22. She then did a similar job developing the kitchen at The Star at Ingatestone.

Now based at The White Hart, she works closely with her two sous chefs, James and Andrew. "They are both really stable, my rocks in the kitchen. I'm so proud of how well we are doing as a team. Working with Liz providing the food offer for both pubs is great because she leaves me to create the menus and be creative with the local ingredients. As executive head chef, I split my time between the two although here at The White Hart I'm more hands on."

As if on cue, James lifts a hefty lamb shoulder out of the oven. Pulling back the foil, the kitchen fills with the smell of slow-roast lamb, the richness cut through with the essence of lemon, pomegranate and molasses, added to the mix before roasting, and which gives a uniquely subtle, sweet flavour as it combines with the lamb juices to create a sticky jus. Karen leaves the shoulder to rest as she sears the rack of lamb in a hot pan simply with fresh thyme, before putting it in the oven till it's just done, still pink in the middle. She arranges a two-bone rack with a portion of the shoulder on the plate, alongside creamy dauphinoise potatoes.

Lamb is a favourite with White Hart customers, she says, and it's a dish she'll offer year-round. "In winter we cook rump of lamb with salt-crust baked celeriac and honey-glazed baby carrots with thyme. We also like to use every part of the lamb so in the summer we make lamb koftas serving them as part of a Greek mezze. On Sundays, you'll often find lamb shanks traditionally cooked, roasted with all trimmings, or as a special during the week cooked with warm spices like harissa, cinnamon and star anise, in a tagine adding fresh pomegranate for an on-trend twist.

Salt marsh lamb rack with pulled pomegranate shoulder, dauphinoise potatoes and spring greens

For this lovely combination of slow-braised rich shoulder and pink-seared cutlets, there is nothing like spring salt marsh lamb with its sweetness, and savoury, herbal flavour, but good regular lamb is of course also delicious. Savoy cabbage works well instead of spring greens and if you can't make or find lamb stock, a good chicken stock is the best substitute. Ask your butcher to score the fat of the racks for you. (serves 6)

Lamb shoulder

approx. 1500ml lamb stock
1 lamb shoulder
4 large thyme sprigs
6 large garlic cloves, peeled
Rapeseed oil
1 lemon, thinly sliced
250ml pomegranate molasses

Pre-heat the oven to 150c. Bring the stock to a simmer in a saucepan. Place the shoulder in a deep roasting tin. Chop a quarter of the thyme, seasoning and the garlic together and mix into a paste texture with oil. Rub this all over the top of the lamb shoulder. Pour the stock around the lamb and scatter the lemon in the tin. Pour the molasses over the lamb to coat it. Cover the tin tightly with a double sheet of foil and bake for 5 hours. Remove the shoulder and keep warm. Strain the liquor into a heavy saucepan and reduce to a sticky glaze on a high heat, before keeping warm. Shred the meat well with two forks, removing any gristle or fat. Place in a saucepan and fold in enough glaze to moisten well, cover and keep warm.

Dauphinoise potatoes

I prefer to use Maris Piper potatoes, but King Edwards work well too. Peeling the potatoes is optional; the skins are good for you, but look less pretty on the plate.

750ml single cream
Few thyme sprigs
4 large garlic cloves, thinly sliced
6 large potatoes, thinly sliced

Bring the cream, thyme, garlic and seasoning slowly to a simmer in a very large saucepan. Add the potatoes to the cream. Bring them back to a simmer for a few minutes. Carefully transfer to a heavy gratin dish with enough cream to come up two-thirds of the depth. Bake for 1 hour or until tender in the centre.

Rack of lamb

6 French-trimmed and scored two-bone racks of lamb
Thyme leaves, chopped
4 garlic cloves, crushed to a paste

Pre-heat the oven to 175c. Oil and season the cutlets all over and rub the fat side with thyme and garlic. In a hot, oiled frying pan on a high heat, quickly brown the racks all over and put them in a shallow roasting tray. Bake for 10 minutes and then rest somewhere warm for a further 5 minutes.

Spring greens

2 large heads of cleaned spring greens, stalks removed

Prepare a very large bowl of iced water. Thinly shred the leaves. Bring salted water to a boil in a large saucepan, add the greens and blanch for 2 minutes. Drain quickly through a colander and tip into the iced water, stirring around to cool. Drain again and set aside.

To serve

Unsalted butter
Pomegranate seeds

Place an oiled sauté pan on a high heat, adding two knobs of butter and the greens. Season generously to taste and toss well until heated through.

Onto hot plates, place a neat serving of the pulled shoulder, potatoes and greens before topping with the lamb cutlets and a scattering of pomegranate seeds.

Pan fried mackerel, beetroot tart, dill crème fraîche

A great light lunch, this tart looks nice served in individual portions as pictured above, though this recipe is for a large one to share. Whole sardines or sea bass fillets can replace fresh mackerel. (serves 6)

1 tsp pink peppercorns
300g crème fraîche
1 small bunch of dill, chopped
100g butter
75g caster sugar
6 cooked beets, thickly sliced
300g baby silverskin onions
500g puff pastry sheet
4 mackerel, fillets only

Crush the peppercorns and mix with the crème fraîche and dill, season to taste and chill.

Pre-heat the oven to 190c. Melt the butter and sugar in an ovenproof deep sauté pan on a medium heat without stirring, add the beetroot and onions and heat through. Carefully tuck in the pastry laid over the top. Bake for approx. 20 minutes until the pastry is golden. Remove and keep warm.

Score the skin of the mackerel, before oiling and seasoning. Heat a heavy frying pan or char-grill until smoking on a high heat. Brown the skin of the mackerel for approx. 4 minutes. Carefully flip the fish over, turn off the heat and cook through for a further few minutes.

Carefully invert the tart out of the pan with an upside-down plate. Serve the fish on warm plates with wedges of the tart and dill cream.

Lemon and thyme chicken, heritage tomatoes, fennel & baby leeks

A quick and colourful summer main course, this dish eats well with a good salad and new potatoes. You can butterfly the breasts using a rolling pin, by flattening them out between clingfilm. It's best to marinate the chicken and tomatoes overnight. (serves 6)

100ml rapeseed oil
1 lemon, thinly sliced
Few sprigs of thyme, bruised
6 chicken breasts, butterflied
3 large handfuls of tomatoes
100ml balsamic vinegar
1 bulb of fennel
12 baby leeks

In a bowl mix the oil with the lemon, thyme and pepper, add the chicken and coat well. Separately mix the tomatoes in bite-size pieces with seasoning and the vinegar. Cover both bowls and refrigerate.

Pre-heat the oven to 150c. Halve the fennel lengthways and then into thirds. Oil and season before baking in a deep roasting tin for 1 hour. Remove and turn up the oven to 200c.

In a deep pan of boiling salted water, blanch the leeks for a few minutes. Add the tomatoes and drained baby leeks to the fennel and toss together. Heat through in the oven for a further 15-20 minutes. Cook the chicken on a smoking-hot char-grill or barbecue until browned on one side, flip over and griddle again until fully cooked through.

Serve the chicken on top of the vegetable mixture.

Summer pudding with berries and clotted cream

This quintessential British summer dessert, here with my little twist, is perfect at the height of the berry season. If you want to add more variation, dissolve softened gelatine into the fruit juices and it will set into a lovely jellied slice when you cut it. This is especially useful if you plan to turn the pud out and decorate it before serving. A straight white loaf also works fine. (serves 6)

1 vanilla pod, split and seeds scraped
250g caster sugar
1 brioche loaf, thinly sliced
700g mixed fresh berries
400g clotted cream

Gently simmer the sugar in 400ml water with the vanilla pod and seeds in a saucepan for a few minutes. Add the berries and bring back to the boil. Set aside and allow to cool. Remove the pod.

Use one large glass bowl or 6 individual moulds. Discard the bread crusts and shape slices to line your mould(s), dipping them in the juices as you add them. Add a tablespoonful of berries, then a soaked slice of bread, repeating until the mould is half full. Add a spoonful of clotted cream, then more soaked bread and berry layers until the moulds are full, finishing with bread. Cover snugly and chill for 2 hours before serving.

KAREN ON HER...

DISH I'D CHOOSE WHEN EATING OUT?

I pick the thing which intrigues me, so perhaps flavours I can't imagine would work together, or a dish I've not used before on my menus.

WHY I'M STILL A CHEF?

It's a labour of love, and working in a really busy, successful place is a huge team effort. I don't want to let anyone down. You get such a kick and a great feeling of achievement when you get to the end of the week and you have positive feedback – it's just such a buzz!

FAVOURITE TIME OF YEAR TO COOK?

It has to be the summer when English strawberries and asparagus are available and when the sun is shining. You just seem to get all the best ingredients then.

COOKING TIP?

Most people know to rest meat when it comes out of the oven, but it's also important to rest it for five minutes before you put it in too. Also, when pouring a wet filling into a pastry tart case, put the case on a baking sheet, slide it into the oven and pour while it's there to save carrying it and slopping over the edges.

SIGNATURE DISHES

Starters

Greek mezze: falafel, lamb kofta, halloumi, houmous, beetroot & almond dip, honeydew peppers, pitta

Lambton & Jackson deep-smoked salmon mousse, juniper-smoked salmon, crostini, dill pickled beetroot

Retro king prawn cocktail, Marie Rose sauce, granary bread

Mains

The White Hart steak & ale pie, seasonal vegetables, potatoes

Cajun salmon fillet, braised coriander & lime rice, honey-roast peaches, mango salsa

Stuffed plaice fillet, crab & scallop mousse, seared scallop, pea purée, new potatoes, pickled radish

Puddings

Passion fruit curd brûlée, poppy seed tuile, exotic fruit

Chocolate bark mousse, pistachio moss

Salted caramel tart, peanut butter ice cream

FAVOURITE COOKBOOKS?

I have a ridiculous number! I prefer cookbooks that have a story to them as well as recipes. If the book tells you a little about the region the food comes from, the ingredients and how the chef sources them, then all the better.

MIDNIGHT FEAST?

Cheese is my downfall! I tend to graze quite healthily throughout the day but I could eat cheese day and night quite happily.

FAVOURITE KITCHEN GADGET?

Our Robot Coupe processor which we use so many times a day – as soon as it's washed it's back in use again! Also the Rational oven, you don't realise how good these pieces of equipment are until you have one and then you wonder how ever you managed before.

FAVOURITE PART OF ESSEX?

The Lavers near Ongar takes me back to my roots, and also Matching Green, both really picturesque parts of the county. I also just enjoy finding a country pub with a nice garden to sit in.

MY EARLIEST INSPIRATION?

I lived next door to my paternal grandmother growing up and she produced all food from scratch cooking from morning to night for her nine children!

FAVOURITE INGREDIENT TO COOK WITH?

Pomegranate is something I particularly like, and also molasses which goes particularly well with lamb.

Young at Hart

The White Hart Inn is proud of its public house roots which stretch back 250 years. But while the beamed ceiling, dark wood bar, plaques and artefact-filled cabinets nod to the pub's long history, this is very much a pub for today, having undergone a complete refurbishment since Liz Haines took over in 2002.

The outside is freshly painted, with well-kept gardens, shrubbery and hanging baskets making the approach appealing. A large gravel drive leads towards the substantial dining conservatory and there's even the village post box in the front garden amidst a parade of wooden picnic tables. The pub's boundary is on the village green, a space that Liz and her team look after, keeping it presentable for the whole village to enjoy.

Inside, tables are set elegantly with cloth napkins and sparkling glassware in all three of the separate dining areas, while two comfortable double bedrooms upstairs with views across the pretty countryside mean you can make a night of it if you like.

The pub's annual Beer Festival in July attracts crowds thirsty for a taste of 80 or so real ales and ciders, plus a Pimm's and gin bar. Year-round, the resident beers, Adnams Best and Broadside plus Oscar Wilde and IPA by Maldon-based brewer, Mighty Oak Brewing, are joined by guest beers from all over the country. Grape Passions in Witham and Cellar 12 in Writtle supply the wines, and a gin bar offers nigh on 40 different gins.

The White Hart Inn
Swan Lane, Margaretting Tye, Ingatestone CM4 9JX
W: thewhitehart.uk.com
T: 01277 840478
E: enquiries@thewhitehart.uk.com
/The-White-Hart-Inn-Margaretting-Tye
@whitehartmtye
/Whitehartinnmtye

Accolades: Waitrose *Good Food Guide*; winner, Pub of the Year, *Essex Life* Food & Drink Awards 2016; CAMRA Mid Essex and Chelmsford Recommendation 2016

Covers: 82 inside; 80 outside

Cost: average carte £25; wine from £13.80; pint from £3.60

Open: Monday-Fri L 12-2.30; Tues-Fri D 6-9 (Fri 9.30); Sat L 12-3, D 6-9.30; Sun 12-7.30

Details: open fires in winter; two double bedrooms; private hire available to seat up to 40 people; annual beer festival in July; walks from the pub; parking

CHURCH STREET TAVERN, COLCHESTER
EWAN NAYLON

Too much of a good thing?

Customers – and the owner – of the Church Street Tavern can't get enough of the Mersea Island oysters served up at this popular Colchester spot by head chef Ewan Naylon

"Do you need all these oysters?" Piers Baker, owner of the Church Street Tavern, sweeps through the kitchen and barely waits for an answer from head chef Ewan Naylon before picking a shell from the heap waiting to be prepped.

Ewan isn't too concerned. "When I was in Ireland I loved oysters so much I'd eat them for my starter, main and dessert. Now I think I've over-oystered! I still love to cook with them but I leave the eating to our diners – and Piers."

He's also thrilled to spend time with Richard Haward, seventh-generation oysterman and owner with his wife, Heather, of the famous Company Shed on Mersea Island. At 72, Richard still keeps a close eye on the business from the water's edge, his son Bram now the one to go out on the boat and land the oysters. "Together we get the blame for bringing the tourists to the island!" he jokes. "But you can't please all the people all the time!"

Dredged from the river Blackwater, the oysters are laid on the Hawards' own oyster beds. There they lay over the summer months in warmer waters to fatten and strengthen and take in rich nutrients from the surrounding marshland. This is what gives Mersea Island oysters their distinctive saline taste and silky plumpness.

Once at their prime, they are taken to the processing building – a simple wooden hut next to The Company Shed – that at low tide overlooks the hulls of mud-stranded yachts on the shoreline. There, the oysters are cleaned in large tanks of purified, running sea water before being packed in wooden boxes and either used in the Hawards' restaurant or sold to chefs in Essex and around the world.

Ewan has oysters on his menu all year, the Colchester Natives, a flat round oyster available from September-April (these spawn from June through to August) and Rock oysters which look like the name suggests and are available year round. Back in his kitchen,

"When I was in Ireland I loved oysters so much I'd eat them for my starter, main and dessert. Now I think I've over-oystered!"

he's in his element preparing a 'surf and turf' with sirloin beef and oysters. "It's a classic. The oysters add a distinct rich saltiness, and I use either Dedham Vale or rare breed beef that's been hung for up to 45 days to give it a full flavour. It's a bit special – you can't go wrong with this quality of beef and these oysters. This time of year of course we also have asparagus so this dish is a summery take on a classic."

It's not always an elaborate affair though. Oysters are popular year-round at the Church Street Tavern, prepared simply on ice with lemon, or perhaps in a light tempura batter and served with a punchy wasabi mayonnaise.

Ewan loves to cook his bold-flavoured, colourful, Mediterranean-influenced menu through the summer months. "It's frustrating to have to wait, but I love working with summer produce – aubergines, courgettes, tomatoes – and I'll only use these ingredients when they are in season. I also love all the summer fruits; the colours you can create on a plate are stunning. Summer is definitely my favourite time to cook; you get all the good stuff! Going through the winter trying to write a colourful menu when stuck with just a pear or an apple can bring challenges!"

Ewan grows chillies, tomatoes, runner beans and courgettes at his home. "If I have a glut I'll bring them to the restaurant but mainly I grow to cook at home. I love going to pick-your-own farms too on a sunny day, then coming home and cooking what we've picked."

Simple starters such as Violetta di Chioggia artichokes, ricotta, radicchio and walnuts, or a plate of bresaola with Taleggio, rocket and pine-nuts typifies his style. He might follow this with a gutsy seafood stew with aioli, or Mersea Island lamb chops with asparagus, girolles and bone marrow. Puddings could include a strawberry bavarois with pineapple salsa, or a classic baked Alaska with elderflower, honey and nougat.

Ewan started his chef career a bit by accident, working as a kitchen porter at a hotel on the ski slopes of Tignes in France. "I did A-level psychology, design technology and IT then at the end of the exams I was over-studied; I knew I didn't want to do that anymore so I took some time out. In Tignes it was just me and the head chef and sous chef so when the sous broke his shoulder I was asked to step up and was really thrown into cooking!" He was hooked, came back to the UK and took jobs in this country and France and Spain that would progress his career. "I always chased the best restaurants in town for a job. It was worth it; I always had to work really hard, but if you're in a good kitchen you learn from the best."

He's glad now to be settled in Essex, where he met Jess, a wedding event manager. "It's great because being in hospitality too, she understands the hours chefs put into their job!"

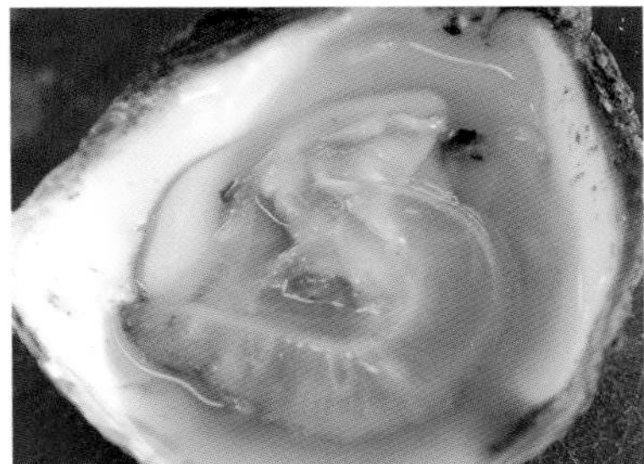

Rolled hereford sirloin, poached native oysters, girolle mushrooms, bone marrow and oyster hollandaise

A stylish take on steak for an elegant dinner party. The oysters add their essence of the sea to complement the meaty and creamy textures of the beef, marrow and the sauce. We match the grand 'surf and turf' flavours with asparagus and zesty crisp-fried pangrattato crumbs for textural and flavour contrast.

Rolling the beef achieves even cooking throughout. Any good butcher will do this for you but pre-cut sliced steaks would be a fair substitute. Ask your butcher to extract some bone marrow for you too. (serves 4)

Oyster hollandaise

5 native oysters, opened, juices retained
Half a lemon
2 egg yolks
100g clarified butter, warmed

In a glass bowl, suspended over a saucepan of simmering water, whisk together the oyster juices, a squeeze of lemon juice and yolks continuously until the mixture thickens and doubles in volume, then remove the bowl.

Off the heat, very slowly whisk in the butter a little at a time, incorporating well before adding more. Once all added, you should have a fairly thick, velvety sauce. Finely chop the oysters (or pulse in a processor) and fold them through the hollandaise. Season to taste and leave in a warm place until needed.

Pangrattato

50ml olive oil
2 garlic cloves, minced
Crumbs from 3 medium slices of white bread
Zest of 1 lemon and juice of a half
2 salted anchovy fillets, chopped
Pinch of dried chilli flakes
2 tbsp flat leaf parsley, chopped

Pre-heat the oven to 200c. In a hot frying pan over a medium heat, add the oil and cook the garlic for 1 minute, then stir in the crumbs, before mixing through the remaining ingredients. Turn up high and fry for 3 minutes, stirring well. Transfer to a shallow roasting tin and bake for 5 minutes until crisp and crunchy. Season with salt and reserve.

To serve

16 asparagus spears, trimmed
Olive oil
4 2cm deep sirloin steaks, taken from fridge 1 hour ahead
Unsalted butter
Few sprigs of fresh thyme
4 garlic cloves, flattened
400g clarified butter
12 native oysters, shelled
50g bone marrow, diced
200g girolle mushrooms
1 tbsp tarragon, leaves chopped

Blanch the asparagus in boiling salted water until just al dente and drop into iced water. Drain and set aside.

Over a high heat, cook your steaks in a hot oiled heavy frying pan, adding a few slices of butter, the thyme and garlic. Turn them over every 30 seconds until cooked to your liking (medium-rare taking roughly 4 minutes), basting as they cook. Remove to a warm plate to rest somewhere hot.

Heat a griddle pan on a high hob. Oil and season the asparagus before grilling for 3 minutes, turning to brown all over. Meanwhile heat the clarified butter in a medium saucepan over a low heat, when hot but not simmering, add in the oysters and gently poach without it bubbling for 3 minutes. Also at the same time, stir-fry the bone marrow and mushrooms for 2 minutes in a hot sauté pan with a knob of butter, seasoning as you go, finishing by folding through the tarragon.

Serve the rested steaks, asparagus and mushroom mixture on hot plates, finishing with the hollandaise, poached oysters and a sprinkle of the pangrattato.

Chickpea farinata pancakes

A summertime favourite I often cook when I have an abundance of ripe home-grown tomatoes, transformed into a delicious balsamic- and basil-marinated salad – perfect along with marinated mozzarella cheese and olive tapenade. (serves 4)

100g chickpea or gram flour
½ tsp fresh yeast
½ tsp caster sugar
1 egg
½ tsp baking powder
1 sprig rosemary, finely chopped
Unsalted butter
Olive oil

Whisk the flour, yeast, sugar, egg with a pinch of salt and 100ml of lukewarm water in a bowl until smooth. Cover and prove for 1 hour in a warm place. Add the baking powder and rosemary, mixing in well. Allow to sit for 10 minutes. Heat up 1 tbsp of oil and a knob of butter in a large frying pan on a medium heat. When sizzling, pour in separate small ladles of the batter and fry until browned on one side, carefully flip over and cook through. Keep warm under kitchen paper while repeating until the batter is used up. Serve when the batch of pancakes are all cooked.

Fish molee

A Keralan fish curry cooked in coconut milk, this spicy fragrant southern Indian dish is always popular. We serve it with pineapple salsa, cauliflower 'rice' and poppadoms. Any firm meaty fish works well, monkfish is ideal but I also use local Mersea cod. (serves 4)

Vegetable oil
1 large onion, thinly sliced
2 garlic cloves, minced
2 green chillies, finely diced (seeds optional)
2 tsp turmeric
1 tsp ground coriander
1 tsp ground cumin
3 cloves, ground
4 curry leaves
300ml coconut milk
400g firm fish fillet in 5cm cubes
Handful coriander leaf, shredded

Heat 1 tbsp vegetable oil in a deep sauté pan on a medium heat and cook the onion until soft but not coloured.

Add the garlic and chilli and cook a further 5 minutes. Add turmeric, coriander, cumin and cloves and cook for 2 minutes. Stir in the curry leaves, coconut milk and 1 tsp sea salt and bring up to a simmer. Cook for 20 minutes. Add the fish and simmer until it's cooked through, about 5 minutes. Adjust the seasoning and sprinkle with the coriander before serving.

Hendrick's gin and mint pannacotta

Light and refreshing, this summer dessert is definitely one of the Tavern's eye-catching signature dishes, served as it is, rather unusually, with gin syrup-soaked cucumber 'spaghetti'. Candied lemon adds zest. (serves 6)

Half a cucumber
500g caster sugar
150ml Hendrick's gin
200ml water
1 cucumber
3 gelatine leaves
1 litre double cream
4 sprigs of fresh mint
100g caster sugar

Liquidise the half cucumber into a juice and bring to a simmer in a large saucepan with the sugar, gin and 200ml cold water to make a syrup. Remove from the heat, cool and chill. 'Spiralise' the whole cucumber and fold into the syrup. Macerate for 4 hours or overnight.

Meanwhile soften the gelatine in cold water for 15 minutes. In a wide saucepan over a medium heat, warm the cream and mint to a simmer. Remove and infuse for 20 minutes. Return to the heat and stir in the sugar to dissolve before whisking in the gelatine along with the gin. Sieve into a large jug. Refrigerate, stirring well every 10 minutes, until it just starts to set on the edges. Pour into suitable moulds and leave to set in the fridge overnight.

Unmould onto cold plates, garnished with the cucumber and syrup.

FAVOURITE KITCHEN GADGET?

I wouldn't be able to survive without my Thermomix. It broke a couple of weeks ago and it was a nightmare!

DISH OF MY CHILDHOOD?

Roast dinner. Mum cooked every day and we had a roast every Sunday even in the summer when it was scorching hot. My Dad would say 'it's Sunday so we have to have a roast'. Whenever I cook a roast dinner it makes me think of home with everyone all there together.

COOKERY TIP OR CHEF'S CHEAT?

To open your oysters pop them into a warm oven for 3 or 4 minutes – it makes the oysters loosen their grip. It will save you wrestling with them. Also, if you have a glut of home grown tomatoes just put them in the freezer - the skins fall off easily when they defrost so you can cook with them.

SIGNATURE DISHES

Starters

Cod ceviche, fennel, orange, chilli, pomegranate, coriander

Bresaola, taleggio mousse, rocket pesto, pine nuts

Marinated violetta artichokes, burnt walnut pesto, herbed ricotta, radicchio

Mains

Hot & sour aubergine, flatbreads, soused onions, cumin & coriander yoghurt, toasted almonds

Seafood stew, crab aioli, garlic focaccia

Barbecued leg of lamb, roast fennel & tomato salsa, smoked aubergine & cumin crème fraîche

Puddings

Strawberries & cream – vanilla pannacotta, prosecco jelly, strawberry sorbet

Douglas fir bavarois, ginger-poached pear, meringue

Chocolate pavé, espresso semifreddo, chocolate & hazelnut soil

DREAM TRAVEL DESTINATION?

I'm off to see my sister who lives in India in October so I'm excited to visit all the spice markets with her and sample all the street food. She's lived there for the past six years so she sends me cookbooks and spice blends which I love experimenting with at home.

EWAN ON HIS...

FAVOURITE COOKBOOKS?

I have all of Nathan Outlaw's and Raymond Blanc's. Jess doesn't seem to mind my vast collection as they are all in the spare room. As long as they get put back on the shelves of the book cases she's all right with it. I have a few of Ottolenghi's too.

FAVOURITE PART OF ESSEX?

Frinton as Jess's parents have got a beach hut there. I also like Wrabness. I just love being by the beach.

MIDNIGHT FEAST?

I'm just not hungry at that time so I normally sit down and have a couple of beers. I put the radio on to unwind for a couple of hours before finally going to bed.

BEST RESTAURANT I'VE EATEN IN?

Nathan Outlaw's, I've eaten there a couple of times and I met him but I didn't tell him I was a chef. I like his food because it looks simple but you can taste that there's a lot of skill.

Bank on it

Step not that far from the crowds of Colchester, down a narrow lane just off Head Street, and you'll find a foodie haven just waiting to be discovered. Church Street Tavern – housed in a former savings bank – opened in 2014 with a trendy ground floor bar and stylish first floor restaurant, and has been a hit with locals since day one.

The restaurant, owned by Piers Baker who also owns the popular Sun Inn at Dedham, celebrates the best of Essex produce in a relaxed, informal space. Head chef Ewan Naylon and his team are determined to use ingredients which are of the season and bursting with native freshness, whether it's vegetables from a local farm or fish from inshore day boats on the Essex coast.

For warmer days there's a small alfresco seating area, while the ground floor is the place for a quick bite from the simple bar menu of soup, sandwiches and salads, or cocktails in the evening. Head upstairs where the full à la carte is offered alongside a pre-theatre menu till 7.15pm. There, a vibrant and eclectic mix of paintings, drawings, photographs, books and objets collected by Piers and other members of the team when on their respective travels, fills the space, with a colourful mural of culinary herbs and vegetables on the far wall being the eye-catching focal point.

Church Street Tavern
3 Church Street, Colchester C01 1NF
W: churchstreettavern.co.uk
T: 01206 564325
E: office@churchstreettavern.co.uk
/ChurchStTavern
@ChurchStTavern
/churchsttavern

Accolades: Waitrose *Good Food Guide*; *Michelin*

Covers: 80 upstairs; 20 downstairs

Cost: average carte £28.50; light lunches and pre-theatre menus available; wine from £16; pint from £3.50

Open: Wed-Fri L 12-2.30, Sat-Sun L 12-3; Wed-Thu D 6-9.30, Fri-Sat D 5.30-10

Details: vegetarian, vegan and gluten-free options; children's menu (weekends and school holidays); wine dinners; private hire available; wheelchair access; parking nearby

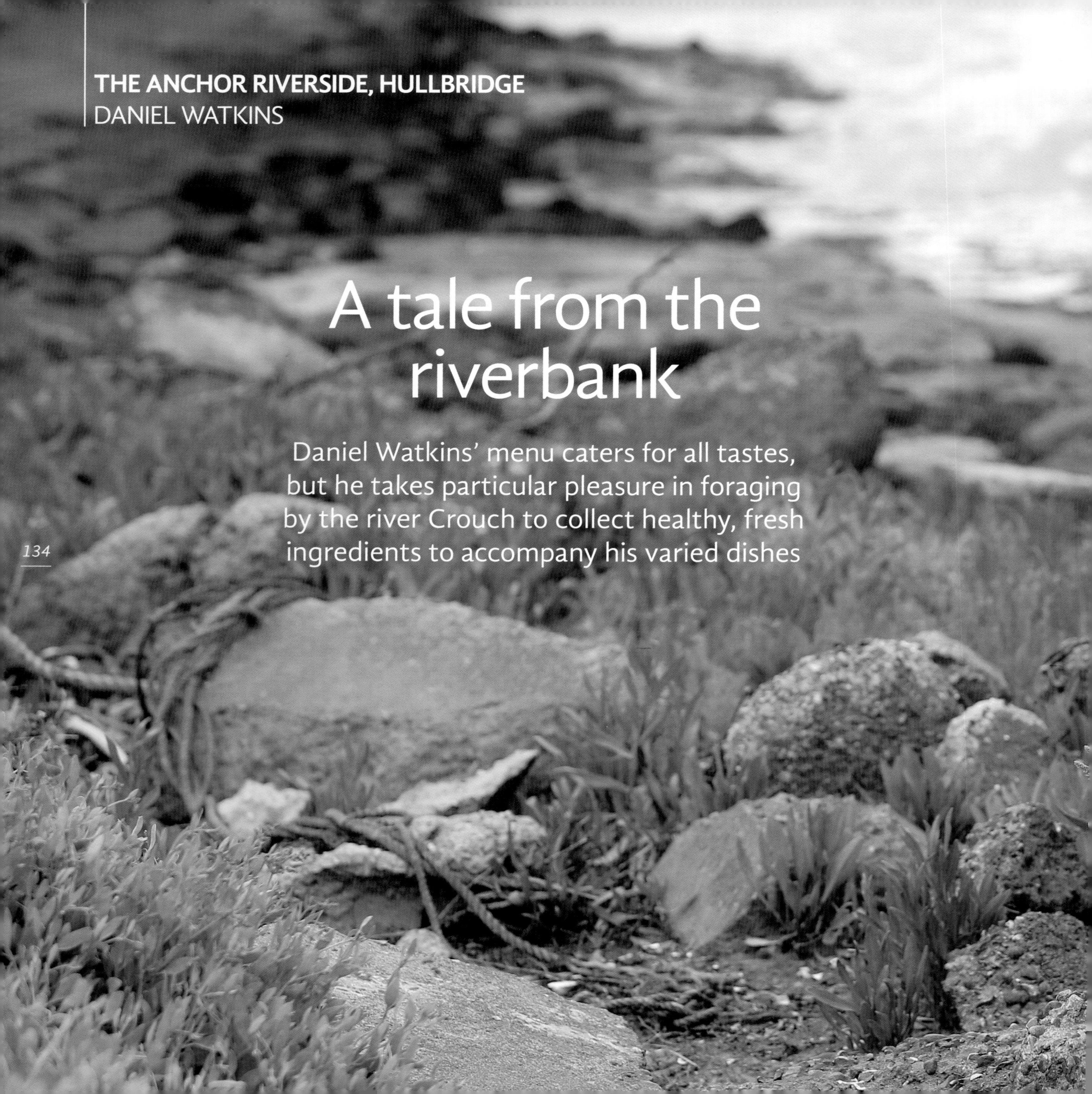

A tale from the riverbank

Daniel Watkins' menu caters for all tastes, but he takes particular pleasure in foraging by the river Crouch to collect healthy, fresh ingredients to accompany his varied dishes

BOSS

Once upon a time, there was a supremely versatile chef. He created a menu with the likes of sirloin on the bone or Moroccan-spiced lamb for meat-eaters, steamed halibut or tempura monkfish for pescatarians, a line-up of tempting desserts including a deliciously retro knickerbocker glory, a full menu for children, plenty for snackers, and even a dedicated menu for vegan guests. The latter is not surprising, because while Daniel Watkins, executive head chef at the Anchor Riverside in Hullbridge, cooks for all tastes, he himself is vegan.

"My household has been vegan and gluten-free for the past two years ever since our little boy, Freddie, was diagnosed as autistic," Daniel explains. "Sad as it sounds, since we made that change, we've eaten very, very well – there's no sugar or processed foods in the house, and certainly no more cheese on toast and a Snickers bar for me as a snack after service! I've lost a lot of weight, my cholesterol is fine, I don't get fatigued any more. I don't eat after 8pm at night, and I practise yoga twice a day too. Most importantly we've seen an improvement in Freddie's wellbeing."

It's not surprising, then, that Daniel wants to take us foraging for edible plants, scouring the banks of the river Crouch for the sea vegetables that add flavour, colour and texture to his dishes. "I create dishes using ingredients other than plants of course – and I taste them all too – but I really enjoy foraging and using what I find out and about. I'm lucky that the owners here have given me a pretty free rein with the menu. The first 10 years of my career, I was cooking fairly standard dishes, but here I feel my food has been able really to take off."

Daniel learnt to identify edible plants by reading *The Forager Handbook* by Miles Irving and thanks also to a couple of apps he downloaded, though he insists that even now he'll only pick the plants he is really familiar with. We head to the riverbank. Swans keep a close watch in the background as Daniel picks purslane, sea aster, samphire, sea rosemary, and sea beet. "You can eat all of the sea beet," he explains, "the green flower spikes, the reddish stems, even the roots which are like beetroot. It's great in salad – purslane is too – and sea aster and samphire are fantastic to dress up a fish dish."

With a wicker basket full of fresh waterside greens, we head back to the kitchen. Daniel poaches a fillet of turbot in a simple stock with fresh herbs and star anise, before turning his hand to the sea vegetables to make a pesto. He blanches the washed green leaves before drenching them in iced water to stop them cooking further. He then pan-fries them for a few minutes with just a little butter and Maldon salt before blitzing them with rapeseed oil, pine nuts and fresh garlic to produce a fabulously fresh pesto. "Rather than

"You can eat all of the sea beet, the green flower spikes, the reddish stems, even the roots which are like beetroot."

conventional basil-based pesto, this version has a salty edge making it a good accompaniment for fish," he says. He uses chef's tweezers to tease the turnip tagliatelle into a neat spiral, and sits it next to a spoonful of pesto topped with the turbot. He finishes the dish with kombu. "Kombu is a type of kelp used in Asian cooking, and it gives an umami profile to the stock, giving you a round, balanced flavour," he explains as he scatters fresh herbs, sea purslane, sea beets, samphire, and sea rosemary generously over the plate.

It's an enticing dish, made even more attractive by the stoneware plates Daniel loves to use. "Some are from [catering supplier] Goodfellows, made by Studio Mattes in Belgium – they made the plates I'm using today. A lot of companies offer me knives and kitchen equipment, but it's mainly the plates. I have so many I could do with running a Greek night!"

When he's not collecting sea vegetables himself, picking wild garlic in nearby woodland, or cutting herbs and edible nasturtiums, viola and calendula from his own beds at the Anchor, Daniel calls on a couple of local growers with allotments. "They bring me hens' eggs, corn on the cob, beetroot, spinach, parsley, courgettes, runner beans, squashes... all sorts, all organic and delivered to the kitchen door."

Daniel gained his experience working in hotels in London's West End, and was also hired for Directors' Dining before heading out to Essex to run the Waterfront in Harwich and then moving to the Anchor. "I've worked in some really cool places, but I've been more excited about the last seven years here than all the rest. I'm lucky that the owners keep refurbing the property, and it's the same with the menu. I'm constantly changing it and looking to do better dishes."

And while he is clearly happy with where the Anchor is now, he insists there's still room for improvement. "I have a massive respect for what we are doing here now, but I've always said we are only 60% there. I want to continue to take this place forward. Who knows, eventually I might even produce a cookbook of my own!"

Poached turbot, sea green pesto, turnip tagliatelle, buttered herbs

Fish and coastal vegetables such as sea beet, purslane, aster or samphire are a perfect combination. I urge you to try foraging safely for edible greens from the seashore, but caution and careful identification are essential. A regular pesto recipe would suffice but won't deliver in the same way on the palate. You can find the dried kombu and dashi in good supermarkets, Asian stores or online. The parmesan rind in the stock adds the sixth flavour, umami savouriness. We have pictured it with a lemon and yuzu dressing and some of our own herbs for a contrast. (serves 4)

Sea green pesto

50g pine nuts
80g sea beet leaves
50g parmesan, grated
150ml rapeseed oil
2 garlic cloves

Toast the pine nuts in a hot frying pan on a low-medium heat till golden, stirring constantly to avoid burning. Tip into a processor and process to crumbs.

Add the leaves, cheese, oil and garlic and purée smooth. Season to taste and decant before chilling.

Turnip tagliatelle

For this you need a Japanese mandolin or spiraliser to create ribbons of turnip. If not, slice the roots very thinly and then cut into thin matchsticks.

3 orange-sized turnips in ribbons

Bring a large saucepan of salted water to the boil, drop in the turnip and boil hard to blanch for 30 seconds before draining into a colander. Place under a running cold tap to cool and then drain before setting aside.

Poaching stock

50g dried kombu
10g dashi powder
1 bay leaf
1 garlic clove
1 parmesan rind (optional)

Place all the ingredients into a pan. Gently bring to the boil and simmer for 5 minutes.

To serve

You will need to juggle finishing off all the elements.

4 150g turbot fillet portions
2 large handfuls sea vegetable leaves
2 thick slices of butter
4 tbsp double cream

Just before serving, sprinkle the fish with salt on both sides and set aside in a colander for up to 30 minutes to firm up. When ready to cook, prepare a large bowl of iced water. Bring the stock to the boil and blanch the sea vegetables for 30 seconds, before removing with a slotted spoon, draining and then stirring through the iced water. Drain off and set aside. Keep the stock simmering, drop in the fish and gently heat until just cooked through and flaking.

Meanwhile heat 1 slice of butter and the cream in a heavy sauté pan and add the turnip, toss through with tongs to coat until hot and season generously to taste. Loosen with a little of the stock if necessary.

Melt the remaining butter in a frying pan on a high hob until foaming before tossing through the sea vegetables to heat through. Remove the fish from the stock with a fish slice and sit on a clean tea towel to drain.

Using tongs, place the turnip onto hot plates, topped with the fish, scatter on the sea vegetables before finishing with the pesto.

Asian-cured salmon

This is an oriental version of the famous Scandinavian gravadlax, raw fish marinated in a flavoured sugar-salt mix to cure it overnight. We keep the classic familiar flavour with our sweet-sour dill-pickled cucumber on the side along with oyster mayonnaise. (serves 6 for a starter)

250g Maldon sea salt
375g caster sugar
2 star anise, ground
1 tsp coriander seeds, ground
zest of 1 lime
zest of 1 lemon
500g piece of fresh skinless salmon

Mix the first 6 ingredients well together in a food processor.
In a deep roasting tray, lined with double sheets of clingfilm, make a bed of one third of the salt mix to fit the size of the fish. Lay on the salmon skinned-side down and pack the rest of the salt on top. Wrap up the fish tightly with the clingfilm. Put another tray on top, then severall heavy tins. Refrigerate overnight.

To serve, wash the fish under the cold tap, dry with a clean tea towel and then kitchen paper. Slice down the fish vertically into fine slices and arrange on cold plates.

Grilled asparagus, goats' cheese, hazelnuts and nasturtiums

Cultivating nasturtiums is well worth it – their peppery flowers and zingy flavour and colour make an interesting dressing (the young leaves are great in salads too). Rocket or watercress makes a good dressing instead, just adjust quantities to suit your taste. We add a crisp goats' cheese wafer and a green mayonnaise made with charred asparagus to the dish. (serves 4)

150g nasturtium flowers
110ml rapeseed oil
1 tsp good French mustard
25g ice
Splash cider vinegar

Liquidise all the ingredients together and season to taste before chilling.

2 bunches asparagus spears, trimmed
Rapeseed oil
100g goats' cheese, crumbled
2 tbsp hazelnuts, toasted and crushed

Oil and season the spears.
Heat a char-grill or barbecue until smoking and griddle all over until charred for a few minutes. Transfer to a bowl and toss with oil and seasoning to taste.

Serve on warm plates, drizzled with the dressing and scattered with the cheese and nuts.

Millionaire's shortbread

Kids big and little will love this rather rich dessert, perfect if you have a sweet tooth. For the caramel cream filling, I use a milk jam mousse but here I suggest you use ready-made caramel and softly whipped cream. We finish it with a little gold leaf and home-made chocolate 'oreo'. (serves 4)

50g egg yolk
50g caster sugar
125ml double cream
125ml milk
120g dark chocolate, grated

Whisk up the yolks and sugar in a food mixer. Bring the cream and milk to a simmer in a heavy saucepan and whisk in a slow drizzle into the egg. Return to the pan, stir constantly over a gentle heat till steaming. Set aside and cool for 15 minutes before adding the chocolate and then mix well. Decant to a bowl and chill.

125g butter, diced
180g plain flour
60g caster sugar

Pre-heat the oven to 170c. Beat all three ingredients in a mixer for 3 minutes, clingfilm the dough and chill for 30 minutes. Roll out thinly and cut into shapes before baking on parchment-lined metal trays until cooked and light-golden.

I tin ready-made caramel
275ml double cream, softly whipped

Arrange the shortbread, chocolate, caramel and cream on cold plates.

DANIEL ON HIS...

WHAT INFLUENCES ME?

I eat out a lot. I particularly enjoy Nordic cuisine, but I also love Sat Bains' food, and I find Japanese cooking fascinating too. I take a little bit of everything, but I still like to cook in a clean, simple, tidy manner, and I teach my team not to put things on the plate that don't need to be there. We also try not to waste anything – for example, the cucumber skins we don't use, we dry and grind down and add to the dish rather than peel them and simply throw the skins away.

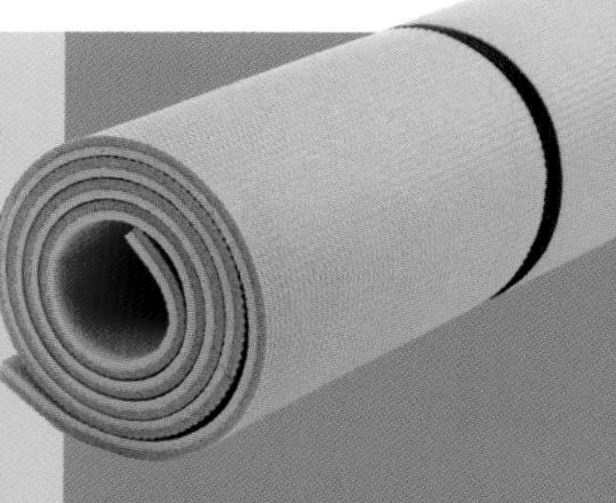

WHERE I'M HAPPIEST?

Alone in the dark somewhere; 'chef' is the most used word in this kitchen! Seriously, I do hide some days when I'm at work – we have a couple of sheds at the back of the restaurant! When I'm out with my family of course I'm hugely happy, but I also love to practise my yoga, just for the stillness and the quiet.

DISH OF MY CHILDHOOD?

My mum brought us up vegetarian so I can't say something like the aroma of roast pork! Saying that, veggie roast dinners where always good and my mum was always making apple pies and crumbles, I seem to remember.

BEST DISH I'VE EVER EATEN?

I've been to Restaurant Dill in Reykjavik a few times. Normally, it's 10 courses of Nordic local, organic food. I've eaten smoked goose heart and reindeer, lots of different pickling and fermenting techniques, sea truffle and catfish. I just fell in love with the place!

SIGNATURE DISHES

Starters

Tandoori scallops, lime pickle, mint yoghurt, cauliflower, peanut crumb

Smoked brisket in a steamed bun, pickles, radish, xo mayonnaise

Moroccan-spiced lamb, harissa mayonnaise, yoghurt, flatbread

Mains

Tempura monkfish, sweet potato dhal, mango, peanut crumb, masala mayonnaise

Apple & cider glazed pork belly, apple, caramelised turnip, herb dressing

Sweet potato mee rebus curry, cauliflower, romanesco, asian nut granola, rice noodles, miso

Puddings

Glazed lemon tart, steeped raspberry

Sticky toffee pudding, vanilla ice cream, toffee sauce

Millionaire shortbread, crémeux, caramel mousse, hazelnut, tonka bean ice cream

WHO WOULD YOU LIKE TO COOK FOR?

Because I find him incredibly interesting, I'd love to have cooked for Abraham Lincoln. Kelly Brook too, but not for the same reason!

FAVOURITE COOKBOOKS?

I have a massive collection, my favourite is Sat Bains' *Too Many Chiefs Only One Indian*, and I love René Redzepi's *A Work in Progress*, and *North: the New Nordic Cuisine of Iceland* by Gunnar Gislason who owns Restaurant Dill in Reykjavik. Those are well-used favourites.

BIGGEST EXTRAVAGANCE?

My Nessmuk knife. The handle is made from 2,000-year-old bogwood.

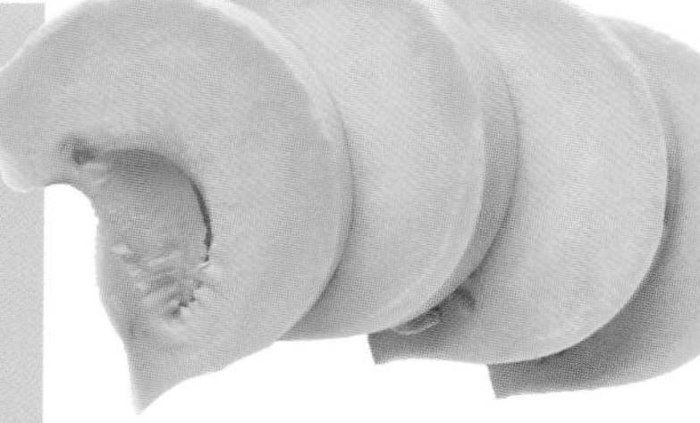

FAVOURITE TIME OF YEAR TO COOK?

Autumn, and perhaps a little bit of spring. I love slow-braising and cooking with squashes and roots.

FAVOURITE KITCHEN GADGET?

Dehydrators and my Thermomix, but I love my Yakitori Japanese barbecue too. The asparagus I did today was done on there.

WHY I'M A CHEF?

I fell into it, but then fell in love with it. I also loved photography. I left college with experience in both under my belt, so I could have gone either way. Now I cook food and photograph it.

Take me to the river

The Anchor Riverside, set at the point where the river Crouch meets the shore at Hullbridge, takes a bit of finding, but you'll be glad you made the effort. The restaurant holds a *Michelin* Bib Gourmand, and is the sort of place that combines stylish dining with a more informal family- and dog-friendly environment with ease.

The building is flooded with light, both in the main restaurant and the Orangery with its floor-to-ceiling windows that open back fully, weather permitting. In the warmer months, this is a place to linger into the evening and enjoy stunning, uninterrupted views as the sun sets over the moored boats on the water at the bottom of the garden.

The galley-style kitchen (workplace for Daniel Watkins who has headed up the kitchen here since 2010, and his brigade) is visible from the glamorous main restaurant with its cream leather seating, well-spaced bare wood tables, and four booths that are ideal for small gatherings wanting a bit of privacy. Outside, there are rattan sofas on a suntrap terrace, while from the back of the restaurant there's direct access through a picket fence to the riverside, and a well-tended, dog-friendly garden. Here there are various seating areas, and an outside bar (in addition to the large indoor cocktail bar) and cookhouse, with enough space for up to 150 diners. All around the grounds are beds of herbs and edible flowers which the chefs use in their cooking.

Alongside Daniel's menu, the wine list romps through perennial favourites, and there is a good selection of locally-brewed ales including Brewers Gold from nearby Crouch Vale Brewery, Anchors Aweigh (Woodforde's) and several from Braintree-based Bishop Nick Brewery.

The Anchor Riverside Pub & Restaurant
Ferry Road, Hullbridge SS5 6ND
W: theanchorhullbridge.co.uk
T: 01702 230777
E: info@theanchorhullbridge.co.uk
/theanchorhullbridge
@AnchorRiverside
/chefdanielwatkins

Accolades: Waitrose *Good Food Guide*; *Michelin* Bib Gourmand; winner, Outstanding Experience award, *Exquisite Essex* Excellence Awards 2015

Covers: 150 inside; 300 outside during summer

Cost: average carte £35; wine from £20.95; beers from £3.80

Open: Restaurant Mon-Sat L 12-3; D 6-9.30; Sun 12-8. Bar menu Mon-Fri 3-9; Sat 3-6.

Details: gluten-free and vegan menus; cocktail bar/lounge; beer garden; wheelchair access; parking

Love a duck

Richard Lewis wears his unshakeable passion for duck on his sleeve – literally – and shares his pleasure in cooking the bird with customers at his stylish country pub

Some chefs just say they love an ingredient, others may put their name to a promotional campaign supporting it, but not quite as many will wholeheartedly commit to the feeling by inking their love forever into their skin. Richard Lewis's short-sleeved whites reveal the 'I heart duck' tattoo with a chilli pepper – a nod to his fondness also of fiery oriental cooking – underneath it, and a few other food-related designs on his forearms. "I had the duck tattoo done in 2016. I liked the 'I heart NY' ones so I thought it would be fun to do a take on that."

Duck is rarely off the menu at The Green Man, the pub-restaurant in Lindsell, near Dunmow, that Richard has run since spring 2014 with business partners Scott Reid and Chris Turnell, who is also restaurant manager. It might appear on the tapas menu in a confit duck and foie gras terrine served with brioche and a plum and apple chutney, or as a smoked duck starter, or as 'duck and waffle'. "For that dish, the duck is marinated in five spice," Richard explains, "then we confit the leg, and it's served crisped up with a homemade waffle, mustard maple syrup and a fried egg. It goes down very well!"

Richard is keen to head down to Great Clerkes Farm in the north Essex village of Little Sampford, just minutes from The Green Man. Simon Hughes is in charge there, the third generation to rear free-range ducks and other poultry on the farm. "We produce over 5,000 ducks and geese across both of our busiest Easter and Christmas periods," he says.

"All our birds are reared here free-range from day-old chicks and we look after every aspect of their lives to ensure the highest welfare standards. There are a couple of ponds and the birds can literally roam wherever they like," he explains. It's an attractive sight, his Aylesbury-cross ducks wandering happily around the farmyard, each one a pristine white contrast to the black barns and lush green fields that surround the farm. They are fed on home-grown wheat supplemented by special duck pellets made by Marriage's Mills.

Despite his love of ducks, Richard has never held one before. Naturally wary, the birds bid a hasty retreat on our arrival until one of the Feast crew adds duck-wrangling to his list of skills, and Richard finds himself face to beak with a beautiful white bird with Simon's terrier, Morph, insisting on being part of the picture too.

Back in the kitchen, Richard portions the whole duck to create a neat breast and leg ready to roast and confit. With three pans spitting and sizzling on the stoves, and the leg in the oven, Richard seasons the duck breast and puts it skin side down into the hot pan, rendering the fat until it turns golden brown, before finishing the meat off in the oven, then letting it rest and slicing it.

He plates up the tender pink breast alongside the leg and livers, finishing with creamy mash, caramelised onions, braised Savoy cabbage, and a glistening jus. He's pleased with the end results. "I'm surprised my mum's not also here," he jokes. "She's been dropping 'is the photoshoot today?' hints for ages now!"

This is the sort of 'classical with a contemporary twist' cooking that Richard likes best, and when it's not a duck dish, he'll be using locally-reared pork from Priors Hall in Great Dunmow, pigeon, plus game in season shot by local gamekeepers.

Richard learnt his trade in Essex, sharing stoves with the French chefs at the Churchgate Street hotel in Old Harlow. "Eighty per cent of the chefs there were French. They were a bit hard on you as a young chef. I used to get shouted at regularly, but it gave me a good grounding. So I suppose I'm French-trained!" He invariably tucks a nod to the orient into his cooking, however. "There's only so many times you want to peel a potato! I like to do Thai, Korean and Japanese dishes, and we also do tapas from a different part of the world which we change every two months – the oriental tapas is always the most popular, though."

Richard worked in Dunmow then Bishop's Stortford before going into business with Chris Turnell and running an outside catering company and providing agency chefs for other restaurants. "I probably worked at 40-50 different places setting up restaurants for other owners. It really helped us when opening our own restaurant because we had seen first-hand what was good and bad." Richard and Chris then joined forces with Scott Reid, and when The Green Man came on the market, the trio decided to buy it.

Three years on, and having moved from Dunmow to Thaxted with his girlfriend Lucy and their young daughters, Pip and Tilly – "it's so peaceful, the first time we've had a full night's sleep in two years!" – things seem to be falling into place for Richard. How long will it be before Richard adds a green man to the inks on his arms?

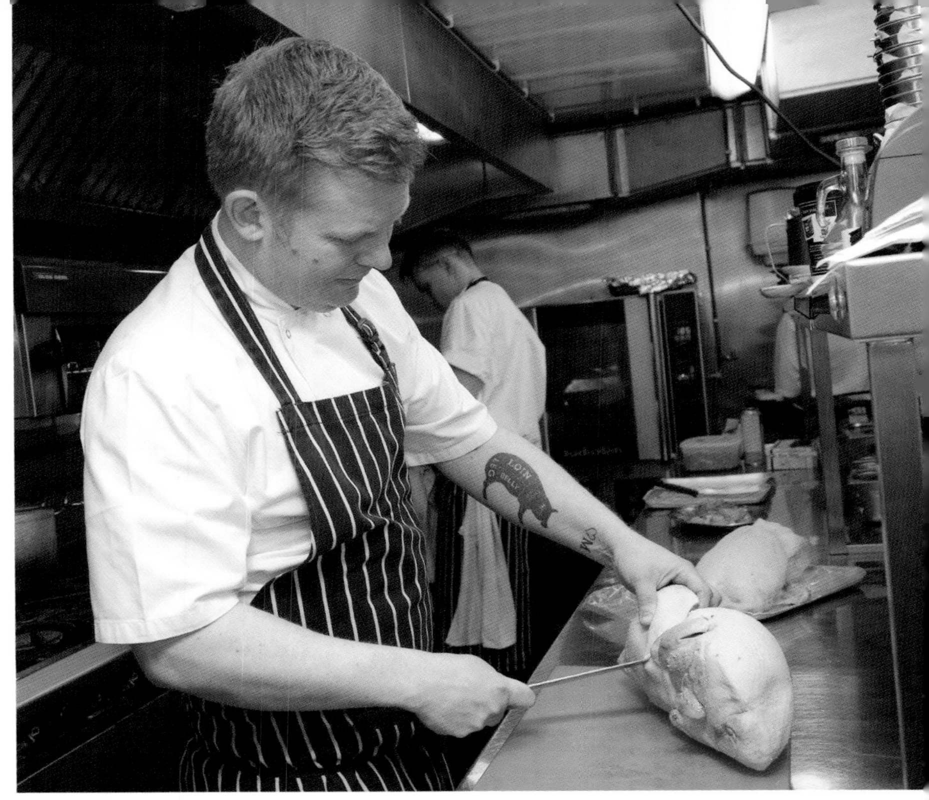

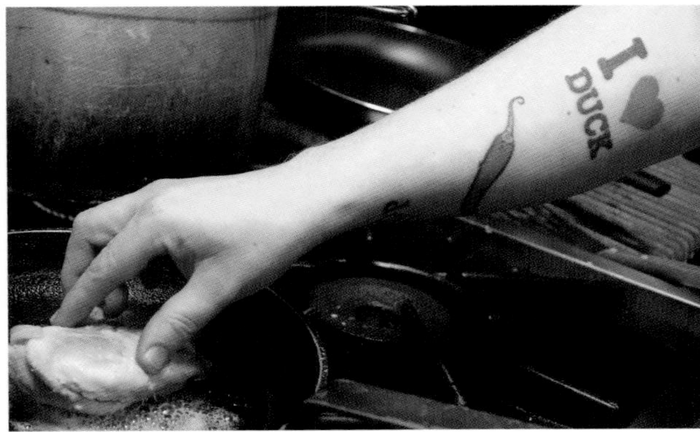

Trio of duck: roasted breast, confit duck leg and duck livers

I love duck as my tattooed arm declares permanently. And this, one of my all-time favourite meat dishes after 12 years of cooking it, uses nearly all the duck and it is a signature staple on the Green Man menu. I love the varying flavours and textures of how the recipe cooks the three different cuts.

We chefs do like serving our duck breast pink and the livers rare so they are juicy and succulent but if you do want to cook them through, try not to dry them out otherwise they will go rather solid and rubbery. I like to serve this plateful of glorious farmyard duck with silky potato mash and quick-braised Savoy cabbage. Prepare the duck legs ahead of time, starting 48 hours before required.

Confit duck legs

4 duck legs, oven-ready
1 bulb of garlic, cloves roughly chopped
1 good sprig of thyme, chopped
200g duck fat

Put the duck into a close-fitting container, rub generously all over with salt, garlic and thyme, cover and refrigerate overnight.

The next day pre-heat the oven to 120c. Remove the legs from the fridge, transfer to a snug roasting dish and cover with the duck fat. Cover with foil and bake for 2-3 hours. Remove from the oven, check the meat is tender and flaking, cool, then store the legs refrigerated in the fat.

Caramelised onions

Knob of unsalted butter
10 white onions, finely sliced
50g caster sugar
Splash of balsamic vinegar

Place the butter in a heavy lidded frying pan over a low-medium heat, melt and then add the onions. Cook these down over the lowest heat until soft, stirring occasionally. Add the sugar and balsamic, bring to a gentle simmer and then turn right down again, stirring every few minutes until golden and caramelised.

Red wine jus

1 medium onion, celery stick, carrot and small leek, all roughly chopped
Good local rapeseed oil
200ml red wine
600ml good veal or beef stock

Fry the vegetables in a hot saucepan with a little oil until light golden. Pour in the red wine, bring to a rolling boil and reduce to half the volume. Add the stock, reduce to just one third volume and a gravy-like texture. Cool and sieve the jus, discarding the vegetables.

To serve

4 duck breast portions, skin scored
4 duck livers, cleaned and dried

Pre-heat your oven to 200c. Place the duck legs in a roasting tin and bake for 20 minutes to crisp up. Season the breasts on both sides. Heat up a small frying pan on a high hob and pan-fry the breast skin-side down until golden-brown then turn over and roast in the oven for around 8 minutes or to your liking. Remove to a carving board somewhere warm to rest. While the breast is resting, heat an oiled frying pan and sauté the livers for about a minute each side, being careful not to overcook them.

Slice the breast and arrange on hot plates with the leg, liver and onions and chosen vegetable. Drizzle with gravy.

Creamy glazed rice pudding with Tiptree raspberry jam

Mine and my Dad's favourite on a winter's day! Great for a family Sunday lunch because you can make it in advance and then glaze and serve when required. (serves 4)

500g short grain rice
500ml rich whole milk
500ml double cream
200g caster sugar
2 vanilla beans, seeds scraped and pods
Zest of 2 oranges, removed with peeler
1 cinnamon stick
Pinch of ground nutmeg

Place all of the ingredients in a heavy saucepan, heat gently to simmering point, stirring well, and cook over a low heat for 20-25 minutes until the rice has softened and absorbed the liquid. Discard the vanilla pods, cinnamon and orange zest and place into a dish or individual pots. Cool and refrigerate.

Golden caster sugar to glaze
Tiptree raspberry jam

Scatter with a good layer of caster sugar and using a chef's blowtorch carefully glaze the tops like a brûlée.

Serve with lots of jam on the side.

Rustic ham stew and dumplings

This is a perfect dish for a cold night in as a hearty supper or have it as a great soup starter. (serves 4)

2 ham hocks
1 head of celery, 1 onion,
1 leek, 4 carrots, all chopped
1 bulb of garlic, halved
Few sprigs of thyme

Place all the ingredients in a large stockpot, cover with water and simmer for 4 hours, keeping the water level topped up to cover the meat. Carefully remove the hocks and set aside. Strain the stock, cool and refrigerate. When cool enough to handle, pick the meat from the bones in chunks, and refrigerate.

100g self-raising flour
50g suet
Pinch of salt
Chopped parsley

Mix together in a large bowl and lightly bring together with sufficient cold water to form a firm but soft dough. Roll into walnut-sized balls.

1 swede, 3 carrots, 2 potatoes, all diced
Handful of defrosted peas

Pour the stock into a large saucepan, add the diced vegetables and simmer for 15 minutes until cooked. Add the dumplings and cook for another 10 minutes. Add the ham and peas, bring to a simmer, adjust the seasoning and serve.

Roast cod with sauté new potatoes, chorizo, samphire and red pepper pesto

A lovely easy summer dish great for dinner parties. (serves 4)

1 medium jar of roasted red peppers
50g grated parmesan
50g toasted pine nuts
Handful of rocket
200ml of good local rapeseed oil
4 thick cod fillet steaks
12 cold, cooked new potatoes
125g mild or spicy chorizo sausage
400g samphire

For the pesto, pulse the first 5 ingredients in a food processor until a coarse sauce texture (or use a handblender).

Pre-heat the oven to 180c.
In a medium-hot oiled ovenproof frying pan, pan-fry the seasoned cod steaks skin-side down until the skin is crisp and golden. Turn over and cookfor 8 minutes or so.

Thickly slice the new potatoes and chorizo. In another frying pan, sauté the potatoes until lightly-golden, add the chorizo and fry for another minute or two. Place in the centre of warm plates, drizzle around with pesto and top with the cod steaks and samphire.

DISH OF MY CHILDHOOD?

My mum's lamb stew and dumplings which inspired the ham hock stew I've prepared today. Also, we used to have caravan holidays in France as children, and we'd eat mussels and chips – that dish is what inspired me to become a chef!

MUSICAL KITCHEN?

Definitely! We like rock music and Magic FM with plenty of 70s, 80s and 90s music. It does help to get you through when you've been working 15 hours!

FAVOURITE LOCAL RESTAURANTS?

The Flitch of Bacon in Little Dunmow, and Smith's in Ongar. We used to enjoy going to London to eat too, but now that we have two children aged six months and two years, we don't go out!

MIDNIGHT FEAST?

Peanut butter on toast – crunchy of course!

BEST RESTAURANT I'VE EATEN IN?

One would be Restaurant Story in London or Le Chateaubriand in Paris. Before we had children, we drove around France on a foodie tour and I really wanted to eat at Frenchie on the Rue du Nil in Paris, but it had shut for the August break sadly.

SIGNATURE DISHES

Starters

Deep-fried sweet & spicy Korean chicken wings

Tian of crab, avocado purée, toasted ciabatta

Honey roasted figs, blue cheese mousse, roasted hazelnuts

Mains

Pan-fried sea bass, paella-style risotto, crispy squid, red pepper coulis

Pan-fried calf's liver & bacon, mashed potatoes, spring greens, onion gravy

Grilled lobster Thermidor, home-cut chips, mixed salad

Puddings

Oreo cheesecake

Apple & sultana strudel crème brûlée

Morello cherry Eton mess, Chantilly cream, chocolate shards

RICHARD ON HIS...

FAVOURITE TIME OF YEAR TO COOK?

Spring and summer, definitely. I like to cook with bright colours at that time of year, the greens and reds of the salads and tomatoes just jump off the plate.

FAVOURITE KITCHEN GADGET?

I'm not very gadget-orientated but I use my ice cream machine every week; we make all our ice cream. Our Japanese green tea and white chocolate is fantastic, but I also love simpler flavours too like coffee or honeycomb.

FAVOURITE PART OF ESSEX?

West Mersea or Frinton because I like to take our children, Pip and Tilly, to the sea, and I also love Thaxted where I live.

COOK'S TIP?

Salt white fish like hake or cod for three hours before cooking it to firm up the flesh and draw out any water.

RECENT FOODIE DISCOVERY?

I've recently discovered gochujang, a Korean chilli paste which is phenomenal. It's smoked and fermented in barrels underground for six months.

Three men and their pub

When Richard and his business partners Chris Turnell and Scott Reid bought The Green Man in early 2014, they wasted no time sprucing it up, reopening for business, and turning it into the popular spot that it is today. For some, it's a local pub ideal for an informal meal and a drink, for others a destination restaurant with full à la carte menu, for others still a welcome spot to bring the children who can play happily in the vast garden.

The 100-seat restaurant with its white cloths, comfortable purple and cream seating and fresh flowers on every table looks out over a terrace with rattan furniture in summer, and across the extensive gardens. In winter, a heated marquee extends the space. In the pub area, the look is more traditional with exposed beams, flag floors, open log fires in winter, and bare tables which can be dressed to accommodate more diners if necessary.

The Green Man is – of course – painted white. Flanked on all sides by rolling farmland and surrounded by the pretty villages of Thaxted, Great Bardfield and Stebbing, it is a charming place. It was not always quite so well-presented, however. Fire razed the building to the ground some 30 years ago, but a generous local farmer donated the beams from an old barn on his land and enabled the rebuild to retain a delightful old-fashioned feel.

The Green Man
Mill End Green, Lindsell, Dunmow CM6 2DN
W: greenmanlindsell.co.uk
T: 01371 852285
E: info@greenmanlindsell.co.uk
/greenmanlindsell
@GrnManLindsell

Covers: 70 inside; 30 in the bar; 100 outside

Cost: average carte £30; wine from £19.95; pint from £3.40

Open: Tues-Fri L 12-3; D 5-9.30; Sat 12-10; Sun 12-6

Details: alfresco tables; private hire available; wheelchair access; dogs allowed in rear garden; parking

The simple things in life

Cameron Marshall loves to put vegetables centre stage on his menu, especially when he can use just-picked produce from nearby supplier, Remfresh.

Sometimes, the simplest things are the best – a perfect strawberry in June, the first taste of baby-pink rhubarb as winter relents, the crunch of a just-picked carrot. This chimes with Cameron Marshall, owner and head chef of the Boathouse Restaurant, Dedham.

The restaurant clings to the river Stour in a landscape so achingly, timelessly, beautiful that it has seduced visitors and been the subject of countless pictures ever since local boy, John Constable, first put brush to canvas in the early 19th century. It's a setting that has charmed and delighted without ever being anything other than what it naturally is – just like that perfect June strawberry.

"I like to keep flavours simple and uncomplicated, and these vegetables will be perfect with the meat," says Cameron, back in his kitchen with a basket bursting with baby fennel, leeks, carrots, turnips and beetroot. With a shoulder of lamb from Andrea Hale at Millfields Rare Breeds already cooking slowly, Cameron trims the fennel and carrots, and blanches them quickly before putting the fennel in to roast, and glazing the carrots and shallots with butter, a touch of seasoning and a clove of garlic in a sizzling pan. He covers the vegetables with a salt crust to ensure they cook evenly and gently, and they join the fennel in the oven. "This variety of carrot will add a contrasting dash of vibrant purple to the final dish," he explains. He lets the lamb rest before plating up carefully, arranging the colourful vegetables around the meat, and finishing with a glossy, rich bordelaise sauce.

The vegetables are from Remfresh, the Ardleigh-based supplier of baby vegetables to the restaurant trade. Started in 1975 by Elaine and Ronald Smith, Remfresh grows produce on its 12-acre site, selling to chefs not only in Essex but up and down the country, including a weekly delivery to Cornwall. "My husband used to drink in the Black Horse in Stratford St Mary, and so did local chefs," Elaine recalls. "He got talking to them and they kept saying how difficult it was to get good quality baby vegetables in Essex. So he started to grow baby beans, carrots and lettuces, and we just went from there."

The Remfresh range has adapted over the years to accommodate food fashions. "It's hard to say what our bestseller is because everything goes, but certainly our beetroot is popular early in the year. We grow it undercover which means we can get it to chefs a little earlier than other suppliers can." The couple's son, Neil, works with Elaine managing the poly-tunnels. "I start everything inside," he says, "then I take the beet, leek, and fennel outside as they prefer not to be too hot. The carrots and turnips stay inside. Over the years, we've got to know what grows best inside and outside."

It's a beautifully simple business – the Smiths listen to their chef clients, keep alert to trends, and plant accordingly – and it's a relationship that has worked well for Cameron for years. "We do so many different things with them and we just love what they grow, particularly the turnips and fennel. I use the fennel in dishes like this one today, or I'll make a fantastic pesto with the tops. It's simple but tastes delicious."

If not putting a call in to Remfresh, Cameron scours Essex for ingredients for his à la carte and set menus that sing with Mediterranean and Asian flavours. Pan-seared peppered tuna steak, with crispy Parmentier potatoes, baby vegetables and a lime and ginger emulsion, or cod marinated in five spice and treacle and served with coriander egg noodles, teriyaki sauce and toasted sesame are both popular dishes, ditto smoked haddock with leek and potato mash, a poached duck egg, and cauliflower and saffron coulis.

"I started cooking when I was seven, when mum went out on a Saturday afternoon I'd experiment making tarts and bread."

It's a style that Cameron has adopted over decades being obsessed with food. "I started cooking when I was seven," he says. "When mum went out on a Saturday afternoon I'd experiment making tarts and bread." He went on to take a catering course at Wirral Metropolitan College, worked in various hotels, then moved to Jersey to work in the kitchen at the Grand Jersey hotel and spa in St Helier. There, he met Claire and six years later the couple moved back to England, first to Cheshire before taking on the Boathouse in 2002, their first restaurant.

"At first we just served teas, cakes, pizza because we had no money to do anything else," Cameron says. Within less than a year of ploughing all profit back into the building, however, they were able to install a new kitchen and update the rest of the building inside and out. A flood in their first week of opening was a painful setback, but they picked themselves and the business up, going on to create a place that will no doubt continue to captivate for many years to come.

Confit lamb shoulder with heritage carrots, sauté baby vegetables and bordelaise sauce

This is a no-fuss dish for a smart supper because you can prepare a lot of it in advance, or even finish it completely and reheat as required. Ask your butcher to debone your lamb shoulder but if needs be, it is not too difficult a task at home as there are just two bones to separate and remove. If a potato dish or starchy side is required, keep it simple, something like pommes boulangère, a baked gratin layered with stock and onions, is delicious. (serves 4+)

Lamb

1 whole deboned lamb shoulder, medium-sized about 1.5kg
Goose fat (and/or rapeseed oil)
Small bunch of rosemary branches
Small bunch of thyme sprigs
1 whole garlic bulb, skin left-on and split horizontally

Pre-heat the oven to 180c. Rub 50g of sea salt well in all over the lamb and chill overnight. Rinse the shoulder and dry thoroughly with a clean tea towel. Place the herbs, garlic and lamb in a deep, snug roasting tin and cover completely with goose fat (and/or oil). Tightly cover with foil and bake for 3-4 hours until completely tender. Remove the meat to a hot plate and keep warm under loose foil.

Baby vegetables

2 large handfuls of baby vegetables, such as fennel, leeks, carrots, courgettes etc

Blanch the baby vegetables in boiling salted water until al dente, drain and set aside.

Heritage carrots

1kg of mixed heritage carrots
Small bunch of thyme sprigs, leaves only
Olive oil

Simmer the carrots whole in a large pan of salted water for 4-6 minutes and then drain. Pre-heat the oven to 200c. Toss the carrots well in a shallow roasting tray with generous salt and pepper to taste, thyme and oil. Cover tightly with foil and bake for 30 minutes until tender. Keep warm until required.

Bordelaise sauce

1 tbsp unsalted butter
200g shallots, finely chopped
2 garlic cloves, minced
Few sprigs of thyme, chopped
1 tbsp Dijon-style mustard
1 tbsp Worcestershire sauce
300ml rich beef stock
200ml good drinkable red wine

In a small frying pan, melt the butter over a gentle heat, add the shallots, garlic and thyme, and soften. Stir in the mustard, Worcestershire sauce, stock and red wine before boiling on a medium heat until reduced by a third in volume. Season to taste and keep warm. If a thicker gravy is preferred, combine 2 tbsp cold water with 1 tbsp cornflour in a small bowl, then gradually add the paste to the gravy, whisking constantly over a gentle heat until the desired consistency is reached.

To serve

Slice the lamb carefully into thick slices and garnish on hot plates with the carrots, baby vegetables and sauce.

Duck liver parfait

In the restaurant, we serve this delicious pâté starter with toasted brioche, sweet apple butter and red onion jam. (serves 4+)

60g onions, diced
3 pinches of dried thyme
2 garlic cloves, crushed
50ml good brandy
150ml good port
400g unsalted butter
400g duck livers, trimmed
5 medium eggs

Pre-heat the oven to 130c.

In a large deep saucepan, boil the onions, thyme, garlic, brandy and port together over a high heat until reduced by a third in volume and set aside to cool. Melt the butter in a small saucepan on a low heat and set aside.

Liquidise the livers with the cooled onion mixture, add the eggs one at a time and process until the mixture is silky-smooth. With the motor running, slowly pour in the butter, then season with 1 tsp salt and generous pepper.

Decant the mixture into your chosen parchment-lined mould/s. Cover loosely with foil. Put the mould/s into a deep roasting tray and add boiling water to the tray up to two-thirds level. Bake for 45-60 minutes in the centre of the oven. Remove carefully from the water and allow to cool for 30 minutes before chilling overnight.

Wild mushroom and spinach ravioli

A really tasty vegetarian starter or light lunch, especially if you have safely foraged your own fungi. We serve this with a caper and red onion butter. (serves 4)

250g mixed wild mushrooms, in bite-size pieces
1 large onion, finely diced
2 garlic cloves, crushed
Olive oil
Good pinch of tarragon leaves, shredded
100g baby spinach leaves
100g cream cheese
500g ready-made pasta sheets
1 egg, beaten

Soften the mushrooms, garlic and onion with 1 tbsp of oil in a hot large frying pan over a medium heat, then add the tarragon and spinach, cooking until it has dried out, for about 5-10 minutes. Set aside to cool.

Beat in the cream cheese and seasoning to taste.

Cut approx. 8cm circles out of the pasta with a cutter (rolling thinner first if needed). Put 1 tbsp of filling in the centre, brush the edges with egg and then top with another circle before sealing well. Place separately onto a floured tray.

Cook the ravioli in a large pan of salted boiling water over a high heat for 4-5 minutes until floating. Drain, season and serve.

Orange & lemon polenta cake

A delicious afternoon tea or supper dessert, served here with fresh strawberry compote and clotted cream. (serves 6+)

200g soft unsalted butter
200g caster sugar
200g ground almonds
100g fine polenta
1½ tsp baking powder
3 large eggs, beaten
1 orange and 1 lemon, zest and juice separate
125g caster sugar

Pre-heat the oven to 180c. Line and butter a 23cm cake tin.

Cream the butter and sugar in a mixer until pale, then beat in the almonds, polenta and baking powder. Add the eggs slowly, keeping the mixer on a high speed before adding the zest. Pour the mix into the prepared tin, level, and bake for about 20 minutes.

To test if done, insert a knife into the centre of the cake – if it comes out clean the cake is ready, if it doesn't, continue baking and check regularly. Set aside to cool in the tin.

Dissolve the sugar in the juice over a gentle heat. Prick the warm cake lightly all over and pour over the hot syrup. Cool completely in the tin before removing carefully.

FOOD NOSTALGIA?

A place which takes me back to another time is Bohemia in St Helier, Jersey. Claire and I went there two months after it first opened under Shaun Rankin. We enjoyed an amazing tasting menu and I remember the petits fours were served in a Christian Lacroix box!

FAVOURITE PART OF ESSEX?

Anywhere along the Essex coast. We have our own boat that we like to take out. We love Doug [Wright's] place, the Chelmondiston Red Lion, on the way to Shotley though we used to go to his restaurant when he was in Kelvedon for fish and chips.

MIDNIGHT FEAST?

Cheese, ham and cucumber sandwich.

PERFECT DAY OFF?

It starts at 5.30am getting up with our son Tommy, then a good dogwalk, going to the gym, enjoying a lovely breakfast cooked by Claire and then we all go out for the day. We love Christchurch Park in Ipswich, a fantastic spot.

WHERE I'M HAPPIEST?

At home with our boy Tommy, my wife Claire and our dogs, two chocolate brown Labradors, Matilda and Mabel.

SIGNATURE DISHES

Starters

Smoked haddock chowder, rarebit croûton

Chilled watermelon, crumbled feta cheese, crispy Parma ham, port syrup

Duck liver pâté, braeburn apple brandy butter, crispy crostini

Mains

28-day aged ribeye steak, leek & stilton gratin, mashed potatoes, red onion jus

Braised shoulder of lamb, broad beans, turnips, minted new potatoes, dijon dumplings

Moules marinières, skinny fries, salad, crusty bread

Puddings

Amaretto cheesecake, marinated cherries, chocolate ganache

Blood orange granita, crushed meringue, mango coulis

Café crème parfait, butterscotch sauce, toffee walnuts

CAMERON ON HIS...

RECENT FOODIE DISCOVERIES?

Brining and curing – we now do anything from pork fillet to asparagus.

CHEF HERO?

Nick Dodd because he was my first head chef. I worked under him at what was then the Trusthouse Forte Belsfield hotel in Windermere [now the Laura Ashley The Belsfield hotel]. We are still in touch regularly all these years later. At the time he was just 23 and in charge of the kitchen of a 200-bedroom hotel! I'd love to cook for chef Nico Ladenis. From the very beginning he was self-trained and he just got the whole ethos of cooking simple but fantastic food.

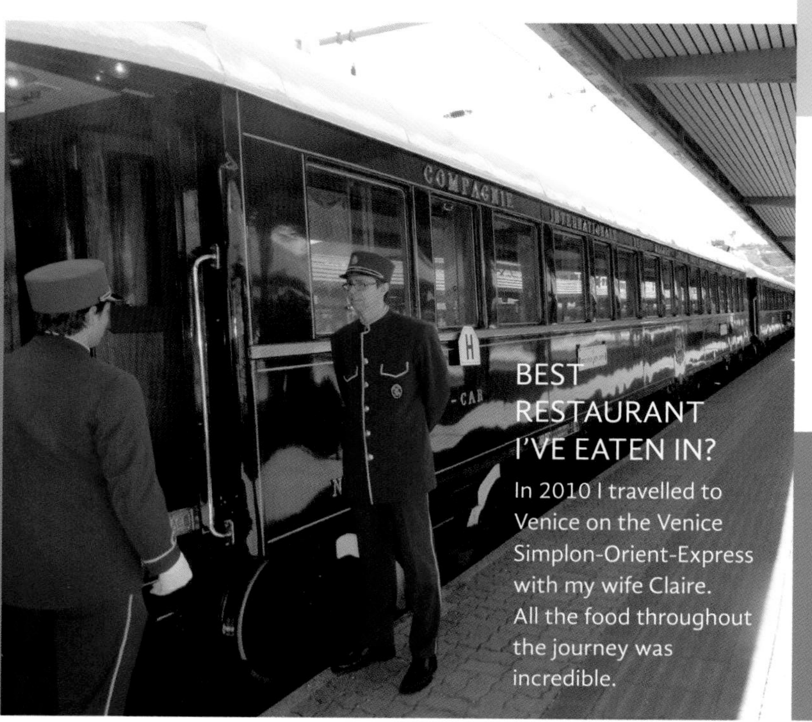

BEST RESTAURANT I'VE EATEN IN?

In 2010 I travelled to Venice on the Venice Simplon-Orient-Express with my wife Claire. All the food throughout the journey was incredible.

CHILDHOOD AMBITIONS?

As a child, I wanted to be a lorry driver or an ice cream man! Later, if I hadn't become a chef I might like to have been an actor.

BIGGEST EXTRAVAGANCE?

We're having a brand new walk-in fridge put in this summer, and we're all looking forward to its arrival and being able to walk into it!

Row, row, row your boat

It was back in 2002 that Cameron and Claire Marshall first came across the Boathouse on the banks of the river Stour. Originally a boatyard – if you look up from your table you can still see the original cubbyholes where boat-builders kept their tools – it had been turned into a tearoom, and the couple knew immediately that they had found the right place for their first restaurant.

Running it at first as a simple tearoom, Cameron and Claire eventually refurbished the property fully to create the sleek, shiny vessel it is today, with its toes dipping into the willow-edged water, and that iconic herd of cattle grazing and dipping their toes into the shallows on the opposite bank. Beyond the lush pasture, there are far-reaching views of the Dedham countryside and the village's church tower.

There are nods to the property's boat-building past with polished wood panelling, and a vaulted roof high enough to house a hull, and of course the smartly varnished rowing boats for hire on the water outside. New windows, a smart glass partition separating the bar and extended kitchen from the main restaurant, and a cream wood conservatory at the opposite end create a sense of space and airiness inside, while outside there are wooden tables and chairs under ancient horse chestnut trees, and (new for 2017) a garden room complete with sail canopy that is ideal for small family gatherings.

The Marshalls extended their business in 2014 to open an informal restaurant and tearoom, Kitchen@Thorpeness, overlooking the boating lake in the Suffolk coastal village of the same name.

Boathouse Restaurant
Mill Lane, Dedham, Colchester C07 6DH
W: dedhamboathouse.com
T: 01206 323153
E: dedhamboathouse@aol.com
/DedhamBoathouse
@BoathouseDedham
/dedhamboathouse

Accolades: winner, Destination Dining, *Essex Life* Food & Drink Awards 2013

Covers: 80 inside; 60 outside

Cost: carte average £35; wine from £14.50; pint from £4.50

Open: Tues-Sun L 12.30-2.30; Tues-Sat D 6.30-9.30

Details: alfresco dining; Garden Room available for private hire; 'row and dine' nights; live music nights; wheelchair access; parking

A feathered nest

Terence and Caroline Howard have found work-life balance at The Creek, and relish offering simple, carefully prepared dishes using local ingredients such as free-range chicken from Park Hall Farm.

Terence Howard very nearly turned his back on cooking as a career when a sleepless 36-hour stint in The Savoy kitchens as a rookie chef fresh from Waltham Forest College nearly did for him. "I'm proud of the fact that I was the College's first student ever to go to The Savoy. I spent almost a year there but those 36 hours made me think 'I'm not cut out for this'."

Thankfully for the people of Essex and further afield, Terence had second thoughts. More positive experiences elsewhere led him back to the stove and an early career cooking in some iconic London spots: the Groucho Club in Soho, Home House on Portman Square, Mayfair's Washington hotel, and latterly as executive head chef at the Reform Club on Pall Mall.

Watching him now talking and smiling as he deftly portions a chicken in the meticulously ordered kitchen of his rural Essex pub, he is a million miles away from those early city days – and a happier man for it. He loves that his commute is to climb the stairs to his home above the pub that he shares with his wife, Caroline, and their children Gabrielle (13) and Theo (9). He loves that by buying the lease back in November 2014 of what was then called The Flag Inn, he realised a long-held dream to own his own restaurant, and he loves to offer local diners food that's "somewhere in the middle of fine dining and gastro-pub".

Fine dining training dies hard, and there are plenty of elements of that style at The Creek, as the couple renamed their restaurant. Prawn and brown crab cocktail is a popular starter, while mains might include roast breast of Gressingham duck with fondant potatoes and a carrot and thyme purée, or pan-fried sea trout with caviar and smoked bacon Caesar salad. Favourite puddings are sticky toffee, or lemon tart with raspberry ice cream. "We want to do a taster menu night in the future so that I can really show guests what we can create, but people don't always like to experiment when they come out for dinner. Our menu needs to appeal to all types of diners every day."

Chicken is a perennial favourite, and Terence is happy to have Park Hall Farm just down the road in St Osyth. Although still predominantly an arable farm, Park Hall is also home to award-

"We love to offer local diners food that's somewhere in the middle of fine dining and gastro-pub."

winning self-catering holiday accommodation created from a former stable block, and a business that supplies free-range eggs and chicken to local restaurants. Trish Ford manages this side of the enterprise while her husband, David, runs the farm. The hens roam freely, pecking their way idly across the farm's 400 acres, at night roosting on the rafters in a fox-secure straw-filled barn. Some are rare-breed, producing colourful eggs in all different sizes, others are classic brown farmyard hens. "Whatever the size of the egg or breed, the yolks are always the brightest yellow because of the hens' healthy way of life," Trish says.

Trish was thrilled when Terence and Caroline came to The Creek – and the appreciation appears to be mutual, the Howards delighted to have such a supplier close by. "For me, The Creek opening was a blessing," says Trish. "My guests have only ever come back from a meal there full of compliments." She delivers poultry and eggs to the kitchen every week, and the meat is a popular staple on the menu, perhaps confit and served with butternut squash purée, fresh spring greens and fondant potatoes, or as a starter of beer-battered fillets served with potato salad, apple coleslaw and zingy pineapple salsa. On our visit, Terence prepares a simple roast chicken breast with root vegetable mash, pommes purée, wild mushrooms and a slice of crispy bacon. "It's the classic flavours of mushrooms, bacon and chicken," says Terence, as he sears the breast in a sizzling pan, spooning over the buttery juices as the skin colours, "but delivered in a more innovative style." He finishes the chicken in the oven, and after resting it a little, slices the meat into an attractive portion, and plates it up with a shard of crisp bacon, a swipe of potato and pile of squash.

It's simple food, with few components, no fuss, but great flavour – just as Terence wants it to be. "I get vegetables from Ross & Wheatley in Clacton, our meat comes from the butchers Wrights of Frinton, and we have fish delivered daily from Direct Seafoods. It's great to have Trish down the road too of course. In London, I had 41 suppliers to choose from, and even if there's far less choice out here I'm OK with that. I just plan my menus ahead more which makes you more organised and ultimately probably a better chef!"

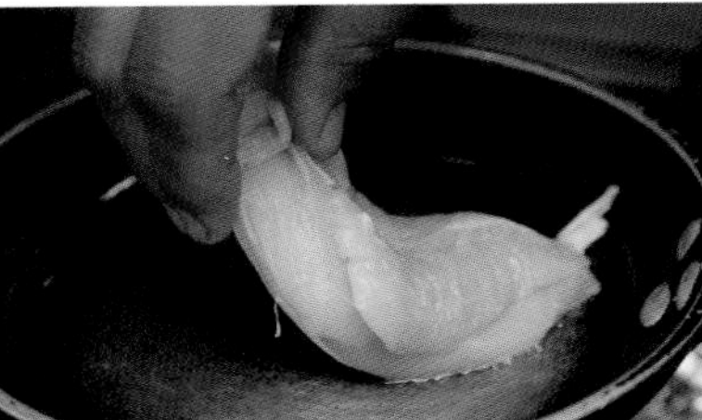

Roast rare breed chicken, new potato purée, root mash, wild mushrooms and crispy bacon

A simple family Sunday lunch dish with a twist and also a popular hearty supper choice with our Creek diners. New potatoes have a real sweetness when puréed and this is complemented by the rustic mash while the wild mushrooms and bacon add a rich, savoury edge.

Most elements in this dish can be prepared in advance, and either kept warm or reheated as required.

Root mash

4 handfuls of prepared root vegetables in chunks eg swede, squash, turnip, parsnip, carrot
I white onion, finely chopped
Few large cloves of garlic, finely chopped
Sprigs of rosemary and thyme
Unsalted butter

Pre-heat the oven to 200c. Tip the root vegetables into a large roasting tray, season well and toss with the onions, garlic and herbs. Drizzle with a little water, add a few knobs of butter, cover with tin foil and bake until tender. Remove, discard the herbs and carefully mash the root mixture with a potato masher or pulse in a processor into a coarse texture. Adjust seasoning, cover and keep warm.

Potato purée

200g peeled new potatoes
1 large clove garlic, finely chopped
1 small onion, finely chopped
50ml double cream

Finely chop the new potatoes and simmer them in a lidded saucepan with the garlic, onion and cream until cooked. Remove and blend in a liquidiser until smooth. Season to taste, cover and keep warm.

Roast chicken

4 boneless free-range chicken breasts
Rapeseed oil
Unsalted butter

Pre-heat the oven to 200c. Season the chicken breasts on both sides, place in a hot oiled ovenproof frying pan on a medium heat. Cook until browned on one side, then flip over carefully. Add a good knob of butter and baste with the juices using a spoon for a minute. Transfer the pan to the oven and bake until cooked through and the juices run clear in the middle of the meat when pressed with a knife. Remove and keep warm until required.

Crispy bacon

4 rashers smoked streaky bacon or pancetta

Pre-heat the oven to 160c. Line a baking tray with greaseproof paper, lay out the bacon rashers on it and then top with more paper and another tray. Bake until well-coloured and crispy, then remove.

Wild mushrooms

100g fresh wild mushrooms, cleaned

Cut or tear the mushrooms into bite-size pieces. Take a hot, oiled, deep sauté pan and fry the mushrooms over a medium-high heat until lightly browned and cooked through but retaining some 'bite'.

To serve

Ensure all the elements are hot. Make a bed of the root mash and potato purée on different sides of warmed plates. Top with the carved chicken, scatter with the mushrooms and finish with the bacon rashers.

Pigeon breast, asparagus, runny egg, rhubarb and smoked salt

Another quick and easy recipe, suited to a light early summer lunch. I urge you to try the pigeon breasts rare if you haven't before as it is the best way to enjoy them. You can fry them for longer in the pan but the meat will toughen as it cooks through. (serves 4)

8 asparagus spears, trimmed
1 rhubarb stick
4 pigeon breasts, oven-ready
4 large free-range eggs
Maldon smoked sea salt
Unsalted butter
Rapeseed oil

Blanch the asparagus for a few minutes in boiling water, drain and set aside. Create rhubarb shavings by running a potato peeler down the stick lengthways and set aside. Heat an oiled frying pan and quickly sauté the asparagus over a high heat. Set aside.

Season the pigeon breasts and fry for no more than one minute on each side, without moving them, to keep the meat pink. Rest them somewhere warm.

Fry the eggs in a hot oiled frying pan with a little melted butter over a medium heat until cooked to your liking. Serve the carved pigeon on warm plates with the asparagus, scattered with the rhubarb and topped with the egg. Finish with a sprinkling of smoked salt.

Surf & turf of beef fillet and brill with shellfish marinière

A rather grand version of the steakhouse favourite. Juggle preparing the marinière while the beef and fish are cooking. (serves 4)

4 100g fillet steaks
4 portions of brill
Rapeseed oil
2 shallots, finely chopped
2 garlic cloves, finely chopped
Unsalted butter
Good dry white wine
4 handfuls of raw shellfish
200g tenderstem broccoli
Double cream
Lemon halves
Soft herbs, finely shredded

Preheat the oven to 200C. Brown both sides of the beef and the fish in two separate hot, oiled, ovenproof frying pans. Bake until the fish is cooked through and the beef done to your liking, then keep somewhere warm.

Soften the shallots and garlic with a little butter and oil in a hot saucepan on a low-medium heat. Add a glug of wine and simmer, carefully add the shellfish and the sliced broccoli, cover and boil until cooked through and/or the shells open. For mussels and clams in shells, only cook closed, raw ones and only eat open, cooked ones.

Stir in double cream to make a sauce and finish with lemon juice, herbs and seasoning to taste. Put the beef and fish on warm, deep plates and garnish with the shellfish and sauce.

Pork, date and onion faggots

This is one part of an elegant pork duo we offer, alongside roasted pork tenderloin, dauphinoise potato, butternut squash purée and baby turnips, finished with caramelised apple and sage. For a simple supper, these faggots eat well with buttery mash and greens. Either ask your butcher to mince your pork and liver or pulse in a processor. (serves 4)

400g boneless pork, minced
100g pork liver, minced
50g dates
1 small onion
1 garlic clove
4 sage leaves
Unsalted butter
Rapeseed oil
150ml chicken jus or gravy
50ml good red wine

Pre-heat the oven to 200c. Place the mince and liver in a mixing bowl. Finely chop the dates, onion, garlic and sage before mixing with the pork along with a little seasoning. Quickly test the flavour by frying a teaspoonful in a hot frying pan until cooked through and then adjusting the seasoning.

With damp hands, roll the mixture into golf-ball size faggots before chilling for 30 minutes. Pan-fry the faggots in a hot, oiled, ovenproof frying pan over a high heat, browning on all sides. Add the jus and wine and bring to a simmer. Transfer to the oven for 5-10 minutes until fully cooked through. Remove and serve on warm plates.

TERENCE ON HIS...

FOODIE INFLUENCES?

I'm classically trained, but I like to put my own twist on things. When I started in the industry, it was all about fusion food so I like to use that influence. You'll always find shellfish on my menus which is odd because I'm allergic – I like working with shellfish, love the way it looks and smells, and I wish I could eat it!

FOOD HEROES?

I like Sat Bains' cooking, I think he's phenomenal. Also Nathan Outlaw who is very, very simple with his food in comparison with other Michelin-starred chefs.

DISH OF MY CHILDHOOD?

My parents were fantastic cooks, so my mum's macaroni cheese and pork stuffing bring back strong memories. Her crumbles were to die for!

HOW I MET MY WIFE?

Caroline and I met at a snooker hall – she was behind a door and I opened it suddenly and almost knocked her out! We've been together for 15 years and married for five. Now that I've moved to Essex I'm in a couple of pool leagues and I won my division in the first season. There used to be a pool table and darts board when we bought the premises and we sometimes get locals who call in asking where they have gone.

SIGNATURE DISHES

Starters

Home-marinated olives, warm Brightlingsea bakery bread, chorizo, crackling sticks, balsamic oil, whipped garlic butter & smoked Maldon sea salt (to share)

Smoked salmon, crayfish, avocado, soft quail's egg, horseradish cream, crostini

Cream of cauliflower soup, pork belly lardons, sautéed wild mushrooms, croûtons, truffle oil

Mains

Fillet of sea bass, crushed potatoes, green beans, walnuts, white wine cream, crispy sage & leek

Roast medallion of sirloin beef, baked macaroni cheese, peas, chorizo, spring onion

Roast loin of cod wrapped in parma ham, lobster sauce, braised fennel, polenta & spring onion mash

Puddings

Chocolate brownie, chocolate sauce, honeycomb, chocolate ice cream, shortbread crumbs

'The Creek' split: caramelised banana, salted caramel ice cream, crème Chantilly, salted caramel, roasted walnuts

Bramley apple & local rhubarb crumble, crème anglaise, Chantilly cream

CHILDHOOD AMBITIONS?

Well the only thing I was good at during my time at school was Home Economics. Thankfully I enjoyed it too, so I decided to do it as a career. But working under Anton Edlemann at The Savoy as a young chef almost destroyed me!

MIDNIGHT FEAST?

Once a week, I'll have a really good ribeye steak after work. Mind you, the other day for some reason I just fancied a Findus Crispy Pancake, with tinned spaghetti hoops and a couple of Trish's fried eggs for good measure!

FAVOURITE PART OF ESSEX?

We both love Dedham, it's absolutely beautiful. We've not yet taken a boat out though I hope on our next visit we will. Epping reminds me of my childhood and we'd like to visit Jahdre [Hayward] at Haywards – trouble is he's closed on the days that I have off!

WHAT DRIVES ME?

In all honesty, cooking is the only thing I can do. If I didn't do this I don't know what I'd do. I'm not driven by accolades or success. That's not my thing; for me it's all about the food and having your own restaurant. I'm happy living that dream.

A river runs through it, almost

Terence and Caroline Howard's restaurant, bar and lounge is set in a beautiful 17th century Grade II-listed building in the village of Great Bentley, a few wiggling country lanes from the Colne Estuary and the tidal inlet, Flag Creek, after which the building was originally named. The Howards renamed the property The Creek after instantly falling in love with it back in 2014. The creek in question flows behind the pub and there are spectacular views across the salt marsh, mud flats and reed beds, a fantastic spot for Terence to relax and ponder his next menus changes.

In their two short years of ownership, the Howards have made a name for themselves for offering food with flair and a dash of classical style, but simplified and served in relaxed surroundings. Romantic pictures of the creek taken in different photographic styles and lights decorate walls, there's a cosy wood burner in the bar, and the restaurant has a contemporary feel with smart dark wood tables brightened up with olive green, cream and chocolate brown leather seating.

Customers can choose from specials chalked up on a board, a set lunch menu, or full à la carte at lunch and dinner. A compact wine list is curated by family-run enterprises, G&G Gallo in Braintree and Grape Passions in Witham, with care taken to offer wines that can't be store-bought in order to give customers something of a sense of occasion, Terence explains. The couple's focus is entirely on their restaurant, though Terence has made numerous television appearances, including cooking live on UKTV's *Market Kitchen* with Tana Ramsay, and preparing mock turtle soup with the Hairy Bikers.

The Creek
Flag Hill, Great Bentley, Colchester CO7 8RE
W: thecreekgreatbentley.co.uk
T: 01255 317950; 01206 586435
E: contact@thecreekgreatbentley.co.uk
/Thecreekgreatbentley
@thecreekpub

Accolades: winner, Chef of the Year, *Essex Life* Food & Drink Awards 2016

Covers: 54

Cost: carte average £30; wine from £15.95; bottled beers from £3.50

Open: Wed-Sat L 12-2 (2.30 Sat), D 6-9 (9.30 Sat); Sun 12.30-3

Details: alfresco tables; separate bar area; private dining for ten; wheelchair accessible; parking

Game on

Phil Utz revels in the rich autumnal flavours of game – especially locally shot partridge – as much as his customers at The Hoop pub enjoy eating it

Phil Utz may have a background rooted in top-end hotels, preparing and cooking the most luxurious ingredients for high-spending customers, but his welcoming 450-year-old country pub in Stock, near Ingatestone, is much more 'him'.

He does love a party, though, and the game dinner that celebrates the end of every shooting season is an event fixed in the Hoop diary. "We organise it every June for all the gamekeepers who run local shoots, their partners and the beaters," says Phil. "I'll create a menu of, say, venison with beetroot and ceps, or braised beef cheek and cavolo nero with matching wines for each course – and a good time is had by all!"

Keith Weaire who runs a flooring company when he's not organising the local shoot as a hobby, is always on the guest list. He (with his devoted black Labradors, Echo and Pip) is our guide for a day out in the countryside around the hamlet of Nounsley, a place of rolling fields, some water and a smattering of woodland that create an ideal habitat for partridge. Keith regularly brings friends here to shoot so knows the area well.

"My brother got me into shooting years ago," says Keith. "He was a gamekeeper for Earl Spencer. I once went shooting with the Earl and my brother, and from that day on I have loved everything about the sport. I also like to put my guns away at the end of the season, though, and look forward to the dinner at the Hoop – it's always a great social event!"

Phil likes the idea that the dinner is perhaps also a nod to The Hoop's centuries-old history. "I'd like to think a similar relationship might have gone on many years ago with the gamekeepers coming here after a day's shoot and that we are perhaps carrying on a long-held tradition," he says. Keith is certainly doing his bit to keep the custom going, bringing guests to the pub after a day's sport, and himself being a loyal customer of 15 years. He'd like to get Phil out more: "He's walked around with us on a few occasions; trouble is he's too busy in his kitchen to do it often!"

Partridge from the shoots will find itself on The Hoop menus in various guises – perhaps pheasant and partridge tempura as a bar snack, or pheasant pithivier with a chestnut mousse, or the pot roast partridge dish that Phil prepares today. After butchering the bird himself Phil adds seasoning and herbs. He sears the crown for a minute and a half each side to colour it before sloshing in generous amounts of red wine, and adding a mirepoix. He covers it with foil and puts it in the oven for ten minutes, careful not to overcook the meat. He wraps the confit legs in wafer thin filo pastry to create the croustillant, and then wraps them again in thinly-sliced strips of potato before crisping them up in a smoking-hot pan. The Anna potato and celeriac work well alongside in terms of flavour, colour and seasonality.

It's a delicious plate of food, but essentially a simple one that fits with the no-frills, no-fuss approach to cooking that Phil enjoys so much. "My cooking is always seasonal, casual, perhaps with some Italian influences – I love how they cook things so simply in Italy – along with the French and English traditions, but none of it I'd call fine dining! Downstairs, we do bar food, all fresh-made, home-cooked favourites like beer-battered cod and crushed peas and our chunky chips, or Holt's of Witham sausages with mash and onion gravy. Upstairs, it's a little more refined but I still do dishes like belly of pork with chorizo jam, or sautéed baby squid with bok choy, or Goosnargh duck with an onion tarte fine." He loves using local ingredients of course such as Lathcoats Farm strawberries, or even locally foraged puff balls or ceps brought in by Albert Kitchen, who used to own the pub, and lives locally.

"My cooking is always seasonal, casual, perhaps with some Italian influences – I love how they cook things so simply in Italy."

Phil started his cooking career at the Lanesborough hotel on London's Hyde Park Corner working under renowned chef Paul Gayler for over 10 years. "I learnt a lot from Paul," Phil says, "and I also met Michelle while working there. I was a pastry chef, she was a commis pastry chef. She then went travelling but thankfully came back, and the rest is history!" From the Lanesborough, Phil moved to Brocket Hall, Hatfield, working at their acclaimed restaurant, L'Auberge du Lac, and then to the Bear in Stock, just around the corner from The Hoop. He and Michelle took over The Hoop some 10 years ago, Phil running the kitchen, and Michelle front of house in between looking after their 17-month-old son, Albert.

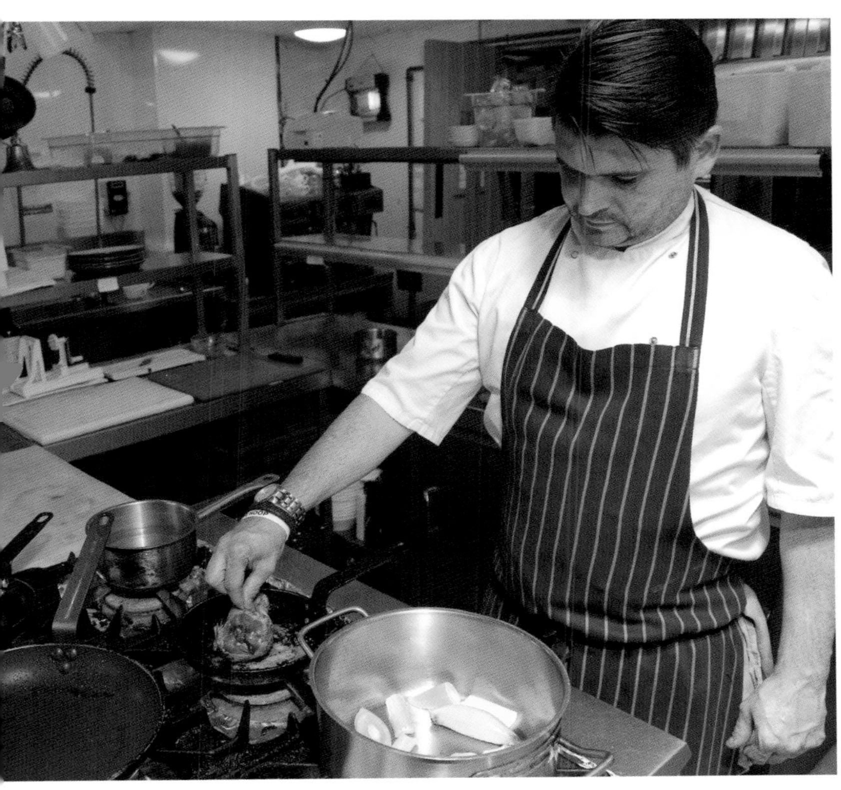

Pot-roasted partridge breast, croustillant leg, anna potato, crispy pancetta, celeriac purée and baby leeks

This hearty early winter main course is chef-friendly and the partridge, potato and celeriac elements can be made ahead and reheated. If you would like more vegetable content, it eats well with either slow-cooked sweet-sour red cabbage or quick-wilted savoy cabbage.

Partridge breasts

Rapeseed oil
4 partridges, oven-ready and legs separated
Half an onion, chopped
3 carrots, chopped
2 celery sticks, chopped
4 sprigs thyme
1 bay leaf
200ml red wine

Pre-heat the oven to 200c. Heat up a heavy ovenproof casserole on a high heat, pour in a glug of oil and add the vegetables, thyme and bay leaf and stir regularly until coloured well all over. Take off the heat and keep warm.

Heat another oiled frying pan on a high heat until smoking, brown the partridges for a minute or two on each side. Add to the casserole with the wine, cover and bring to a simmer before baking for 20 minutes.

Croustillant legs

8 partridge legs
1 bay leaf
4 thyme sprigs
2 garlic cloves
400ml rapeseed oil
1 sheet filo pastry
25g butter, softened
1 large potato, spiralised into spaghetti
25g butter
Oil for frying

Pre-heat the oven to 120c. Place the first five ingredients into a lidded hobproof casserole dish. Heat up, cover, and cook for an hour until the meat falls from the bone. Remove the legs and cool before shredding off the meat. Season well to taste and roll into 4 balls. Wrap each one in a square of filo pastry and brush with butter and set aside. Blanch the potato briefly in boiling water before draining and putting in iced water. Drain, and dry on a tea towel before placing in a bowl and stirring through a splash of oil to coat. Take 4 or 5 strands, wrap round a filo ball, and repeat. Heat up your deep fryer to 180c and fry the balls for 4-5 minutes until crispy. Drain on kitchen paper, season and keep warm.

Anna potato

8 medium potatoes, sliced very thinly
500g butter, clarified

Pre-heat the oven to 180c. Brush a heavy 15cm ovenproof frying pan with some butter. Arrange a fanned layer of potatoes on the bottom and then butter and season before repeating to a depth of 2.5cm. Put onto a medium heat to brown for a few minutes and then bake for about 1 hour until cooked through. Remove and check the potato cake is loosened and any butter poured off before placing a board on top and carefully turning over to remove the potatoes. Cut into quarters and keep warm.

To serve

50g butter
300g celeriac, chopped
8 baby leeks
4 pancetta slices, grilled until crisp

In a large saucepan, heat up the butter and add the celeriac. Cook until just colouring, cover with water and then simmer until soft. Meanwhile, simmer the leeks in salted water until just soft, drain and keep warm. Drain and purée the celeriac with seasoning to taste in a processor until smooth.

Carve the partridge breasts onto four hot plates and garnish each with a croustillant ball, potato wedge, celeriac, pancetta and leeks before finishing with the braising liquor.

Herb-crusted cod, shellfish ragù, tomatoes and fennel

A great springtime fish lunch, you need to juggle the seafood cookery simultaneously to finish the dish. (serves 4)

100g flat-leaf parsley, chopped
100g fresh breadcrumbs
Zest of half a lemon
2 fennel bulbs, thinly sliced
25g butter
100ml fish stock
200ml dry white wine
400g chopped tomatoes
Juice of 1 lemon
4 150g cod fillet portions
800g mussels and clams, closed in the shell
12 shelled king prawns

Pre-heat the oven to 200c.
Process the parsley, crumbs, zest and seasoning until fine. Soften the fennel with the butter in a hot, deep lidded sauté pan on a low heat, add the stock, wine and tomatoes, turn up and simmer for 15 minutes. Finish with the lemon juice and seasoning to taste. Keep warm.

Pre-heat the grill. Brown the seasoned cod in a hot, oiled ovenproof frying pan on a high heat, turn over and then cook for 5 minutes. Remove and keep warm. Add the mussels and clams to the fennel and simmer well for four minutes until the shells open, discarding any still closed. Add the prawns and cook through before seasoning. Coat the cod with the crumbs and grill until lightly browned. Serve the stew, topped with the cod in warm soup plates.

Gooseberry and apple crumble tart

For this elegant take on a nursery pudding, you will need a sweet egg-enriched pastry base (choose ready-rolled for speed), blind-baked until light-golden in individual springform tart tins. (serves 4+)

4 cooking apples, diced
200g gooseberries, hulled
1 vanilla pod, split and seeds scraped
100g caster sugar
300g butter
75g icing sugar
300g plain flour

Pre-heat the oven to 180c.
In a deep sauté pan on a medium heat, cook the apples and gooseberries with the vanilla pod and seeds gently until the apples break down. Remove and stir in the sugar.

For the crumble, cream the butter and icing sugar in a mixer until pale, then add the flour. Spread onto a large baking sheet and bake until light-golden throughout, stirring occasionally as it cooks. Allow to cool.

Fill the pastry cases still in their tins with the fruit until three-quarters full, top with crumble and bake for 10-15 minutes.

The Hoop brown sauce

Who needs a squeezy bottle of ready-made stuff when you can make your own? This just cries out for a fat bacon butty for breakfast, but it's equally great with sausage and mash and of course, proper butcher's beef burgers sizzling on the barbecue! (makes lots)

1 tbsp rapeseed oil
1 medium onion, chopped
2 cooking apples, peeled and chopped
125g chopped dates
800g tinned plum tomatoes
80g soft brown sugar
3 tsp black treacle
200ml malt vinegar
4 tsp worcestershire sauce
2 tsp mustard powder

Add the oil to a hot frying pan on a low-medium heat and then stir in the onion, cooking until softened but not coloured. Add the apple and dates and cook until softened. Fold in all the other ingredients, bring to a simmer and cook gently for 40 minutes until thickened and well-reduced. Purée in a processor until smooth, decant, cool and then store in the fridge.

COOKERY TIP?

Instead of taking skins off tomatoes in boiling water, just blow torch them and the skins will just fall off.

AMBITIONS AS A CHILD?

I wanted to be a chef. Everyone is a chef in the family – my dad, sister, cousin, uncle. Since I was about five I wanted to work in the kitchen. I remember my dad used to do private functions – our living room would be full of teapots when he had just done an event, and I wanted to follow in his footsteps!

FAVOURITE KITCHEN GADGET?

My Thermomix! It's so versatile, you can do everything with it, it's a great bit of kit. I'd like to get a Pacojet which is similar but the blade goes ten times faster.

FUNNY CULINARY MOMENT?

We used to keep a bowl of chocolate on top of the bakers' ovens at the Lanesborough to keep it melted. You guessed it! I tipped the whole bowl over me...

WHY I'M STILL A CHEF?

Every day is different. You never know what to expect, and you are also forever learning.

FAVOURITE TIME OF YEAR TO COOK?

I love the winter, the flavours and versatility of the veg, the hearty dishes, the stews – just good, real cooking!

ULTIMATE DREAM?

I'd love to own a freehold, and I'd like to run a B&B with four or five rooms in a countryside setting, and not under too much pressure!

PHIL ON HIS...

BEST DISH EVER EATEN?

On our mini-moon we went to Portofino in Italy and we had linguini with black truffles, parmesan and ceps. The dish came to the table in the frying pan with the oil and then they tipped it into a giant parmesan hollowed out, then stirred it inside the parmesan and scraped it out for us to eat. We were sitting by the sea looking at the boats with a glass of wine, and it was just lovely.

SIGNATURE DISHES

Starters

Salt beef terrine, mustard mayonnaise, pickles, toasted sourdough

Scottish smoked salmon, shallot, chives, egg white & yolk, capers, crème fraiche, toasted rye bread

English beetroot & goats' cheese salad, candied walnuts

Mains

Roast fillet of beef, watercress, pickled shallot salad, triple cooked chips, béarnaise

Roast rack of lamb, petits pois à la française, mint jelly

Trout, clams, pancetta and croûton butter, samphire, lemon

Puddings

Individual treacle tart, vanilla ice cream

White chocolate, lime, cocoa sorbet

Warm chocolate fondant, salted caramel ice cream

DISH OF MY CHILDHOOD?

Mum's lamb stew. To be honest, I never really liked it that much, although I did like her stodgy dumplings.

FAVOURITE COOKBOOKS?

I buy them for the sake of buying them and I use them to get ideas. I have hundreds and hundreds – we've had to buy extra shelves to accommodate them all!

Drinking in tradition

They say that old habits die hard, and that's certainly the case with The Hoop free house in Stock, owned by Phil and Michelle Utz since 2006. The building was originally three weavers' cottages, and was converted into a pub – or ale house as it would have been called then – some 450 years ago. It's been going strong ever since.

Some of the building's original timber frame is used ornamentally, and the old-world look inside The Hoop continues as a mark of respect for its long heritage – this isn't a place to find fruit machines, non-descript music or satellite TV. It is a real ale pub with a solid wood bar, plenty of bar stools and a chunky brass bell to call 'time gentlemen'. Exposed beams and open brickwork fireplaces are a feature, there is some original wooden planked flooring, and the bumpy walls are simply white-washed.

Downstairs is the place for no-frills pub food with home-cooked favourites and a no-booking policy, while upstairs in the recently renovated Oak Room is where chef-owner Phil Utz offers his more refined à la carte menu. The vaulted ceiling makes the room feel spacious, and a striking chandelier gives sparkle – there's a little bit of glamour about this space, especially with the pristine white cloths, gleaming glassware and soft purple velvet seating.

The annual Hoop Beer Festival, held every late May bank holiday weekend, is another tradition set to continue, it would seem. The two-day event is a chance to try over 100 real ales and 80 ciders, as well as feast on an all-day barbecue and hog roast.

The Hoop
21 High Street, Stock, Ingatestone CM4 9BD
W: thehoop.co.uk
T: 01277 841137
E: thehoopstock@yahoo.co.uk
/thehoopstock
@TheHoopStock
/thehoop

Accolades: Waitrose *Good Food Guide* (Oak Room); AA one rosette

Covers: 40

Cost: average carte £30; wine from £16.00; pint from £3.20

Open: Oak Room Tue-Fri L 12-2.30; Tues-Sat D 7-9; Sun 12-3. Bar food Mon-Fri L 12-2.30; Mon-Fri D 6-9 (Fri 9.30); Sat 12-9.30; Sun 12-5

Details: Private dining for 40 (seated) or 50 (buffet) in the Oak Room; annual beer festival; wheelchair access (ground floor only); parking nearby.

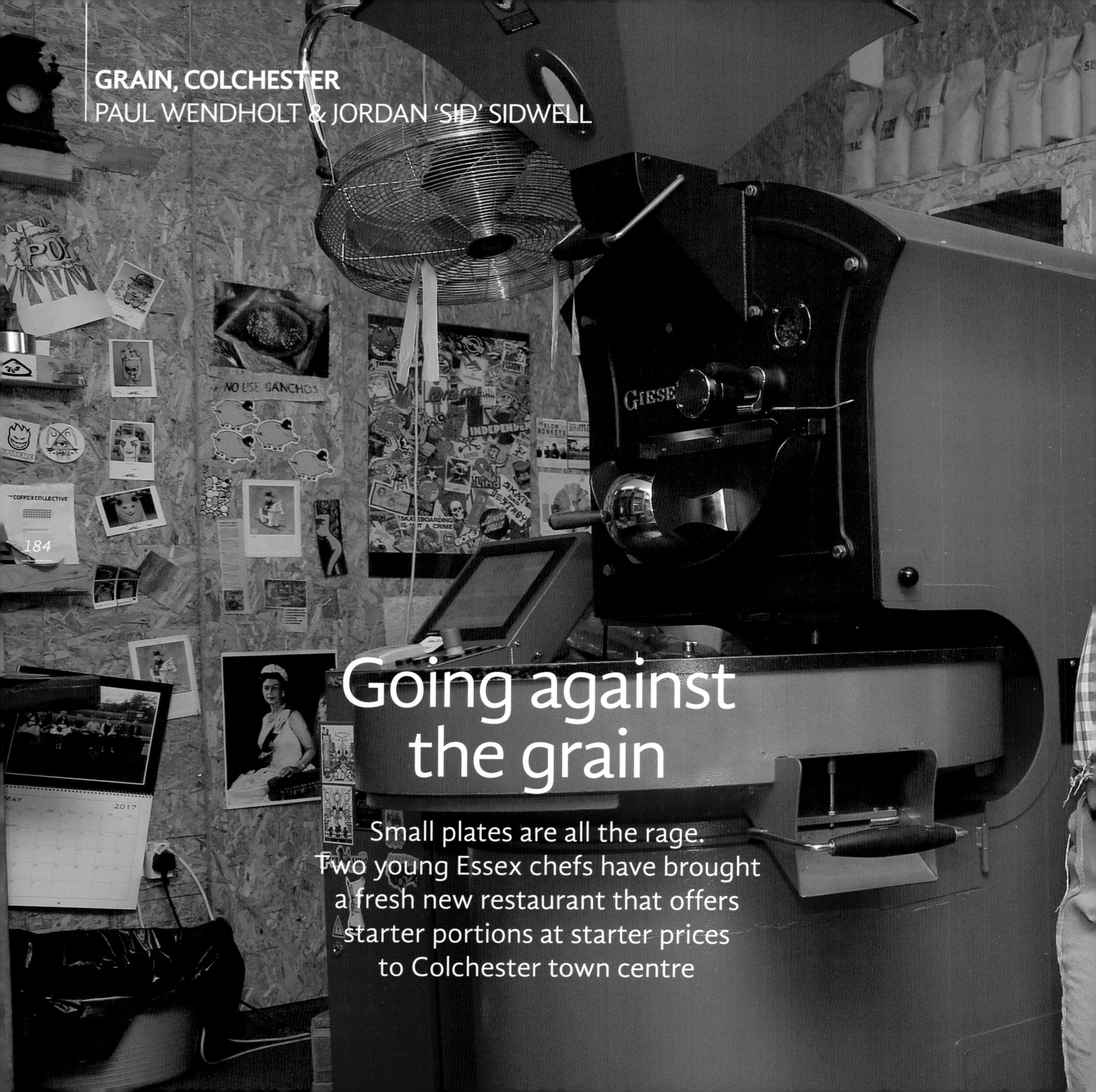

Going against the grain

Small plates are all the rage. Two young Essex chefs have brought a fresh new restaurant that offers starter portions at starter prices to Colchester town centre

MOFO DELUXE
PREMIUM
ORIGIN JANUARY 2017
FINCA

GRAIN PAUL WENDHOLT & JORDAN 'SID' SIDWELL

If it wasn't for 167 Kickstarter backers and their £11,290 whip-round, Grain would not exist, co-owners and chefs Paul Wendholt and Jordan 'Sid' Sidwell would probably be working at others' stoves, and Colchester would not have this relaxed, youthful spot tucked away down North Hill to shake up the town's dining scene.

As it is, Paul and Jordan have opened their own place to considerable local applause, bringing a fresh, new small-plates restaurant (starter sized, starter priced) to the heart of England's oldest recorded town. Both Essex-born and with early careers in Essex restaurants under their respective belts, they met at Wivenhoe House hotel in Colchester back in 2012. "I met Paul [Boorman, executive chef at Wivenhoe House] at the *Essex Chronicle* Chef of the Year final in 2009. He gave me a card and said 'if you ever need a job give me a call'. I eventually ended up working with him at Wivenhoe House which is where I met Jordan." The pair hit it off, worked elsewhere (Jordan went to Switzerland for a bit, Paul opened a bar-restaurant in Chelmsford), and when the time was right joined forces to run a 30-day Kickstarter campaign to create Grain which finally opened in summer 2017.

Offering food from many parts of the world, this is a place for the likes of polenta-dusted snapper, bang-bang chicken with slaw, roast and confit duck, or milk chocolate s'mores. "I'd say it's global," says Paul. Jordan, who finds inspiration from Netflix programmes such as *Chef's Table* and *The Mind of a Chef*, agrees.

They have produced more dishes in the six months since opening, they say, than either ever has before. "We are full of ideas! Initially, we'd change the menu every week, but then we realised that customers were coming back with friends and asking for particular dishes. Our one-hour egg and the crispy pork was creating its own following on social media – we even had an Asian couple who ordered using pictures they'd downloaded from Instagram!" Now, the dishes evolve rather than change rigorously every week. Diners are encouraged to order perhaps three of the starter-sized savoury plates each, followed by something from the sweet selection menu, or of course to have as many or as few as suits their appetite, and whatever combination of sweet and savoury takes their fancy.

Paul and Jordan's determination to use local suppliers led them to Remfresh at Ardleigh, and Anglia Produce for fruit and vegetables sourced from local farms. Pyefleet Pure oysters supplied by the Colchester Oyster Fishery are another favourite, as is meat from Frank Wright, a local Colchester butcher.

The Essex coffee-roasting company, Mac & Me, also fits the Grain ethos. "As soon as we contacted them they were like 'come and meet us and see how we roast the coffee and see the freshness of the beans we are importing'," says Jordan "They were so into it, we just knew we'd found the right supplier. Their coffee is smooth and rich, ideal not only to serve to our customers, but also to use in recipes."

Mac & Me is run by Grant Whitaker, Damian Barrett and David Macdonald from the roastery in a simple barn complex in Writtle, just outside Chelmsford. Initially a coffee import business, the three started to roast their own beans in small batches for local trade customers back in 2013 developing a barista training wing alongside the roastery. Damian explains: "We are genuinely interested in the customer, which is why we want to show them the importance of the ethical side of our business and the beans we roast. We work with restaurant owners and show them what makes a good cup of coffee, from getting the freshest beans, to the freshest roast, and we also teach them how to make a really good cup of coffee."

Grant met Paul and Jordan at Grain when he delivered their first order. "I remember thinking they are really young and brave with this new concept which they were hell-bent on doing! Once I stepped inside Grain though, I thought they'd lucked out. It's perfect for them."

Back in Colchester, whites on and with the 'Grain'-stamped bag of Mac & Me's Homeblend coffee to hand, Paul makes the coffee parfait, adding bubbling, golden coffee sugar syrup to the egg yolks, whisking furiously all the while. He folds in coffee-infused whipped cream, then lightens the mixture with Italian meringue. "You wouldn't think it would necessarily work," he says. "Obviously coffee and chocolate works well, but they are very rich so by serving the parfait with passion fruit you cut through some of the sweetness." With dashes of passion fruit purée on the plate first, Paul carefully places a rocher of chocolate mousse topped with the tiniest sprinkle of Maldon sea salt on top, finishing the plate with two pieces of the coffee parfait and fine gratings from a freshly-roasted coffee bean.

The coffee pops up elsewhere on the Grain menu. "I use it in our meat rubs for our pulled pork," says Jordan. "It has a really savoury, earthy taste, not at all like coffee. You can also use the coffee grounds with celeriac in a salt crust, or try a shot of espresso in barbecue beans – it gives an amazing depth of flavour!"

Espresso coffee parfait, milk chocolate and passion fruit

One of our most popular desserts, first impressions might make coffee, chocolate and passion fruit seem an odd combination but it does work. The sharpness and fruitiness of the passion fruit cuts through the richness of the milk chocolate and the roasted caramel notes of the coffee. Use the equivalent weight of pasteurised egg yolks and whites for this recipe if at all vulnerable. Please note the parfait recipe calls for distinct caution as it uses molten sugar and therefore should only be attempted by confident cooks.

Parfait

350g double cream
35g coffee beans
150g sugar
1 shot of good espresso
2 whole eggs and 2 yolks
2 egg whites
100g sugar

Bring the cream and coffee beans to a simmer and set aside for 2 hours before sieving into a bowl and chilling in the fridge. Simmer the sugar, espresso and a little water together to 120c (using a sugar thermometer). Whisk the eggs and yolks in a food mixer until fluffy, continue whisking while very gently pouring in the espresso until the mixture cools to room temperature. Whisk the chilled coffee cream into soft peaks and fold together with the espresso mix. Whisk the whites in a food mixer to soft peaks. Boil the remaining sugar and a little water to 118c and very carefully pour in slowly while whisking to make an Italian meringue. Fold half of it into the coffee mix vigorously, then fold in the other half with a spatula gently to combine. Place in clingfilmed moulds and freeze for at least 8 hours.

Chocolate mousse

100ml double cream
20g honey
160g milk chocolate, broken up
185ml double cream

Dissolve the 100ml cream and honey together in a heavy saucepan over a high heat, remove and pour over the broken-up chocolate in a large bowl. Leave for a few minutes, then stir until melted together, smooth and glossy. Whisk the 185ml cream to firm peaks and fold well through the chocolate mixture. Chill for a few hours until set.

Biscuits

115g softened butter
60g caster sugar
20g soft dark brown sugar
150g plain flour
¼ tsp bicarbonate of soda
¼ tsp salt
2 tsp cinnamon
1 tsp nutmeg

Pre-heat the oven to 170c. Beat together the butter and both sugars in a food mixer until light and fluffy. Add all the dry ingredients and mix until it becomes a soft dough. Spread thinly onto a baking paper-lined tray (or use silicone sheet). Bake for 12-15 minutes until the biscuits are golden and browning around the edges. For a uniform shape, cut the edges whilst still warm. Cool and store in an airtight container.

Passion fruit

2 passion fruit
Caster sugar

Halve the fruit, catching any juice, and empty the flesh into a bowl, along with any juice off your cutting board. Weigh a jug and sieve the fruit into it, using a ladle to help push through all the juice. Calculate the weight of the juice and add it with 10% of its weight in sugar into a heavy saucepan. Bring to a boil and cook until reduced by a third before decanting into a bowl and chilling.

To serve

Dark chocolate
Coffee beans

Remove the parfait from the moulds by dipping the outside in boiling water quickly and decanting onto cold plates. Leave to soften for 10 minutes at room temperature. Place a spoonful of mousse alongside, dress with the passion fruit sauce and broken-up biscuits. Finally grate over a little chocolate and coffee bean.

Baked duck egg, chorizo and patatas bravas

If we had the time at the restaurant, this would be our perfect breakfast every morning! But it is also great for brunch, lunch, or a quick midweek supper. (serves 4)

1 bunch flat leaf parsley
100ml olive oil
200g chorizo sausage (diced or torn depending on your mood)
8 cooked new potatoes
20 cherry tomatoes, halved
4 fresh duck eggs (at room temperature)

Blend most of the parsley leaves with the oil in a liquidiser until smooth and refrigerate.

Pre-heat the oven to 175c.
In a hot oiled frying pan, sauté the chorizo until crispy, then remove it with a slotted spoon. Brush the oil from the pan around four ramekins and set aside. Heat the pan and any remaining oil on a medium heat, add the potatoes and cook, stirring regularly, until golden. Fold through the chorizo, tomatoes and the remaining parsley. Cook for a few minutes and season to taste before setting aside somewhere warm.

Break the duck eggs into the ramekins and bake for 3 minutes, remove and top with the pan mixture. Return to the oven for a further 2 minutes. Leave to stand until the egg has just cooked through. Dress with the parsley oil and seasoning before serving.

Mackerel ceviche with cucumber and dill

Full of summer flavours, we also garnish this classic Peruvian-style marinated raw fish starter with charred cucumber. (serves 4)

3 large lemons, juiced
50ml white wine vinegar
Sprig of dill
Fennel and coriander seed
Small bunch of dill leaves
Extra virgin olive oil
Cucumber, diced
Lemon halves for squeezing
4 boneless mackerel fillets

Simmer the juice and vinegar with the dill sprig, a pinch of each seed, 100ml water and a pinch of salt for two minutes. Decant the liquor into a jug, cool and chill overnight.

Blend the dill with sufficient olive oil until smooth and pourable. Set aside. Mix the cucumber with seasoning and a little lemon juice before drizzling with olive oil. Slice the mackerel fillets into long strips and marinate in the liquor for 4 minutes before draining. Lay out the fish on cold plates with the cucumber and a drizzle of dill oil.

Potato bread and crème fraîche butter

Churning your own butter is so easy with a food mixer, and tastes delicious with this simple potato bread, halfway between a crumpet and a white loaf. The loaf toasts brilliantly and keeps well. (serves 4+)

250g full fat crème fraîche
300g strong white flour
300g dry mashed potato (from baked potato is best)
1 sachet (7g) fast action yeast (or 20g fresh yeast)
15g salt
10g malt extract
20ml rapeseed oil
75ml golden ale
Butter or rapeseed oil

Whisk the crème fraîche with 2g of fine salt at a medium speed on an electric mixer. The cream will thicken, then begin to split into fat solids and buttermilk. Reduce the speed and when the fat starts to clump together, remove from the machine and strain through a sieve into a bowl. Refrigerate until needed.

Place the next 6 ingredients in a mixer bowl and add 50ml of ale and mix with a dough hook for 10 minutes slowly. Cover the bowl with clingfilm and leave at room temperature for an hour. Knead the dough for 1 minute to knock out the air. Shape and place into a greased loaf tin, Prove again for an hour until almost doubled in size. Pre-heat the oven to 185c. Bake for 30-40 minutes until the loaf is golden and hollow-sounding when tapped underneath.

PAUL AND JORDAN ON THEIR...

MENTOR?

Paul Boorman was a real mentor for me, especially in my early career. Also, the chefs I worked with in Switzerland. I concentrated on pâtisserie which over there is broken down into à la carte pâtisserie, confectionery and konditorei (bakery), so it's very, very professional, a real art. You get a far more in-depth understanding of that one area. *– Jordan*

CHILDHOOD AMBITIONS?

When I was little I wanted to be a pilot, but then I decided there was too much work involved, so I became a chef. How little I knew. *– Paul*

CHEFFY TIP?

If you want to do breaded chicken, or in fact breaded anything, don't use breadcrumbs. Use Rice Krispies just broken down with a pestle and mortar or a food processor. It will give you a great, tasty crunch. It's not really a shortcut, but it gives you a far better result in my opinion. *– Paul*

FAVOURITE INGREDIENT?

I went to Japan last year and fell in love with their cuisine, so I use miso quite a bit now. I also love grated, crispy goats' cheese – it's grated goats' cheese, scattered thinly over a baking tray and slowly cooked to caramelise. Once it cools it can either be broken into crisps or ground to use almost as a seasoning. It loses its creaminess and is replaced with a salty and crisp-textured cheese. - *Paul*

SIGNATURE DISHES

Savoury

Black pudding, one-hour egg, hash brown, mushroom ketchup

Crispy pork, cashew, sesame, yuzu

Prawn slider, sweet potato fries, avocado

Confit parsnip, cavolo nero, gingerbread, cranberry

Roast and confit duck, carrot, miso, Jersey Royals

Beetroot, goats' cheese, raspberry, mint

Sweet

Caramelised banana, peanut butter, malt, vanilla

Sticky toffee apple pudding, bonfire caramel

Milk chocolate s'mores

IF I COULD COOK FOR ANYONE?

Stephen Fry, just because when I hear him talking about food I get the impression he's a real foodie but not pretentious about it. He's such an interesting guy. Hopefully he'd enjoy what we're doing here, and if he could tweet about it that would be good too! *– Jordan*

IF NOT A CHEF?

I'd love to be a food writer, to go to other restaurants, try their food and write about it – I could see myself doing that! Perhaps something to consider for the future. *– Jordan*

BEST DISH I'VE EVER EATEN?

The ones which are amazing are the ones when you don't quite know how they've done it. In Copenhagen I ate in a one-Michelin star restaurant, Relae. It was a simple dish of mushrooms, with a mushroom purée, raw and cooked mushrooms and salsify. So simple but the end result was incredible. *– Paul*

WHERE AM I HAPPIEST?

Anywhere with a glass of wine in my hand! Seriously though, I love to be outside enjoying the Essex sunshine and now with our own restaurant I've taken more of an interest in wine and Champagne. We regularly finish our shift and sit out in the courtyard and taste the latest samples delivered to us by our wine supplier. *– Jordan*

A kick start in business

Owning your own Kickstarter-enabled restaurant as a young chef would be daunting enough, without throwing in one or two other factors – as Paul Wendholt knows only too well. "Jordan was in Switzerland when I came across this restaurant, so I was sending him pictures and negotiating on behalf of both of us. He was out of the country for the whole acquisition process – but we got there in the end!" Not content with managing the purchase, Paul has also married his fiancée Laura, moved house, and become a dad for the first time – all within the space of 18 months.

Inside Grain, favourite cookbooks by some of the world's finest chefs, including Daniel Humm (Eleven Madison Park), Dan Doherty (Duck and Waffle), and Massimo Bottura (Osteria Francescana) are housed in wooden wine boxes made into makeshift book shelves; there's a small wooden bar with stools to match, chunky wooden tables and chairs, and industrial-style lighting that all add to the simplistic look. It all fits with the no-frills approach to the food. A central courtyard with its own fireplace is a sheltered, secluded spot at the heart of the restaurant, while a private dining room is used on busy nights to accommodate diners. On the first floor, in contrast to the simpler ground-floor style, are flamingo-pink velour sofas, a popular spot to relax with a pre- or post-dinner drink.

Grain
11a North Hill, Colchester CO1 1DZ
W: grain-colchester.co.uk
T: 01206 570005
E: info@grain-colchester.co.uk
/graincolchester
@grainrest
/graincolchester

Accolades: Waitrose *Good Food Guide*

Covers: 40, plus courtyard dining

Cost: average carte £27; wine from £21; beers from £4

Open: Weds-Sun L 12-2; Tues-Sat D 6.30-9 (Fri-Sat 9.30)

Details: private dining for up to 10; alfresco tables; wheelchair access; town centre location; parking nearby

THE VINE, GREAT BARDFIELD

STEPHEN MANN

Pork talk

A chance conversation at the bar of The Vine led to a happy chef-supplier relationship between Stephen Mann and Greg Coe

If you go down to the Vine on the August bank holiday, don't be surprised to find yourself sharing the pub garden with a few frisky rare breed pigs. "We have a beer festival here that weekend every year," says chef-owner, Stephen Mann, "and Greg [Coe, pork supplier] brings six of his rare breed pigs to race in the garden. It's great fun; we had around 600 people in watching last year and we raised £3,500 for Guide Dogs for the Blind. They asked us to name one of their puppies, so we called him Bardfield – of course!"

The relationship between Stephen and Tanya Mann and Greg 'The Egg' Coe goes back three years, ever since Greg dropped into the bar one day and got talking with Stephen about his rare breed pigs, his free range hens (hence his nickname) and how he used to work at The Vine many years ago washing up. These days Greg stays front of house, forward of the bar, and when he's not chatting to the other locals he's selling his free range produce to them, particularly on a Friday night.

Pork from Greg Coe's Kitchen Farm features regularly on the Vine menu, maybe as a peanut-crusted pork with candied walnuts, pork crackers and peanut sauce, or a ham hock terrine with peas, or with gherkins served with apple and cauliflower pickle.

Stephen loves to work with the pork from Greg's farm. "Pork is so versatile and this particular meat is so tasty and we like to support our local economy too. Our customers love the dishes we create using this particular rare breed pork."

Greg is keen to show Stephen his animals, so we head to the farm in nearby Bardfield Saling. "I used to work in construction," Greg explains, "but I got fed up with commuting on the M11, so bought a few acres and some hens back in 2002." Since then, he has expanded the farm to a full 52 acres and, as well as the hens and a flock of rare breed Soay sheep, he rears his pigs, crossing Tamworth Large Blacks with Oxford Sandy and Blacks to create gloriously inquisitive animals with thick coats of coarse black hair – and, above all, great-tasting meat. "They produce delicious pork, a really rich flavour because they've lived for nine to twelve months in a field." Greg also grows some of the food for his animals himself: "I grind up my own barley or wheat which I grow here on the farm, and soya protein which I buy in, for the lactating sows I use Badminton Feed from Baileys which is 300 yards up the road from us."

"When I decided to go into farming, I wanted to go back to the old ways," Greg says. "My pigs are born in arks out in the field which have a bed of warm straw. They spend all their life out in open farmland, and they can do that because of their coats – they are bred to live outdoors." When eventually they are slaughtered it's at Humphreys which is just 15 minutes away from Greg's farm.

When he's not looking after his animals and hens, Greg delivers his produce to the nearby villages, finishing up on a Friday night at The Vine selling to their customers. "It's back to the old days, delivering to my customers and rearing the animals the way it used to be." He clearly cares for his animals. "You know when pigs are

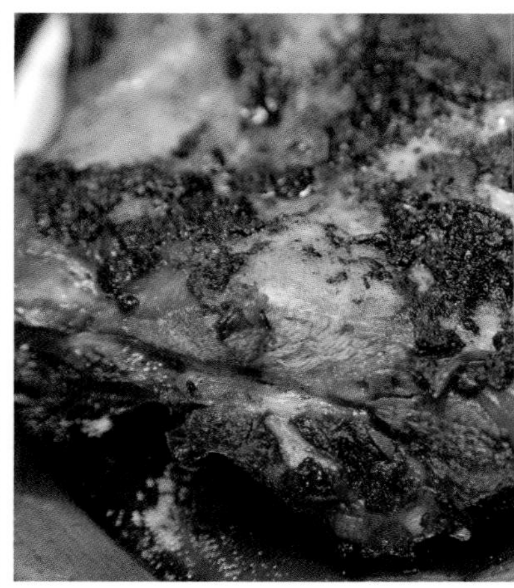

happy because their curly tails go completely straight," he says – and indeed they did, every time Greg threw another scoop of meal in their direction. "It's so nice seeing them in their own environment," says Stephen. "It's important for me to know where our ingredients come from. Being able to see where and how they are reared has been great especially when they live so close by."

Back at The Vine, Stephen shows his sous chef, Georgia Boon, how to bone the pork belly before the two of them rub pungent sage leaves and salt into the skin and place the meat into a roasting tin on top of plenty of freshly chopped onion. They slosh dry cider round the joint, and put it in the oven for at least three to four hours, allowing it to steep and to cook long and slow.

This is the sort of cooking Stephen likes best, a traditional style which will often use the whole animal. "I suppose I'd describe it as 'English with a twist'. My mother was an atrocious cook and because Dad preferred my cooking, at the age of ten I was cooking for the whole family. I learnt everything from my grandmother Emily who I called Nanny James. I used to spend the summer holidays with her and loved watching her cook."

With 30 years' experience working in the hospitality industry under his belt, Stephen opened The Vine with his wife Tanya in 2009. "We used to host food and wine pairing dinners at home for 10-14 guests every weekend. Our friends kept saying we should run a pub – and here we are! I think we've managed to create a country pub that serves good real ale and fantastic wines, and that is also a place where we share our love of good food made using locally-sourced ingredients."

As for the best wine to pair with the slow-cooked belly, Tanya suggests a white wine, a Pinot Gris from the MacMurray Estate, Sonoma, California. "It has a very complex aroma spectrum. It's peachy yet spicy with a rounded pleasant body and is refreshing too. It's so good and we sell it exclusively here at The Vine."

Slow-cooked pork belly with onion and cider sauce served with mash and tenderstem broccoli

This fairly inexpensive cut of pork makes a very tasty weekday supper or homely centrepiece for a family Sunday lunch. Potato-wise for the mash, go for the floury varieties like Maris Piper or King Edward if you can and for the broccoli, the regular large-headed calabrese type eats fine but I prefer the long tenderstem or purple sprouting sort. If you cook the pork belly ahead of time, which works well, you do need to reheat it uncovered in the oven until piping hot. Time the potato and broccoli to coincide with the meat and sauce being ready to serve, they really don't like hanging around. (serves 6)

Pork belly

Bunch fresh sage
Few tbsp good local rapeseed oil
2kg piece pork belly, skin removed
3 large white onions
500ml good dry cider

Pre-heat the oven to 160c. Thinly shred the sage and mix with enough oil to make a paste. Rub all over the pork belly.

Slice the peeled onions thickly, scatter on the bottom of a large deep roasting tray and place the pork on top. Pour the cider over the meat. Wrap the tin tightly with a double sheet of foil and cook for 3-4 hours or until very tender. Remove the pork from the tray onto a hot serving plate, loosely cover with foil, and allow it to rest somewhere warm such as the back of the hob.

Pour the contents of the tin into a large saucepan and boil until well-reduced to a syrupy consistency, stirring regularly to prevent the onions from sticking. At this point, you can strain the liquor to remove the onions if preferred. Keep the pan hot.

Mashed potato

1.5kg potatoes, peeled
150g unsalted butter
75ml single cream

Cut the potatoes into golf ball-sized chunks and bring to a boil in a lidded saucepan of cold, salted water.

Simmer for 10-15 minutes until tender in the middle when tested with a sharp knife. Drain into a colander and return to the pan, putting back on the low heat for a few minutes to steam dry. Place the butter and cream in another small pan over a low heat until melted together. Meanwhile, mash the potatoes until smooth and then fold in the butter-cream mixture carefully. Season to taste and beat until mixed well together.

Broccoli

24 tenderstem or sprouting broccoli florets
Knob of unsalted butter

Bring the florets to the boil in salted water and simmer until tender, about two minutes for tenderstem and probably double that for sprouting broccoli. Drain well, return to the pan, season to taste and add the butter before gently tossing a little to glaze.

To serve

Onion-cider reduction from the pork
2 heaped tsp wholegrain mustard
100ml double cream

Stir the mustard and cream into the reduction, bring to a simmer and season to taste. Meanwhile, carve the pork belly into thick slices and place on a warm serving platter. Serve with the sauce in a jug, alongside the mash and broccoli.

Yellowfin tuna sashimi with bloody mary jelly

A stylish starter, which sounds far harder to make than it is, one to wow your friends and family with. The freshest tuna from a good fishmonger is key. (serves 4+)

3 leaves of gelatine
250ml tomato juice
10ml good vodka
Worcestershire sauce
Tabasco
1 avocado, flesh only
1tbsp crème fraîche
500g yellowfin tuna fillet
Juice of half a lime

Soften the gelatine in cold water for 10 minutes. Mix together the tomato juice, vodka, a dash of worcestershire sauce, and tabasco and warm up in a pan, seasoning to taste. Remove from the heat and whisk in the drained gelatine. Place in a storage container and chill until set. Slice the jelly into tiny squares.

Blend the avocado until smooth with the crème fraîche and season to taste.

Carve the tuna into small cubes, then pipe on the avocado mix and finish with the jelly.

Blackened salmon with sugar snap peas

A good light lunch dish with a dressed salad and warm homemade bread. Some prefer the salmon very lightly-cooked in the centre – it's up to you. (serves 4)

3tbsp black treacle
90ml warm water
4 100g salmon fillet portions
2 large handfuls of sugar snap peas
Knob of unsalted butter

Mix the treacle with the water until blended. Place the salmon in a snug container, pour over the treacle mix and leave to marinate for 30 minutes. Drain well in a colander. Prepare a saucepan of boiling salted water for the peas.

Heat a large, oiled frying pan over a medium-high setting and put the salmon in skin-side down. Beware, it will spit! While it cooks, simmer the peas for a few minutes. Turn over the fish once browned and continue to fry on the other side until just cooked through. Drain the peas and return to the saucepan with seasoning to taste and butter, tossing to glaze. To serve, put some of the treacle on a warmed plate, place the salmon on top and finish with the peas.

Steak sauce, the best and easiest

This is a flexible friend, a Saturday supper staple perfect with steak, chips, peas and crispy onion rings. Adjust the quantities to suit how many you are feeding. You can add wholegrain mustard or piquant blue cheese to change the flavours. (serves 2)

1 medium red onion
Good local rapeseed oil
4 rashers smoked streaky bacon
2 portobello mushrooms
Glug of drinkable brandy
Double cream

In a large deep frying pan over a medium heat, sauté the onion in a little oil until soft and just browning. Empty into a dish and keep warm. Finely shred the bacon and roughly slice the mushrooms. Heat the pan on a high setting, add a little more oil and stir-fry the bacon and mushrooms until browning well. Return the onions and then taking the pan away from the heat, stir in the brandy and enough cream to give a good serving of sauce. Once all the ingredients are combined, bring the sauce to a simmer and season to taste before serving alongside your perfectly cooked, juicy steaks.

STEPHEN ON HIS...

BEST RESTAURANT I'VE EATEN IN?

The Fat Duck at Bray, which was just an amazing experience. They showed us all round as they recognised Tanya so their sommelier wanted to ask her lots of questions. I had sweetbreads and then with the seafood dish they gave me headphones and put shells on the plate to take the whole experience to another dimension.

ULTIMATE DINING DESTINATION?

I would love to go to China to sample their food.

FAVOURITE TIME OF YEAR TO COOK?

Christmas! I just love it. I have fostered over 40 children and when you're making it special for them it's just a happy time of year. Plus, there's all the abundance of great ingredients.

WHAT I CHOOSE WHEN EATING OUT?

Usually a steak. I tend to prefer old-fashioned food, so I might choose a steak & kidney pudding. Tanya likes to go to fine dining places on our time off but that's just three days a year!

COOKERY TIP?

To quenelle always wrap cling film around the spoon first, that way the food won't stick to the metal.

CHILDHOOD FOOD MEMORIES?

Fighting over the custard skin!

SIGNATURE DISHES

Starters

Deep-fried shredded chilli beef, sweet chilli sauce, spring onions, sesame seeds

Ham hock & pea terrine, apple & cauliflower piccalilli, sourdough toast

Crispy gnocchi, goats' cheese, rocket, sage oil, roasted butternut squash

Mains

Wild mushroom ravioli, mushroom cream sauce, Italian hard cheese

Chickpea, sweet potato & spinach curry

Oven-roasted salmon fillet, chorizo, cannellini beans, tomato cassoulet, tenderstem broccoli

Puddings

Chai tea pannacotta

Chocolate & orange torte

Pear, honey & almond frangipane tart, champagne sorbet

FAVOURITE KITCHEN GADGET?

My kitchen knife – it's where everything starts from – and also 'Granddad' our meat fork which is over 100 years old. My grandfather bought a fork and steel in 1914 with his first wages. He was originally a chef. We still use it here every Sunday.

IF NOT A CHEF?

I would have liked to have been an airline pilot.

FAVOURITE PART OF ESSEX?

Brightlingsea. I have a small motor boat called *Corkscrew*. If I can get down there I am as happy as Larry with a cup of coffee or a gin and tonic.

PERFECT DINNER GUEST?

Nelson Mandela, I could just talk to him about so many different things.

MIDNIGHT FEAST?

A cheese and pickle or sausage sandwich. I'll cook off four sausages earlier in the evening, let them go cold, then enjoy them at 1am with tomato sauce.

A fine pairing

Stephen and Tanya Mann took over The Vine in May 2014, refurbishing it to their standards and creating one of the country's first so-called 'eno-gastro' pubs. While Stephen takes charge of the kitchen, Tanya is the wine connoisseur. Having studied at the Enoteca Italiana Wine School in Siena, Italy, she worked in Selfridges wine department and at the legendary Bordeaux estate, Chateau Margaux, before branching into journalism, teaching and hosting wine tastings.

The wine list at The Vine is a tempting line-up of over 100 bottles, ranging from white rioja and Hungarian dry tokaji to some rare vintage wines. "We purchased all the stock recently of the Barboursville 2010 'Octagon' [from Virginia, USA] which American wine critic James Suckling gave a 90-plus score. We also introduced a new price model for our wines at the Vine, so for example a £25 wine here would set you back say £70 in London."

Expert advice is of course on hand, and staff are always delighted to suggest wines. Not surprisingly, there are regular wine-food pairing evenings hosted by Tanya and often with a guest winemaker – not long before our visit, Ernesto Casetta of the Casetta winery in Piedmont, northern Italy, had presented a range of classic Italian wines.

But you can still enjoy The Vine just for its honest food and its strong 'community' atmosphere. Outside there's a double bay fronted exterior with floral arrangements and potted olive trees. Inside the décor resembles an Edwardian parlour, oak floors, scatter rugs, ornate fireplace, and a welcome bar giving a homely ambience. Dogs are welcome in the bar and there's a separate dining room at the back. The bar itself offers a generous 47 different gins, and 11 lagers and ales on tap.

The Vine
Vine St, Great Bardfield, Braintree CM7 4SR
W: vine-greatbardfield.co.uk
T: 01371 811822
E: steve@stephenmann.me
/VineEnoGastro
@VineBardfield

Accolades: finalist, Harpers Awards 2015; OpenTable Diners' Choice award 2017

Covers: 52

Cost: average carte £25; wine from £15.90; pint from £3.30

Open: all week L 12-3; D 6-9

Details: outside catering service; takeaway menu every evening; regular wine tastings and other events; wheelchair access (restaurant only); dog-friendly; parking

The flour of love

Flour from Marriage's, the Chelmsford-based master millers, is at the heart of Matthew Court's menu at the charming and rural Pig & Whistle Restaurant

THE MASTER MILLERS
CULINARY
FLOUR
FOR LIGHT SPONGES, SCONES & MUFFINS

MARRIAGE'S
Millers
MARRIAGE'S
THE MASTER MILLERS
CULINARY
SELF
RAISING
WHITE
FLOUR

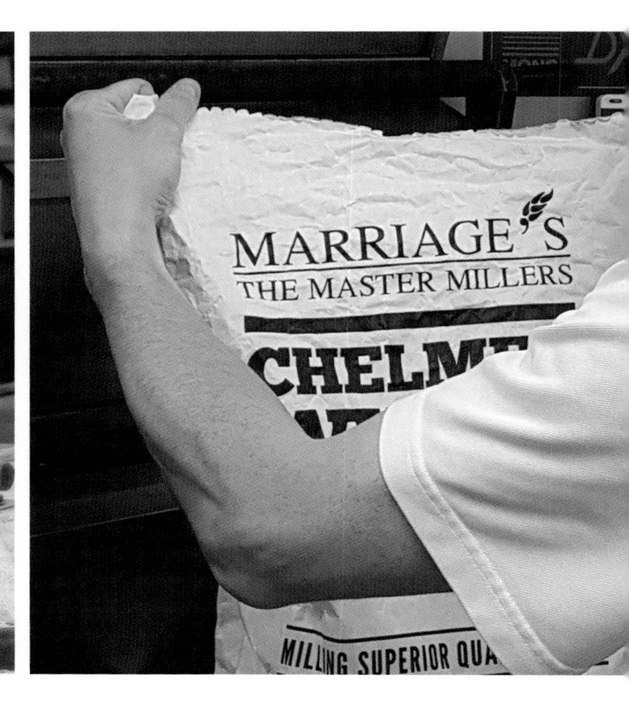

The summer view from Pig & Whistle Restaurant's sun-trap terrace is of rippling ears of wheat. The crop stretches off into the distance, the field framed by clumps of trees, until the vast East Anglian sky dips to meet it. It's quite a picture.

For Matthew Court, head chef at this peaceful countryside restaurant just ten minutes from busy Chelmsford, the crop is vital. Just weeks after our visit, it will be harvested, taken to Marriage's to be milled, and in due course find its way back to Matthew's larder as a staple ingredient for his modern European menu.

"I use Marriage's flour all the time," he says as he prepares the chocolate dessert for the photoshoot. "It's in this sponge, it's in the batter for our freshly prepared fish and chips, I use it seasoned to coat calamari which I serve with a red onion salsa and basil and garlic mayo, I use it to make arancini, and of course in loads of desserts."

Matthew is familiar with the Marriage's product, but this is his first visit to the factory at Chelmer Mills. Run by the Marriage family, Essex millers since 1824, the company is now in the hands of George Marriage and his daughter, Hannah, fifth and sixth generation millers respectively. "As soon as we arrived and were clothed from head to foot in protective white suits I realised there's a lot more to milling flour than I imagined!" Matthew says. "I thought the corn was just harvested, milled and put into sacks – simple as that!"

Although the factory is housed in one of the original mills, inside it is a tangle of machinery, gleaming hoppers, pipes, containers and gantries, some whirring and shaking as grain is tested, sifted, separated, purified, sorted, checked and checked again, before being packaged. Grain that doesn't make the grade is diverted to be turned into livestock feed, while grain that does get through the rigorous filters is passed through giant sieves that grade it from coarse, strong breadmaking flour to the finest of cake and pastry flour.

"We buy as much wheat as we can from farmers within 25-30 miles of Chelmer Mills," says George. "Many are farming families who have supplied Marriage's for generations, but we also use wheat from farms just a few miles away, including the land next to Pig & Whistle Restaurant which we own."

As we collective mourn the absence of traditional millstones, long since quashed under the weight of modern machinery, George shows us a room housing two huge stones. "We produce flour using a combination of traditional techniques and the best modern technology," George says, "and we use these original French burr

"I like to go with the changing trends and seasons. You could say my food is modern European."

stones to mill our stoneground wholemeal flours. They have been milling flour for over a hundred years and play a vital part in the taste and texture of that type," he says.

Matthew can't resist getting his hands into the flour in the Marriage's test kitchen where some 150 loaves are baked every week to make sure each type of flour comes up to scratch. "Having been shown around by George and Hannah, I've seen the milling process first-hand," Matthew says. "It's so complex, and done so expertly and scientifically, all factory-controlled with computers. It's been a real eye-opener!"

Back in his own kitchen, Matthew breaks chocolate into small pieces in a bowl and heats cream and butter in a pan to start making his chocolate sponge. He pours the creamy mixture over the chocolate, stirring the gloriously chocolatey blend till it melts, then whisks in milk before putting it all into the fridge to chill. He turns his attention to the pistachios roasting gently on the stove behind him, then mixes egg yolks with icing sugar in the Robot Coupe, before carefully folding in the sieved flour. He adds more melted chocolate, turns the mixture out and bakes it to a rich, dark sponge.

Matthew has spent his working life near his Chelmsford home having trained initially at Colchester Institute, and going on to develop a cooking style with many global influences. "I like to go with the changing trends and seasons. You could say my food is modern European, with lots of French and Italian influences like the arancini or the sharing antipasti platters, but then in the winter months I also like to include eastern European flavours and dishes such as slow-roasted meats, stews and goulash.

"I read blogs, catering magazines, do lots of research online, find ideas or recipes that I can adapt for my menu here. If something is currently in vogue in London, you can bet it will be here in Essex in the next three months! I don't like to copy anything but instead use what I read as a base to create a dish our customers would want to eat." It goes without saying that Matthew uses local suppliers whenever he can – seafood is from the Little Fish Company in Kelvedon which buys fish landed by small day-boats according to season, while meat, including rare breed, is from butchers Holts of Witham.

Chocolate truffle and fondant

A reworked take on the classic fondant pudding, this is a chocoholic's indulgent dream dessert. We garnish it with red-veined sorrel leaves, white chocolate shards and edible flowers to give a contrast in flavour and textures as well as an extra lift to the presentation! (serves 6+)

Fondant sponge

250g dark chocolate, in chunks
200g unsalted butter, diced
10 egg yolks
250g icing sugar
100g Marriage's plain white flour

Preheat the oven to 180c. Line a shallow baking tin, approx. 32 x 26cm, with parchment paper.

Melt the chocolate and the butter together in a large glass bowl, suspended over a pan of shallow boiling water on a high heat. Next whisk together the egg yolks and the icing sugar until creamy in a food mixer, then fold in the sieved flour until well incorporated. Pour the melted chocolate into the egg mixture, whisking slowly. Pour into the lined tin and knock to remove any air bubbles. Bake for 6-8 minutes, it should be almost cooked throughout but with a little wobble in the centre. Remove, cool and chill. When cold, cut into moon shapes with ring cutters.

Hazelnut cream

300ml double cream, whisked to soft peak
100g icing sugar
200g hazelnuts, crushed finely

Fold the cream and sugar together before stirring in the hazelnuts. Chill until required.

Chocolate truffle

300g dark chocolate, in small pieces
300ml double cream
50g unsalted butter
50ml milk

Heat the cream and butter together in a pan over a medium-hot heat until steaming but not simmering. Pour over the chocolate in a large heatproof bowl and stir until the chocolate is fully melted and incorporated. Finally pour in the milk and combine. Leave to set in the fridge for approx. 2 hours.

Mango purée

2 mangoes, flesh only

Process the fruit in a liquidiser or food mixer until smooth before storing in the fridge.

To serve

Place the moon-shaped fondant sponge on the plate. Using two spoons, shape the truffle mixture neatly into quenelles and place two on the sponge. Fill a piping bag with the hazelnut cream and pipe around the truffle. Decorate with the mango purée (ideally using a squeezy bottle) and any other garnishes before serving.

Oven-baked garlic and parsley cod

A simple fishy pasta dish for a hearty lunch – perfect with a dressed salad and a warm loaf of homemade bread alongside. (serves 4)

1 bunch parsley, finely shredded
4 cloves garlic, minced
250g butter, softened
4 160g portions of cod fillet or loin
400g linguine pasta
Rapeseed oil
16 fresh mussels, cleaned
100g garden peas
100g sundried tomato, finely sliced
200ml white wine
500ml double cream

Pre-heat the oven to 180c. Mix the parsley and garlic into the butter. Place the fish on a baking tray, topped with a tablespoon of the herb butter. Bake for 12-14 minutes.

Meanwhile, cook the pasta in a very large pan of salted boiling water until al dente, then drain and toss with a little oil.

At the same time, warm 2tbsp of oil in a deep lidded saucepan over a high heat and stir in the mussels. Cover for a minute, then add the peas, tomatoes and white wine. Boil hard for 2 minutes to reduce, pour in the cream and boil again for another 5 minutes. Fold in the pasta with tongs and season to taste.

Serve in hot bowls, topped with the cod.

Shiitake mushroom fritters with lemon and basil yoghurt

This crisp, savoury vegetarian starter eats well with a ratatouille-style mix of Mediterranean vegetables, roasted with garlic and tomato. (serves 4+)

50g puy lentils
200g shiitake mushrooms, sliced
Rapeseed oil
100g grated mature cheddar
1 egg
200g natural yoghurt
2 sprigs of basil, leaves only
1 lemon, zest and juice

Simmer the lentils, covered in hot water over a low heat until soft but holding their shape, about 20 minutes. Drain in a colander. Stir-fry the mushrooms in a large frying pan with a little oil over a medium-high heat until softened. Allow to cool for 15 minutes.

Place the lentils, mushrooms and cheese in a food processor, add the egg and seasoning, before processing together until well incorporated into a stiff mixture. Refrigerate to set the mixture.

Mix the yoghurt with the zest and juice in a small bowl, fold in the basil and chill in the fridge. When ready to cook, pre-heat the deep fat fryer to 180c with vegetable oil. Shape the fritter mix with two large spoons and carefully deep fry until golden-brown. Drain on kitchen paper and season. Serve on warm plates with the yoghurt.

Grilled goats' cheese and beetroot salad

A perennial favourite, this light colourful dish makes a good start before a rich meaty main course. Try and source a matured, flavoursome goats' cheese rather than the rindless soft variety. (serves 4)

300g goats' cheese
Balsamic glaze
2 large handfuls of watercress
3 medium beetroot, pre-cooked and peeled
50g pine nuts

After de-rinding the cheese, flatten it between clingfilm sheets to a depth of 1cm and lay on a baking sheet and set in the fridge for 6 hours.

When ready to serve, pre-heat the grill on its hottest setting.

Decorate the plates prettily with the balsamic glaze before laying on a line of watercress sprigs, followed by thin slices of beetroot and a sprinkling of pine nuts. Cut out circles of the cheese, season and lay on a baking sheet before grilling until golden. Remove and allow to set for one minute. Carefully remove with a fish slice and place on the salad.

MATTHEW ON HIS...

ULTIMATE DREAM?

I'd like to make a name for myself. I'd love to think that in the future people would come to my restaurant because they've heard about my style of cooking and that other younger chefs would like to come and work for me for that reason too.

WHY I'M A CHEF?

I was at school and did some work experience in the catering industry and loved it. They offered me a part time job which I also really enjoyed, so when I left school I headed straight for catering college. If I wasn't a chef I'd probably be an engineer or mechanic, definitely something where I worked with my hands.

FAVOURITE TIME OF YEAR TO COOK?

It has to be winter, all that slow braising of meats in rich stocks with root vegetables. I love to produce real, hearty food.

CHEF'S TIP?

Don't overthink your dishes; simplify! And always have your ingredients weighed out and within easy reach so that you can just get on and cook without having to think about it too much.

STRANGEST REQUEST FROM A DINER?

A customer once asked if they could have a ham and leek risotto with mushroom fritters on the top served with a salmon fillet. Admittedly they were all on the menu but as separate dishes! They were basically trying to make their own dish, but this is not a buffet – we write the menus for a reason. You can see why I don't work in an open galley-style kitchen!

DISH OF MY CHILDHOOD?

Lasagne! My dad would always make it, whereas with my mum it was always roast dinners.

FAVOURITE COOKBOOKS?

I'm not massively into actual cookbooks, but I do like to look online for ideas. When I have a break I'm always going online for some future inspiration. On my days off I have my 10-year-old daughter Bethany so I don't get to watch much cookery TV – she's more into animals and dancing!

BIGGEST EXTRAVAGANCE?

I love my Robot Coupe. It makes life a whole lot easier especially with sauces and mayonnaise as it makes them in seconds and saves me doing them by hand.

MUSICAL KITCHEN?

Yes, it helps kill the boredom when you are prepping! We mainly just listen to Radio 1 as they play a really good selection of tunes which get you pumped up.

FAVOURITE INGREDIENT?

I am using a lot more micro herbs to finish dishes at the moment, particularly micro basil.

SIGNATURE DISHES

Starters

Fried calamari, red onion salsa, basil & garlic mayo

Butternut squash arancini, red pesto dressing, watercress, pine nut & radish salad

Thai satay scallops, shredded spring onions, carrot, bean sprouts, coriander, satay sauce

Mains

Jerk chicken, Caribbean rice, pineapple relish, tomato glaze

12oz ribeye steak, chips, slow roasted tomato, portobello mushroom

Vegan beetroot & coriander burger, sesame bun, chips, mustard coleslaw

Puddings

Lemon tart

White chocolate & raspberry cheesecake

Sticky toffee pudding

ANY RESTAURANT IN THE WORLD TO VISIT?

I'd like to visit the ones you see on Facebook like the New York delis and pop-ups that are doing things that other people aren't. A couple of years ago one was crossing doughnuts with croissants to create the Cronut; I'd like to try that.

MIDNIGHT FEAST?

To be honest I normally eat before my shift and on my break, so by the time I'm finished I just want to sleep. I'm too tired to eat!

A rural style

When Brendan Curran bought the 15th century building, home to Pig & Whistle Restaurant, five years ago it was the first time he'd owned a business, even though he had a working life in hospitality behind him. "At first we tried running it as a pub, but it soon became clear that wasn't going to make business sense." So Brendan and partner Justin Mullender restyled the property into a cosy restaurant with linen-clothed tables in four separate areas, original brick fireplaces, lime-washed beams, alcoves twinkling with fairy lights, and wax candles illuminating shelves and mantlepieces. Walls are painted Wedgewood-blue and rich mulberry shades, and colourful Tiffany lamps shed a kaleidoscope of colours through the space.

Brendan left a career as senior cabin crew with an Irish airline to settle in Essex. He is very much front of house, knows how he likes hospitality to be delivered, and ensures his team does it well. "As soon as you walk in, we should be there to greet you – and that includes me," he says.

The exterior is still much as it always has been, though there are plans to spruce that up soon. One side of the restaurant has a flower-filled sun terrace with tables and parasols, more twinkling lights in the evening, and a low wooden fence that separates the property from the Marriage's fields of wheat.

Wines are supplied by Ascot-based Hatch Mansfield, and Street Wines in Colchester. "Neil from Street Wines came in one day to ask directions," Brendan recalls. "He stepped inside and said 'wow!' as soon as he saw the interior, so instead of driving off he stopped, had lunch, and we've been working with him ever since!"

Pig & Whistle Restaurant
Chignal Road, Chignal Smealy, Chelmsford CM1 4SZ
W: pigandwhistlechelmsford.uk
T: 01245 443186
E: info@pigandwhistlechelmsford.uk
/PigWhistleChelmsford
@Pig_AndWhistle
/pigwhistlechelmsford

Accolades: OpenTable Diners' Choice 2017; TripAdvisor Excellence Awards 2015-17

Covers: 72 inside; 27 on terrace

Cost: average carte £24; wine from £17; beer from £3.50

Open: Wed-Sat L 12-3; D 6-9.30; Sun L sittings 12, 3, 6 with last tables at 7; bank holiday Mondays 12-5

Details: alfresco dining; wide range of gins; rural location 10 minutes from central Chelmsford; parking

ESSEX FEAST

FOOD LOVERS' GUIDE

Read on to discover some of Essex's tastiest treats in our 'little black book' of all that is delicious about our great county. Whether you have lived here for decades, just moved in or are a welcome visitor, we hope you enjoy exploring the well-known and perhaps less familiar foodie places listed on the following pages; indeed there are some spots that the locals would really rather keep secret!

It's quite possible that places and things that you love may be missing; omissions made either by oversight or because we just don't know about them. Why not share the knowledge with us by emailing essexguide@feastpublishing.co.uk

Where an address is given it indicates that the place in question welcomes visitors.

OTB indicates just over the border, foodies don't follow county boundaries...

Enjoy...

WHAT TO DRINK

BREWERIES

Centuries of brewing tradition mean Essex's ales need little introduction.

Mersea Island Brewery
Mersea Island Vineyard, Rewsalls Lane,
East Mersea CO5 8SX
www.merseaislandbrewery.co.uk
07970 070399

Crouch Vale Brewery
www.crouch-vale.co.uk
01245 322744

Colchester Brewery
www.colchesterbrewery.com
01787 829422

Maldon Brewing Company and Farmer's Ales
www.maldonbrewing.co.uk
01621 851000

Redfox Brewery
www.redfoxbrewery.co.uk
01376 563123

Brentwood Brewery
www.brentwoodbrewing.co.uk
01277 200483

Hart of Stebbing Brewery
The White Hart, High Street,
Stebbing, Dunmow CM6 3SQ
www.facebook.com/whitehartstebbing
01371 856383

Nethergate Brewery
www.nethergate.co.uk
01787 283220

Saffron Brewery
www.saffronbrewery.co.uk
01279 850923

Silks Brewery
www.silksbrewery.co.uk
01787 275513

Pitfield Brewery
www.pitfieldbrewery.com
01277 890 580

Felstar Brewery
www.felstarbrewery.co.uk
01245 361504

George's Brewery
www.georgesbrewery.com
01702 826755

Harwich Town Brewing Company
www.harwichtown.co.uk
01255 551155

Mighty Oak Brewing Company
www.mightyoakbrewing.co.uk
01621 843713

Round Tower Brewery
www.roundtowerbrewery.co.uk
01245 807343

Wibblers Brewery
Wibblers Taproom & Kitchen, Goldsands Road,
Southminster CM0 7JW
www.wibblers.co.uk
01621 772044

Bishop Nick Brewery
www.bishopnick.com
01376 349605

Billericay Brewing Company and Micropub
52 and 54c Chapel Street, Billericay CM12 9LS
www.billericaybrewing.co.uk
01277 500121

CIDERHOUSES AND PERRY

Our few cidermakers more than make up for their rarity with their quality.

Delvin End Cidery
ciders, mulled cider and cider vinegar
www.delvinendcideryrealessexcider.com
01787 461229

Park Fruit Farm *ciders and cider vinegar*
Pork Lane, Great Holland
near Frinton-on-Sea CO13 0ES
www.parkfruitfarm.co.uk
01255 674621

Carters Cider
Dedham Vale Vineyard, Green Lane,
Boxted near Colchester CO4 5TS
www.dedhamvalevineyard.com
01206 271136

VINEYARDS

East Anglia produces award-winning English wines, taking more trophies than any other region of the UK.

West Street Vineyard
West Street Wine Barn & Visitor Centre,
West Street, Coggeshall CO6 1NB
www.weststreetvineyard.co.uk
01376 563303

Dedham Vale Vineyard
Green Lane, Boxted near Colchester CO4 5TS
www.dedhamvalevineyard.com
01206 271136

New Hall Vineyard
Chelmsford Road, Purleigh CM3 6PN
www.newhallwines.co.uk
01621 828343

Bardfield Vineyard
Great Lodge, off Bardfield Road,
Great Bardfield near Braintree CM7 4QD
www.greatlodge.co.uk
01371 810776

Mersea Island Vineyard
www.merseawine.com
01206 385900

Saffron Grange Vineyard
www.saffrongrange.com
01799 516678

Crouch Ridge Vineyard
www.crouchridge.com
07970 527892

Tuffon Hall Vineyard
www.tuffonhall.co.uk
07968 770138

Sandyford Vineyard
01799 586586
www.sandyfordvineyard.co.uk

SPIRITS AND LIQUEURS

Essex's enthusiasm for distilling is creating interesting and delicious results.

Tiptree *fruit gin liqueurs*
(a Wilkin & Sons Tiptree brand)
www.tiptree.com
01621 815407

Hayman Distillers *gins, sloe gin and liqueurs*
www.hayman-distillers.co.uk
01376 517517

Slamseys Drinks *fruit gins*
www.slamseys.co.uk
07766 584845

55 Above *artisan vodkas and gins*
www.55above.co.uk
0203 500 0755

English Spirit Distillery *Rum, other spirits and liqueurs*
www.englishvodkacompany.com
01787 237896

COLD DRINKS

Ripe berries and orchard fruits make for delicious juices and cordials.

Tiptree *apple, berry & other juices*
(a Wilkin & Sons Tiptree brand)
www.tiptree.com
01621 815407

Park Fruit Farm *wide variety of apple juices*
Pork Lane, Great Holland
near Frinton-on-Sea CO13 0ES
www.parkfruitfarm.co.uk
01255 674621

Spencer's Farm Shop *wide variety of apple juices*
Wickham St. Paul near Halstead CO9 2PX
www.spencersfarmshop.co.uk
01787 267977

Hill Holme Juice *wide variety of apple juices*
www.hillholmejuice.co.uk
01621 891304

HOT DRINKS

Our county has passion and good taste in tea and coffee by the cupful.

H Gunton Grocers *coffee roasters and tea merchants*
81-83 Crouch Street, Colchester CO3 3EZ
www.guntons.co.uk
01206 572200

Mac & Me *coffee roasters*
www.macandmeroasting.co.uk
07775 558190

H R Higgins *coffee roasters and tea merchants*
www.hrhiggins.co.uk
01992 768254

The Coffee Officina *coffee roasters*
www.thecoffeeofficina.com
01279 453385

Modern Standard Coffee *coffee roasters*
www.modernstandardcoffee.com
01375 858407

WHAT TO EAT

PORK

Good soils and fine arable crops for food make for happy herds of delicious pigs.

Wicks Manor Farm *high welfare pork*
www.wicksmanor.com
01621 860629

Priors Hall Farm *high welfare pork*
Lindsell, Great Dunmow CM6 3QR
www.priorshallfarm.co.uk
01371 870256

Primrose Farm *free-range pork*
Hall Road, Great Bromley near Colchester CO7 7TR
www.primrosepork.co.uk
01206 230454

The Rodings Plantery *free-range rare-breed pork*
www.therodingsplantery.co.uk
01279 876421

Deersbrook Farm *rare-breed pork*
www.deersbrookfarm.com
01371 850671

Great Garnetts Farm *high welfare pork*
www.greatgarnetts.co.uk
01245 231331

Park Gate *free-range rare-breed pork*
www.parkgatepleshey.co.uk
01245 237500

New Barn Farm *rare breed pork*
www.newbarnfarm.co.uk
07814 663585

Wildwood Farm *free-range rare-breed pork*
www.wildwoodfarm.co.uk
07811 379597

BEEF

Native cattle breeds and lush pasture make our local beef some of the best.

Beatbush Farm *Aberdeen Angus cross*
www.beatbushfarm.co.uk
01621 741470

Deersbrook Farm *Sussex cattle*
www.deersbrookfarm.com
01371 850671

Park Gate *Red Poll cattle*
www.parkgatepleshey.co.uk
01245 237500

New Barn Farm *Dexter and Red Poll cattle*
www.newbarnfarm.co.uk
07814 663585

Essex Grazing Project *Red Poll cattle*
www.essexgrazing.org.uk
0333 0136867

French's Farm *organic native breeds*
Wigley Bush Lane, Brentwood CM14 5QP
(Wed-Sat)
www.frenchs-farm.co.uk
01277 264317

Reydon Cattle Co. *Hereford cattle*
www.reydoncattle.com
07858 378501

KellyBronze Beef *Little Black Angus cattle*
www.kellybronzebeef.co.uk
01245 223581

Broomhills Farm *native breeds*
www.broomhills-farm.co.uk
01787 269640

Ivy Barns Farm *Hereford cross*
Hatfield Peverel CM3 2JH
www.upsonscountrystore.co.uk
01245 380274

Wick Farm Meats *Limousin/Angus cattle*
Church Road, Layer-De-La-Haye
near Colchester CO2 0EW
www.wickfarmmeats.co.uk
01206 738656

LAMB

Sweet grass gives us some of the best spring lamb, hogget and mutton.

Beatbush Farm *Romney sheep*
www.beatbushfarm.co.uk
01621 741470

The Rodings Plantery *native rare-breed sheep*
www.therodingsplantery.co.uk
01279 876421

New Barn Farm *native rare-breed sheep*
www.newbarnfarm.co.uk
07814 663585

Reydon Cattle Co. *Lleyn-Dorset cross sheep*
www.reydoncattle.com
07858 378501

Layer Marney Lamb *Welsh-Suffolk cross sheep*
www.layermarneylamb.co.uk
01206 331179

Broomhills Farm *native sheep*
www.broomhills-farm.co.uk
01787 269640

Ivy Barns Farm *Jacob-Hampshire cross*
Hatfield Peverel CM3 2JH
www.upsonscountrystore.co.uk
01245 380274

Wick Farm Meats *native sheep*
Church Road, Layer-De-La-Haye
near Colchester CO2 0EW
www.wickfarmmeats.co.uk
01206 738656

POULTRY

The old-fashioned flavour comes from the right breeding and the best feed.

Kelly's Turkeys *free-range bronze turkeys*
www.kellyturkeys.co.uk
01245 223581

Great Clerkes Farm Foods
free-range geese, chickens and quail
www.greatclerkesfarmfoods.co.uk
07968 148896

Beatbush Farm *seasonal poultry*
www.beatbushfarm.co.uk
01621 741470

Great Garnetts Farm
free range bronze and barn-reared white turkeys
www.greatgarnetts.co.uk
01245 231331

Blackwell's Farm
free-range bronze and barn-reared white turkeys
Herons Farm, Colne Road, Coggeshall CO6 ITQ
www.blackwellsfarmproduce.co.uk
01376 562500

Eastwick Hall Farm *free-range bronze turkeys*
www.tastyturkeys.co.uk
01279 423214

Forest Lodge Farm
free-range bronze and barn-reared white turkeys
www.christmas-turkey-essex.co.uk
01277 841083

G & J Barron Farms
free-range bronze and barn-reared white turkeys
www.barronfarms.co.uk
01206 210383

Temple Farm *free-range bronze and other turkeys*
www.sjfrederick.co.uk
01279 792460

Salix Farm *free-range turkeys*
www.salixfarmturkeys.co.uk
01799 586586

Weeks Turkeys *free-range bronze turkeys*
www.weeksturkeys.com
01268 710331

East End Farm *Christmas poultry*
www.turkeyshere.co.uk
01279 793125

WILD GAME

Shooting protects our farming landscape and gives us tasty, great-value natural meats.

Howletts Hall
www.howlettshall.co.uk
07831 758505

Ben Rigby Game
www.benrigbygame.co.uk
01621 741971

Radwinter Wild Game Company
www.radwinterwildgame.com
01799 599883

National Trust Hatfield Forest *wild venison*
Takeley, Bishop's Stortford CM22 6NE
www.nationaltrust.org.uk/hatfield-forest
01279 870678

Spains Hall Estate *wild venison*
www.spainshallestate.co.uk
01371 811596

BACON AND HAMS

Curing and smoking are great traditions of Essex's mixed farming heritage.

Wicks Manor Farm
dry-cured and smoked bacon and hams
www.wicksmanor.com
01621 860629

Hepburns Butchers *dry-cured bacon*
77 Hutton Road, Shenfield CM15 8JD
01277 216656
269 Roman Road, Mountnessing CM15 0UH
01277 353289
www.hepburnsfood.co.uk

Priors Hall Farm *cured and smoked bacon and hams*
Lindsell, Great Dunmow CM6 3QR
www.priorshallfarm.co.uk
01371 870256

Primrose Farm *dry-cured bacon*
Hall Road, Great Bromley near Colchester CO7 7TR
www.primrosepork.co.uk
01206 230454

The Rodings Plantery *cured bacon and gammons*
www.therodingsplantery.co.uk
01279 876421

Deersbrook Farm *cured bacon*
www.deersbrookfarm.com
01371 850671

Great Garnetts Farm *cured bacon and gammons*
www.greatgarnetts.co.uk
01245 231331

Park Gate *cured bacon and gammons*
www.parkgatepleshey.co.uk
01245 237500

Broad Oak Farm *cured and smoked hams*
www.broadoakfarm.com
01279 718316

SAUSAGES

In a county known for good pork, superb bangers are a delicious offshoot.

Wicks Manor Farm *pork sausages*
www.wicksmanor.com
01621 860629

Hepburns Butchers *pork sausages*
77 Hutton Road, Shenfield CM15 8JD
01277 216656
269 Roman Road, Mountnessing CM15 0UH
01277 353289
www.hepburnsfood.co.uk

Millins of Tiptree *pork sausages*
83 Church Road, Tiptree, CO5 0HB
www.millinsoftiptree.co.uk
01621 815796

Primrose Farm *pork sausages*
Hall Road, Great Bromley near Colchester CO7 7TR
www.primrosepork.co.uk
01206 230454

Giggly Pig Company *pork sausages*
132 Petersfield Ave, Harold Hill RM3 9PH
www.gigglypig.co.uk
01708 476124

The Rodings Plantery *pork and lamb sausages*
www.therodingsplantery.co.uk
01279 876421

Deersbrook Farm *pork sausages*
www.deersbrookfarm.com
01371 850671

Great Garnetts Farm *pork sausages*
www.greatgarnetts.co.uk
01245 231331

Park Gate *pork sausages*
www.parkgatepleshey.co.uk
01245 237500

New Barn Farm *pork sausages*
www.newbarnfarm.co.uk
07814 663585

Totham Bangers *variety of types*
www.tothambangers.co.uk
01621 892341

Broad Oak Farm *pork sausages*
www.broadoakfarm.com
01279 718316

Church's Butchers *variety of types*
224 High Street, Epping CM16 4AQ
www.churchsbutchers.co.uk
01992 573231

Churchgate Sausage Shop *variety of types*
Mayfields Farm, Sheering Road, Harlow CM17 0JP
www.churchgatesausage.co.uk
01279 444 812

MEAT PRODUCTS

Tasty meaty treats for speedy meals.

Priors Hall Farm *haslet and scotch eggs*
Lindsell, Great Dunmow CM6 3QR
www.priorshallfarm.co.uk
01371 870256

Millins of Tiptree *variety of pork pies*
83 Church Road, Tiptree, CO5 0HB
www.millinsoftiptree.co.uk
01621 815796

Pyes Farm *meat pies, puddings and pasties*
www.pyesfarm.com
01371 820272

Little Brown Shed Co. *beef and venison jerky*
www.littlebrownshed.co.uk
01799 599883

Wicks Manor Farm *pork and beef burgers*
www.wicksmanor.com
01621 860629

The Rodings Plantery *pork and lamb burgers*
www.therodingsplantery.co.uk
01279 876421

Broad Oak Farm *variety of burgers*
www.broadoakfarm.com
01279 718316

The Lamb Charcuterie Company
www.thelambcharcuteriecompany.co.uk
07867 434004

EGGS

A good full English breakfast calls for freshly laid eggs.

The Egg Shed at Sparlings Farm
free range hens' eggs
Braintree Road, Felsted CM6 3LB
www.sparlingsfarm.co.uk
01371 820281

East End Farm *free range hens' eggs*
Harlow Road, Roydon CM19 5HE
www.turkeyshere.co.uk
01279 793125

Quails In Essex *quails' eggs*
www.quails-in-essex.co.uk
01245 422498

Sarah Green's Organics *free range hens' eggs*
www.sarahgreensorganics.co.uk
01621 778844

The Essex Herb Company *free range hens' eggs*
www.theessexherbcompany.co.uk
07793 317207 (Southend area delivery only)

Ivy Barns Farm *free range hens' eggs*
Hatfield Peverel CM3 2JH
www.upsonscountrystore.co.uk
01245 380274

FISH AND SEAFOOD

*(also see **PLACES TO SHOP – FISHMONGERS**)*
The fruits de mer on Essex's coast are rightly iconic and delicious.

Mersea Island Fresh Catch *fresh fish*
(shop open Tue & Thu 2.45-3.30pm but local orders delivered)
The Jetty, Coast Road, West Mersea CO5 8AR
www.merseaislandfreshcatch.co.uk
01206 385421

Point Clear Bay Fish Company
(Fridays and weekends only)
51 Western Promenade, Point Clear,
St. Oysth near Clacton CO16 8NA
www.facebook.com/pointclearbayfishcompany
07879 846330

Richard Haward Oysters *native and rock oysters*
www.richardhawardsoysters.co.uk
07802 244113

Maldon Oyster Company *native and rock oysters*
www.maldonoyster.com
01621 828699

Colchester Oyster Fishery *rock oysters and shellfish*
www.colchesteroysterfishery.com

Brandy Hole Oyster Company *rock oysters*
www.brandyholeoysters.co.uk
07802 770814

Osborne Bros *cockles and shrimps*
(café and shellfish sales)
Billet Wharf, High Street, Leigh-on-Sea SS9 2ER
www.osbornebros.co.uk
01702 477233

SMOKEHOUSES

The smoking and curing tradition goes back centuries when the aroma of kippers filled the village.

Lambton & Jackson *smoked fish*
www.lambtonandjackson.com
01621 853710

Hanningfield Smokehouse
smoked fish, meats and cheeses
www.hanningfieldsmokehouse.co.uk
01277 840009

Island Smokehouse, East Mersea *smoked fish*
www.islandsmokehouse.co.uk
07542 476772

Hill Top Smokehouse *smoked meats*
Byfords Foods, 29 High Street, Rayleigh SS6 7EW
www.hilltopsmokehouse.co.uk
01449 721998

FOOD LOVERS' GUIDE

Your deliciously indispensable companion to enjoying Essex, edible and otherwise

VEGETARIAN FOODS

Meat-free and vegan cooking shouldn't mean being short on flavour and quality.

Pyes Farm *vegetarian quiches, pasties and pies*
www.pyesfarm.com
01371 820272

Veggielicious *vegetarian meals and home delivery*
www.veggielicious.co.uk
01621 776711

DAIRY AND CHEESE

Dairy farming is key, not least for our new wave of passionate cheesemakers.

Bradfields Farm Dairy
cow's milk, cream and cheeses
Bradfields Farm, Burnt Mills Road,
North Benfleet near Wickford SS12 9JX
www.bradfieldsfarm.co.uk
01268 726207

Shaken Udder *milkshakes and yoghurt drinks*
www.shakenudder.com
01621 868710

Boydells Dairy Farm
sheep's milk, yoghurt, cheese and frozen yoghurt lollies
www.boydellsdairy.co.uk
01371 850481

ICE CREAM

Rich pasture and lots of sunny weather making for happy cows and great milk.

Handmade By Hadley's *ice creams*
www.handmadebyhadleys.co.uk
01787 220420

Only By Nature *frozen yoghurts*
(previously Margaret's Frozen Luxuries)
www.onlybynature.com
01787 224865

The Saffron Ice Cream Company
ice creams and sorbets
www.saffronicecream.co.uk
01799 513 552

Poco Gelato *ice creams, sorbets and frozen yoghurts*
The Scoop Shop, 54-56 Elm Road,
Leigh-on-Sea SS9 1SN
www.pocogelato.co.uk
01702 470019

Caprilatte Ice Cream Company
goat's milk ice cream
Butterfly Lodge Dairy, Mersea Road,
Abberton near Colchester CO5 7LG
www.facebook.com/thecraftygoaticecreamparlour
01206 736850

DESSERTS, CAKES AND BAKERY

Breakfast and afternoon tea calls for fabulous farmhouse baking and super pâtisserie.

Cole's Puddings Ltd. *puddings and mince pies*
(a Wilkin & Sons Tiptree brand)
www.colespuddings.com
01799 531053

Pyes Farm *tarts, puddings and pastries*
www.pyesfarm.com
01371 820272

Tiptree Patisserie *huge array and home delivery*
(a Wilkin & Sons Tiptree brand)
www.tiptreecakes.com
01376 509101

Cupcake Daisy *cupcakes and vintage teas*
www.cupcakedaisy.co.uk
07818 184579

BakeWell *cupcakes, patisserie and bespoke orders*
2 Market Place, Dunmow CM6 1AT
www.youcanbakewell.co.uk
01371 879679

Double S Cakes *miniature and celebration cakes*
www.double-s-cakes.com
07940 459703

Mayfield Farm Bakery *breads, cakes and savouries*
Sheering Road, Old Harlow CM17 0JP
www.mayfieldfarmbakery.co.uk
01279 411774

Herbalicious Muffins *savoury and fruit muffins*
www.herbaliciousmuffins.com
07726 729616

McLaren's *variety of Christmas puddings*
www.mclarenspureandnatural.info
07500 876528

The Gourmet Cake Company
Unit 4, Eckersley Road, Chelmsford CM1 1SL
www.gourmetcupcakes.co.uk
01245 283986

Danbury Fine Foods *bakery*
www.danburyfinefoods.co.uk
01245 403066

The Brentwood Kitchen
Wilsons Corner, Ingrave Road, Brentwood CM15 8AA
www.thebrentwoodkitchen.co.uk
01277 230177

SWEETMEATS

Over coffee or any time of the day, an energy boost or simple luxury, sticky sweetmeats and chocolates hit the spot.

Linden Lady *couverture chocolates*
www.lindenlady.com
01206 330240

Choctails *cocktail-inspired chocolates*
www.choctails.org.uk
07900 264637

Hill St. *avant-garde chocolatiers*
7 Hill Street, Saffron Walden CB10 1EH
www.hill.st
01799 521555

The Grown Up Chocolate Company *wide variety*
www.thegrownupchocolatecompany.co.uk
01279 430293

The Chappel Chocolate House *bespoke chocolates*
www.chappelchocolatehouse.co.uk
07787 506846

Mrs Button's Chocolates
wide variety incl. dairy-free
www.mrsbuttonschocolates.co.uk
01376 573646

Maldon Chocolates
Unit G, Wenlock Way, Maldon CM9 5AD
www. maldonchocolates.co.uk
01621 927090

Candy Carnival *wide variety of fudge*
www.candycarnival.co.uk

VEGETABLES, HERBS AND SALADS

Farmers and market gardeners make great use of fertile soils and a perfect climate.

Sarah Green's Organics *vegetable boxes*
www.sarahgreensorganics.co.uk
01621 778844

Moyns Park Organics
vegetables and vegetable boxes
www.moynsparkorganics.co.uk
07772 457063

FOOD LOVERS' GUIDE

Your deliciously indispensable companion to enjoying Essex, edible and otherwise

The Essex Herb Company
herbs and vegetable boxes
www.theessexherbcompany.co.uk
07793 317207 (Southend area delivery only)

Carpenters Farm *potatoes and asparagus*
St Mary's Road, Aingers Green,
Great Bentley near Colchester CO7 8NJ
www.carpentersfarmshop.co.uk
01206 255365

Fiveways Fruit Farm *asparagus*
Heath Road, Stanway near Colchester CO3 0QR
(May – Oct)
www.fivewaysfruitfarm.co.uk

Wash Farm *asparagus*
Queen Street, Sible Hedingham
near Halstead CO9 3RH
www.washfarm.co.uk
01787 461208

Herbal Haven
Coldhams Farm, Rickling
near Saffron Walden CB11 3YL
www.herbalhaven.com
01799 540695

FRUITS

Orchard fruits, berries and stone fruits, perfect for nursery puds and desserts.

Crapes Fruit Farm
apples, stone fruits, quinces and medlars
Rectory Road, Aldham, Colchester CO6 3RR
www.crapes.wordpress.com
01206 212375

Park Fruit Farm *berries and orchard fruits*
Pork Lane, Great Holland
near Frinton-on-Sea CO13 0ES
www.parkfruitfarm.co.uk
01255 674621

Carpenters Farm *berries and orchard fruits*
St Mary's Road, Aingers Green, Great Bentley
near Colchester CO7 8NJ
www.carpentersfarmshop.co.uk
01206 255365

Lathcoats Farm *apples, berries and stone fruits*
Beehive Lane, Galleywood CM2 8LX
www.eapples.co.uk
01245 353021

Fiveways Fruit Farm
berries, orchard and stone fruits
Heath Road, Stanway near Colchester CO3 0QR
(May – Oct)
www.fivewaysfruitfarm.co.uk
07909 996344

Cammas Hall Fruit Farm
berries, currants and cherries
Needham Green, Hatfield Broad Oak CM22 7JT
www.cammashall.co.uk
01279 718777

Wash Farm *berries, currants and cherries*
Queen Street, Sible Hedingham CO9 3RH
www.washfarm.co.uk
01787 461208

McLauchlan of Boxted
soft fruits and veggies incl. PYO
53 Straight Road, Boxted, Colchester CO4 5RB
www.boxtedberries.com
01206 272275

ORGANIC PRODUCE

Grown and reared without chemicals gives a helping hand to nature.

Moyns Park Organics
vegetables and vegetable boxes
www.moynsparkorganics.co.uk
07772 457063

French's Farm *Organic meats*
Wigley Bush Lane, Brentwood CM14 5QP
(Wed-Sat)
www.frenchs-farm.co.uk
01277 264317

KITCHEN ESSENTIALS

The simple things in the larder are often taken for granted. But without them, our cooking just wouldn't taste the same.

Marriage's Flour
breadmaking and home baking flours
www.flour.co.uk
01245 354455

Maldon Salt Company *sea salt and smoked salt*
www.maldonsalt.co.uk
01621 853315

Drury and Alldis *oils and vinegars*
www.druryandalldis.co.uk
07714 509432

Park Fruit Farm *cider vinegar*
Pork Lane, Great Holland
near Frinton-on-Sea CO13 0ES
www.parkfruitfarm.co.uk
01255 674621

PRESERVES AND HONEY

Sweet ripe fruit taste great, picked in season and conserved in style.

Tiptree (a Wilkin & Sons Tiptree brand)
conserves, marmalades, curds, jams, jellies, etc
Factory Hill, Tiptree CO5 0RF
www.tiptree.com
01621 814529

Thursday Cottage (a Wilkin & Sons Tiptree brand)
jams, marmalades, curds, low sugar etc
www.thursday-cottage.com
01621 814529

Essex Bees *honey, candles and bee products*
www.essexbees.co.uk
07737 942400

Hoyle's Honey
Hoyle's Farm, Princes Gate, Navestock Side
near Brentwood CM14 5SN
www.hoyleshoney.com
01277 733633

PICKLES AND RELISHES

Good meat calls for zingy accompaniments.

Tiptree (a Wilkin & Sons Tiptree brand)
chutneys, sauces, mustards, relishes etc
www.tiptree.com
01621 815407

Jules and Sharpie Preservaments
(a Wilkin & Sons Tiptree brand)
hot jellies, chutney and sauces
www.julesandsharpie.co.uk
01621 814529

Island Smokehouse, East Mersea
pickles, chutneys and wasabi
www.islandsmokehouse.co.uk
07542 476772

SNACKS

Busy lives and eating something on the run or just nibbling over drinks.

Fairfields Farm Crisps *posh potato crisps*
www.fairfieldsfarmcrisps.co.uk
01206 241613

Retrocorn sweet popcorn
www.retrocorn.com
07796 682008

GLOBAL SPECIALITIES

Local ingredients in home cooking combine well with worldly flavours and warm spices.

Spice Queen *dry spice mixes*
www.spicequeenuk.co.uk
07984 593963

Badu's Indian Feast *fresh masala mixes OTB*
www.badusindianfeast.co.uk
07824 345521

DIETARY AND FREE-FROM FOODS

Special diet choices and sensitivity should not preclude enjoyment and indulgence.

Muffin Makery *muffin mixes incl. free-from*
www.muffinmakery.com
07878 816162

Mrs Button's Chocolates *dairy-free*
www.mrsbuttonschocolates.co.uk
01376 573646

PLACES TO BUY

DELIS AND FOOD HALLS

Globe-trotting cuisines and international flavours alongside local ingredients.

The Mistley Kitchen – Retail and Wine
High Street, Mistley near Manningtree CO11 1HD
www.mistleykitchen.com
01206 391024

H Gunton Grocers, Colchester
81-83 Crouch Street, Colchester CO3 3EZ
www.guntons.co.uk
01206 572200

Milly's Deli and Café, Leigh-on-Sea
90 Leigh Road, Leigh-on-Sea SS9 1BU
www.millysdeli.com
01702 474373

Fullers Family Food Hall and Butchers, Dunmow
Bretts Farm, Chelmsford Road,
White Roding near Dunmow CM6 1RF
www.fullersfamilybutchers.co.uk
01279 876189

The Cheddar Vine, Saffron Walden
8a Cross Street, Saffron Walden CB10 1EX
www.thecheddarvine.com
01799 523853

Abigail's Deli, Ingatestone
11a High Street, Ingatestone CM4 9ED
www.abigails.co.uk
01277 355568

Maldon Delicatessen, Maldon
1 Wenlock Way, Maldon CM9 5AD
www.maldondeli.co.uk
01621 842637

The Deli, West Mersea
42 High Street, West Mersea CO5 8QA
www.thedelimersea.co.uk
01206 384753

Village Delicatessen, Wivenhoe
4 High Street, Wivenhoe near Colchester CO7 9BJ
www.wivdeli.co.uk
01206 822824

Deli On The Green, Woodford Green
425 High Road, Woodford Green, Essex IG8 0XG
www.delionthegreen.net
020 8506 1122

The Estuary Gourmet Foods, Leigh-on-Sea
51 Broadway, Leigh-on-Sea SS9 1PA
www.estuaryrestaurants.com/delicatessen
01702 480384

Cake Hole Delicatessen, West Mersea
2 Coast Road, West Mersea CO5 8QE
www.islandartcafe.co.uk
01206 385234

Piatto Delicatessen, Frinton-on-Sea
56 Connaught Avenue, Frinton-on-Sea CO13 9PR
www.piattodelicatessen.co.uk
01255 671648

Green Owl Café & Deli, Buckhurst Hill
44 Queens Road, Buckhurst Hill IG9 5BY
www.greenowlcafe.co.uk
020 8505 4400

Buntings, Coggeshall
18a Church Street, Coggeshall CO6 1UB
www.buntingfoods.co.uk
01376 561233

Oxleys, Dovercourt
141 High Street, Dovercourt
near Harwich CO12 3AX
www.oxleysofdovercourt.co.uk
01255 242604

The Little Kitchen, Epping
180 High Street, Epping CM16 4AQ
www.tlkepping.co.uk
01992 571447

Polignano, Chelmsford
1 Can Bridge Way, Chelmsford CM2 0WP
www.polignano-deli.co.uk
01245 690920

Legend Deli, Southend-on-Sea
16 Market Place, Southend-on-Sea SS1 1DA
01702 808640

Rustic Deli & Bagel Shop, Wickford
9a The Willowdale Centre, Wickford SS12 0RA
01268 561251

The Brentwood Kitchen
Wilsons Corner, Ingrave Road, Brentwood CM15 8AA
www.thebrentwoodkitchen.co.uk
01277 230177

Knead Food Café & Delicatessen, Great Bardfield
The Blue Egg, Braintree Road,
Great Bardfield CM7 4PY
www.kneadfood.com
01371 811801

Angela Reed Café & Bakery, Saffron Walden
5-7 Market Hill, Saffron Walden CB10 1HQ
www.facebook.com/angelareedbakery
01799 520056

Stewart's Deli & Tearoom, Chelmsford
4 Tindal St, Chelmsford CM1 1ER
www.facebook.com/4tindalstreet
01245 265766

Millins of Tiptree
83 Church Road, Tiptree CO5 0HB
www.millinsoftiptree.co.uk
01621 815796

Blue Boar Deli, Abridge
Market Place, Abridge RM4 1UA
www.blueboardeli.co.uk
01992 815354

Elder Street Café & Deli, Debden
Debden Barns, Elder Street,
Debden near Saffron Walden CB11 3JY
www.elderstreetcafedeli.co.uk
01799 543598

The Natural Health Shop, Colchester
27 Sir Isaac's Walk, Colchester CO1 1JJ
www.thenaturalhealthshopcolchester.co.uk
01206 542844

FARM SHOPS

Agricultural diversification has become vital in recent years so support your local farmer.

Barleylands Farm Shop, Billericay
Barleylands Road, Billericay CM11 2UD
www.barleylands.co.uk
01268 288886

Calcott Hall Farm Shop, Brentwood
Ongar Road, Brentwood CM15 9HS
www.calcotthall.com
01277 264164

Hall Farm, Stratford St. Mary
Church Road, Stratford St. Mary
near Colchester CO7 6LS
www.hallfarmshop.com
01206 322572

Priors Hall Farm, Great Dunmow
Lindsell, Great Dunmow CM6 3QR
www.priorshallfarm.co.uk
01371 870256

Blackwell's Farm Shop, Coggeshall
Herons Farm, Colne Road, Coggeshall CO6 ITQ
www.blackwellsfarmproduce.co.uk
01376 562500

Spencer's Farm Shop, Wickham St. Paul
Wickham St. Paul near Halstead CO9 2PX
www.spencersfarmshop.co.uk
01787 267977

Carpenters Farm, Great Bentley
St Mary's Road, Aingers Green,
Gt. Bentley near Colchester CO7 8NJ
www.carpentersfarmshop.co.uk
01206 255365

Upsons Country Store, Hatfield Peverel
Ivy Barns Farm, Ulting Road,
Hatfield Peverel CM3 2JH
www.upsonscountrystore.co.uk
01245 380274

Jacobs Farm Shop, Heybridge
Goldhanger Road, Heybridge near Maldon CM9 4QS
01621 853395

Cammas Hall Fruit Farm, Hatfield Broad Oak
Needham Green, Hatfield Broad Oak
near Dunmow CM22 7JT
www.cammashall.co.uk
01279 718777

Lathcoats Farm, Galleywood
Beehive Lane, Galleywood CM2 8LX
www.eapples.co.uk

Park Fruit Farm, Great Holland
Pork Lane, Great Holland
near Frinton-on-Sea CO13 0ES
www.parkfruitfarm.co.uk
01255 674621

Fryers Farm Shop, Lawford
Harwich Road, Lawford CO11 2JL
www.fryersfarmshop.co.uk
01206 392294

Mitchells Farm Shop, Elmstead Market
School Road, Elmstead Market CO7 7EX
01206 820110

Greenstead Farm Shop, Halstead
Church Road, Greenstead Green CO9 1QY
www.greensteadfarmshop.co.uk
01787 472807

The Veg Box, Southend
76 Lonsdale Road, Southend on Sea SS2 4LR
www.theessexherbcompany.co.uk
07793 317207

The Farm Shop at Poplar Nurseries, Colchester
Coggeshall Road, Marks Tey
near Colchester CO6 1HR
www.poplarnurseries.co.uk
01206 210374

Lord's Farm Shop, Gosfield
13 Petersfield Lane, Gosfield near Halstead CO9 1PU
www.lordsfarmshop.co.uk
01787 477784

Lower Dairy Farm, Nayland
Water Lane, Nayland near Colchester CO6 4JS
www.lowerdairyfarm.co.uk
01206 262314

Old Woodham Road Farm Shop, Battlesbridge
Woodham Road, Battlesbridge, Wickford SS11 7QU
www.facebook.com/
Old-Woodham-Road-Farm-Shop
01268 768704

Burstead Farm Shop, Little Burstead
Tye Common Road, Little Burstead
near Billericay CM12 9SD
www.bursteadfarmshop.co.uk
01277 637150

Manor Farm Shop, Great Baddow
Maldon Road, Great Baddow
near Chelmsford CM2 7DQ
www.themanorfarmshopchelmsford.co.uk
01245 474077

The Farm Shop, Chelmsford
196 Moulsham Street, Chelmsford CM2 0LG
www.thefarmshopchelmsford.co.uk
01245 357 715

Gardeners Farm Shop, Goldhanger
Maldon Road, Goldhanger near Maldon CM9 8BQ
www.gardenersfarmshop.co.uk
01621 788162

Forest Farm Shop & Garden Centre, Hainault
Forest Road, Hainault IG6 3HQ
www.forestfarmshop.com
020 850 02221

Birchwood Farm Shop, Dedham
Birchwood Road, Dedham near Colchester CO7 6HX
www.birchwoodfarmshop.co.uk
01206 323797

Brookelynne Farm Shop, Beaumont
Chapel Road, Beaumont
near Clacton-on-Sea CO16 0AR
www.brookelynnefarmshop.com
01255 862184

Fullers Family Food Hall, Dunmow
Bretts Farm, White Roding near Dunmow CM6 1RF
www.fullersfamilybutchers.co.uk
01279 876189

Wrekin Farm Shop, Althorne
Burnham Road, Althorne near Chelmsford CM3 6DT
www.farmshop.uk.com
01621 786785

Little Mountains Farm, Great Totham
Mountains Road, Great Totham
near Maldon CM9 8BY
www.littlemountainsfarm.co.uk
01621 891215

East End Farm, Roydon
Harlow Road, Roydon near Harlow CM19 5HE
www.turkeyshere.co.uk
01279 793125

Bloom & Veg, Upminster
Central Farm, Aveley Road, Upminster RM14 2TW
www.facebook.com/bloomandveg1925
01708 250096

Ragmarsh Farm Shop and Butchers, Manningtree
Riverside Avenue East, Manningtree CO11 1US

www.facebook.com/ragmarshfarmshopandbutchers
01206 396157

La Vallee Farm Shop, Hockley
Wadham Park Avenue, Hockley SS5 6AL
www.lavalleefarm.co.uk
01702 232641

Walden Local Food, Saffron Walden
stall every Saturday 8.30am - 3.30pm
King Street, Saffron Walden
www.waldenlocalfood.co.uk

FARMERS' MARKETS

Get close to the field-to-fork story.

Barleylands, Billericay
last Saturday 8.30am – 12.30pm
Barleylands, Barleylands Road, Billericay CM11 2UD
www.barleylands.co.uk
01268 290218

Great Garnetts, Dunmow
usually second Saturday 9.30am – 12.30pm
Bishops Green, Barnston near Dunmow CM6 1NE
www.greatgarnetts.co.uk
01245 231331

Wivenhoe *third Saturday 9.30am – 12.30pm*
Wivenhoe Congregational Hall, High Street,
Wivenhoe CO7 9AB
www.en-form.org.uk
01206 367776

Hylands House, Chelmsford *monthly 10am – 4pm*
London Road A414, Writtle, Chelmsford SM2 8WQ
www.chelmsford.gov.uk/hylands
01245 605500

Danbury *first Saturday 9am – 12.30pm*
Danbury Sports Centre, Dawson Field,
Main Road, Chelmsford CM3 4NQ
www.danburysportscentre.co.uk
01245 224515

Blackmore *third Sunday 10am - 1pm*
The Village Hall, Nine Ashes Road,
Blackmore CM4 0QW

Burnham *third Sunday 9am – 12.30pm*
Carnival Hall, Devonshire Road,
Burnham-on-Crouch CM0 8EF
www.facebook.com/burnhamfarmersmarket

Colchester *first Friday 9.30am – 12.30pm*
Colchester Arts Centre, Church Street CO1 1NF
www.en-form.org.uk
01206 367776

Coggeshall *first Sunday 10am – 1pm*
Coggeshall Village Hall, Stoneham Street CO6 1UH
www.facebook.com/coggeshallfarmersmarket

Southend-on-Sea
2nd and 4th Saturdays 9am – 5pm
High Street, Southend-on-Sea SS1 1TJ
www.essexfarmersmarkets.co.uk
01268 733111

Highams Park *4th Sunday 10am – 3pm*
The Avenue, Highams Park E4 9LA
www.essexfarmersmarkets.co.uk
01268 733111

Whetstone *Sundays 10am – 4pm*
High Road, Whetstone N20 9LN
www.essexfarmersmarkets.co.uk
01268 733111

Wanstead *every 1st Sunday 10am – 3pm*
High Street, Wanstead E11 2AA
www.essexfarmersmarkets.co.uk
01268 733111

Loughton *2nd Sundays 10am - 3pm*
High Road, Loughton IG10 1DN
www.essexfarmersmarkets.co.uk
01268 733111

BUTCHERS

Essex's well-bred, well-hung, well-fed farmyard meats need little introduction.

Hepburns, Shenfield & Mountnessing
77 Hutton Road, Shenfield CM15 8JD
www.hepburnsfood.co.uk
01277 216656
269 Roman Road, Mountnessing CM15 0UH
01277 353289

Priors Hall Farm, Great Dunmow
Lindsell, Great Dunmow CM6 3QR
www.priorshallfarm.co.uk
01371 870256

Blackwell's Farm Shop, Coggeshall
Herons Farm, Colne Road, Coggeshall CO6 ITQ
www.blackwellsfarmproduce.co.uk
01376 562500

C Johnson, Upminster & Chadwell Heath
Corbets Tey Road, Upminster RM14 2AH
2 & 3 Tolworth Parade, East Road,
Chadwell Heath RM6 6YU
www.cjohnsonbutchers.co.uk
0208 590 4054

Jon Gold Butchers, Rayleigh
Lubbards Farm, Hullbridge Road, Rayleigh SS6 9QW
www.jongoldfarmshop.co.uk
01268 786434

A Willsher and Son, Colchester
87 London Road, Marks Tey near Colchester CO6 1EB
www.awillsherandson.co.uk
01206 210365

Fowler Bros, Burnham-on-Crouch
Brook Farm, Marsh Road,
Burnham-on-Crouch CM0 8NA
www.facebook.com/thesecretbutchers
01621 782759

French's Farm, South Weald
Wigley Bush Lane, South Weald near Brentwood,
CM14 5QP (Wed-Sat)
www.frenchs-farm.co.uk
01277 264317

Frank Wright & Son, Colchester
43 Crouch Street, Colchester CO3 3EN
www.frankwrightandson.co.uk
01206 573688

Church's Butchers, Epping
224 High Street, Epping CM16 4AQ
www.churchsbutchers.co.uk
01992 573231

Neil Risdon at Cammas Hall Farm Shop, Dunmow
Needham Green, Hatfield Broad Oak
near Dunmow CM22 7JT
www.cammashall.co.uk
01279 718777

Wick Farm Meats, Colchester
Church Road, Layer-De-La-Haye
near Colchester CO2 0EW
www.wickfarmmeats.co.uk
01206 738656

Fullers Family Food Hall, Dunmow
Bretts Farm, White Roding near Dunmow CM6 1RF
www.fullersfamilybutchers.co.uk
01279 876189

John Coleman Butchers, Colchester
Langham Road, Boxted near Colchester CO4 5HU
www.johncolemanbutchers.co.uk
01206 272270

Buntings, Coggeshall
18a Church Street, Coggeshall CO6 1UB
www.buntingfoods.co.uk
01376 561233

Millins of Tiptree
83 Church Road, Tiptree CO5 0HB
www.millinsoftiptree.co.uk
01621 815796

Lothian Meats, Westcliff
233-235 North Road, Westcliff-on-Sea SS0 7AB
www.lothianmeats.co.uk
01702 300061

Primrose Natural Foods, Chelmsford
89 Moulsham Street, Chelmsford CM2 0JF
www.primrose-naturalfoods-juicebar.co.uk
01245 258897

Jon Gold Butchers, Rayleigh
Lubbards Farm, Hullbridge Road, Rayleigh SS6 9QW
www.jongoldfarmshop.co.uk
01268 786434

Philip Splett Meat Emporium, Southend
Burton's Farm, Barling Road,
Barling Magna near Southend SS3 0LZ
www.philipsplett.com
01702 216062

G Leavett Butchers, Tollesbury
85 East St, Tollesbury near Maldon CM9 8SA
01621 869217

Southminster Butchers
3 North St, Southminster CM0 7DF
www.southminsterbutchers.co.uk
01621 772461

Allen and Son, Colchester
13 St Botolph's St, Colchester CO2 7DU
www.butcherscolchester.co.uk
01206 573443

Woodford Meats Farm Shop, Rochford
Bolt Hall Farm, Larkhill Road,
Canewdon near Rochford SS4 3SA
www.woodfordmeats.co.uk
01702 258233

BAKERS

Unsurprisingly in such a great arable county, baking expertise is as strong as our farming skill.

Dorringtons *across West Essex*
17 High Street, Great Dunmow CM6 1AB
01371 874763
23 Cambridge Road, Stansted CM24 8BM
01279 813452
24 High Street, Newport CB11 3PQ
01799 541533
4 Cross Street, Saffron Walden CB10 1EX
01799 522093
www.dorringtons.com

Mayfield Farm Bakery, Harlow
Sheering Road, Old Harlow CM17 0JP
www.mayfieldfarmbakery.co.uk
01279 411774

Bakehouse, Chelmsford
Wyses Road, Chelmsford CM1 3SN
www.bakehousecoffeeshop.co.uk
01245 248245

Braxted Bakery, Little Braxted
Witham Road, Little Braxted CM8 3ET
www.thebraxtedbakery.co.uk
07740 117688

Le Moulin, Hornchurch
18B Station Lane, Hornchurch RM12 6NJ
www.facebook.com/lemoulinpatisserie.hornchurch
01708 472121

Hume's of Halstead
40 High Street, Halstead CO9 2AP
www.humesbakery.co.uk
01787 472375

Cosson's Bakery, Wickford
62 High Street, Wickford SS12 9AT
www.facebook.com/cossonsbakery
01268 766444

Flour and Spoon *home delivery service*
www.flourandspoon.uk
07545 594617

Barke Craft Bakery, Wickford
6 High St, Wickford SS12 9AJ
01268 769855

Grout's The Baker
12 branches across SE Essex incl. Southend, Canvey Island and Rayleigh
www.groutsthebakers.co.uk
01268 511244

De'aths Bakery, Manningtree
7 High Street, Manningtree CO11 1AG
www.facebook.com/breadncakes.manningtree
01206 392600

FISHMONGERS

(also see PRODUCERS – FISH AND SEAFOOD)
With a long famous coastline, our local fresh fish and seafood are a delicious treat.

The Little Fish Shop, Kelvedon
34 High Street, Kelvedon CO5 9AG
www.thelittlefishshop.com
01376 573535

Estuary Fish, Leigh-on-Sea
8 Cockle Shed, Leigh on Sea SS9 2ER
01702 470741
www.estuaryfish.com
www.buy-fish-online.co.uk

Star Fishmongers, Ongar
195 High Street, Ongar CM5 9JG
www.starfishmongers.co.uk
01277 363131

Ken Green Fish, Clacton-on-Sea
34 High Street, Clacton-on-Sea CO15 1UQ
01255 423357

KC Fisheries, Loughton
1 Oakwood Hill, Loughton IG10 3EW
020 8508 4372

Colin Woods The Fishmonger, Brightlingsea
45 High Street, Brightlingsea CO7 0AQ
01206 302215

WINE MERCHANTS

Good food needs great drink, so a fine wine retailer is essential.

Adnams Store, Saffron Walden
1 Market Street, Saffron Walden CB10 1HZ
www.adnams.co.uk
01799 527281

Mr Wheeler, Colchester
Birchwood Road, Dedham near Colchester CO7 6HX
www.mrwheelerwine.com
01206 713560

The Black Dog Wine Company, North Weald
The Cart Barn, Ashlyn's Farm Shop, Epping Road,
North Weald CM16 6RZ
www.blackdogwines.co.uk
01992 525009

The Wine Centre, Colchester
The Causeway, Great Horkesley,
Colchester CO6 4BH
www.thewinecentre.co.uk
01206 271236

Peter Watts Wines, Coggeshall
Wisdoms Barn, Colne Road, Coggeshall CO6 1TD
www.peterwattswines.co.uk
01376 561130

Woodford Wine Room *limited opening*
17 Mill Lane, Woodford Green IG8 0UN
www.woodfordwineroom.co.uk
020 8504 2440

Vino Vero, Leigh-on-Sea
110 Leigh Road, Leigh-on-Sea SS9 1BU
www.vinovero.co.uk
01702 808 251

Liquorice, Shenfield
65 Hutton Road, Shenfield CM15 8JD
www.drinksallsorted.com
01277 500036

The Cheddar Vine, Saffron Walden
wine and cheese deli
8a Cross Street, Saffron Walden CB10 1EX
www.thecheddarvine.com
01799 523853

Fine Wine and Spirits, Harlow
10 High Street, Harlow CM17 0DW
www.fine-online.co.uk
01279 437555

Baythorne Hall, Halstead
Baythorne End, Halstead CO9 4AH
www.baythornehall.co.uk
01440 785680

Joseph Barnes Wines, Saffron Walden
13 Market Row, Saffron Walden CB10 1HB
www.josephbarneswines.com
01799 528019

Promotion Wine, Stoke-by-Nayland *OTB*
Oak Barn Offices, Thorington Street
near Stoke by Nayland CO6 4SP
www.promotionwine.co.uk
01206 338915

BEER AND DRINK RETAILERS

The perfect ales or apéritifs add enjoyment.

Essex Brewery Company *bottled beers*
Norton Field Farm, Norton Lane, Norton Madeville, Ingatestone CM4 0LN
www.essexbrewerycompany.co.uk
07981 953333

Farmer's Yard, Maldon *beer shop*
140 High Street, Maldon CM9 5BX
www.farmersyard.co.uk
01621 854202

Billericay Brewing Company and Micropub
52 and 54c Chapel Street, Billericay CM12 9LS
www.billericaybrewing.co.uk
01277 500121

Wibblers Brewery, Southminster
Wibblers Taproom & Kitchen, Goldsands Road, Southminster CM0 7JW
www.wibblers.co.uk
01621 772044

Mersea Island Brewery
Mersea Island Vineyard, Rewsalls Lane, East Mersea CO5 8SX
www.merseaislandbrewery.co.uk
07970 070399

PICK-YOUR-OWN

Buying direct is a fun way to get the ripest seasonal crops fresh from the fields. nb. Best to check before setting off.

Spencer's Farm Shop, Wickham
PYO berries, orchard fruits and vegetables
Wickham St. Paul near Halstead CO9 2PX
www.spencersfarmshop.co.uk
01787 267977

Carpenters Farm, Great Bentley
PYO berries and soft fruit
St Mary's Road, Aingers Green, Great Bentley near Colchester CO7 8NJ
www.carpentersfarmshop.co.uk
01206 255365

Lathcoats Farm, Galleywood
PYO berries, soft and stone fruits
Beehive Lane, Galleywood CM2 8LX
www.eapples.co.uk
01245 353021

Craner Produce Farm, Broadley
PYO berries and currants
Merryleas, Common Road, Broadley Common near Waltham Abbey EN9 2DF
www.cranerproduce.co.uk
01992 892862

Daymens Hill Orchard, Tolleshunt
PYO apples and pears
Brick House Road, Tolleshunt Major near Maldon CM9 8JZ
01621 815327

Graces Fruit Farm, Wimbish
orchard, stone and soft fruits
Thaxted Road, Wimbish near Saffron Walden CB10 2XP
01371 830387

McLauchlans of Boxted
soft fruit, beans and sweetcorn
53 Straight Road, Boxted near Colchester CO4 5RB
www.boxtedberries.com
01206 272275

Mill Farm, Thorrington
strawberries
Brightlingsea Road, Thorrington near Colchester CO7 8JJ
www.millfarmstrawberries.co.uk
01206 303007

Wash Farm, Sible Hedingham
berries, currants and cherries
Queen Street, Sible Hedingham near Halstead CO9 3RH
www.washfarm.co.uk
01787 461208

GREENGROCERS

Local produce carefully harvested is the basis of any tasty dish.

Green's of Maldon
74 High St, Maldon CM9 5ET
www.greensofmaldon.co.uk
01621 854727

Bumbles Greengrocers, Brightlingsea
24 High Street, Brightlingsea CO7 0AG
www.facebook.com/bumbles.greengrocers
07914 496681

COOKSHOPS AND KITCHENWARE

Good chefs, amateur or pro', need the best cooks' toys.

Adnams Store, Saffron Walden
1 Market Street, Saffron Walden CB10 1HZ
www.adnams.co.uk
01799 527281

Potters of Hockley
4-8 Main Road, Hockley SS5 4QS
www.potterscookshop.co.uk
01702 202727

Smiths of Loughton
132-136 High Road, Loughton IG10 4BG
www.smithsofloughton.com
020 8508 2175

Suttons, Wickford
24 High Street, Wickford SS12 9AZ

www.suttonswickford.co.uk
01268 733497

AGA Cookshops, Chelmsford & Colchester
74-74a Baddow Road, Chelmsford CM2 7PJ
01245 496919
41 London Road, Colchester CO3 9AJ
01206 763473
www.agacookshop.co.uk

Nisbets, Chelmsford
Unit E Army & Navy Parkway,
Chelmsford CM2 7GY
www.nisbets.co.uk
01245 925912

Steamer Trading Cookshop, Brentwood
71 High St, Brentwood CM14 4RW
www.steamer.co.uk
01277 230019

Lakeland, Lakeside & Chelmsford
Lakeside, West Thurrock Way, Grays RM20 2ZP
01708 863860
14, Springfield Road, Chelmsford CM2 6FA
01245 264019
www.lakeland.co.uk

Townrow Department Store, Braintree
63 High Street, Braintree CM7 1JX
www.townrowstores.com
01376 322587

The Emporium, Maldon
85-87 High St, Maldon CM9 5EP
www.theemporiumdirect.co.uk
01621 854225

Bodgers of Ilford
1-12 Station Road, Ilford IG1 4DP
www.bodgersilford.co.uk
0208 478 0116

HOME DELIVERY

Household essentials and culinary delights straight to your door.

Ashlyns *wide range of produce*
www.ashlyns.co.uk
01277 890411

PLACES TO DRINK

PUBS AND INNS

(also see PLACES TO STAY – HOTELS & INNS)
The great Essex pint is a joy; a great brewer, good cellar and passionate landlord are key.

The Compasses Inn, Littley Green
Littley Green near Chelmsford CM3 1BU
www.compasseslittleygreen.co.uk
01245 362308

The Queen's Head, Chelmsford
30 Lower Anchor Street, Chelmsford CM2 0AS
www.queensheadchelmsford.co.uk
01245 322744

The Oyster Smack Inn, Burnham
112 Station Road, Burnham on Crouch CM0 8HR
www.theoystersmackinn.co.uk
01621 782141

Farmer's Yard, Maldon
140 High Street, Maldon CM9 5BX
www.farmersyard.co.uk
01621 854202

The Lobster Smack, Canvey
Haven Road, Canvey Island SS8 0NR
www.thelobstersmackcanveyisland.co.uk
01268 514297

The Olde Dog Inn, Herongate Tye
Billericay Road, Herongate Tye, Brentwood CM13 3SD
www.theoldedoginn.co.uk
01277 810337

The Ale House, Chelmsford
24-26 Viaduct Road, Chelmsford CM1 1TS
www.the-ale-house-chelmsford.co.uk
01245 260535

The White Hart Inn, Grays
Kings Walk, Argent Street, Grays RM17 6HR
www.whitehartgrays.co.uk
01375 373319

Wibblers Taproom & Kitchen, Southminster
Goldsands Road, Southminster CM0 7JW
www.wibblers.co.uk
01621 772044

The Micropub at Billericay Brewing
52 Chapel Street, Billericay CM12 9LS
www.billericaybrewing.co.uk
01277 500121

The Upminster Taproom
1b Sunnyside Gardens, Upminster RM14 3DT
www.facebook.com/upminstertaproom
07841 676225

The Ferry Boat Inn, North Fambridge
Ferry Road, North Fambridge
near Chelmsford CM3 6LR
www.ferryboatinn-northfambridge.com
01621 740208

Mighty Oak Tap Room
10 High Street Maldon, CM9 5PJ
www.mightyoakbrewing.co.uk
01621 853892

Three Wise Monkeys, Colchester
60 High Street, Colchester CO1 1DN
www.threewisemonkeyscolchester.com
01206 543014

PLACES TO EAT

TEAROOMS

A great British institution, whether bone china, crusts off and pinkies raised or not, do make time for tea.

TIPTREE TEA ROOMS
(a Wilkin and Sons Tiptree brand)
Tiptree - The Tea Room,
Factory Hill CO5 0RF
Heybridge - "The Lock" Tea Room,
Basin Road CM9 4RS
Dedham - The Essex Rose Tea House,
High Street CO7 6DE
Writtle - The Lordship Tea Room,
Lordship Road, Writtle CM1 3RS
Saffron Walden - The Courtyard Tea Room,
2/3 Rose & Crown Walk CB10 1JH
Finchingfield - Bosworths Tea Room,
The Green CM7 4JX
Cressing Temple - The Barns Tea Room,
Witham Road CM77 8PD
Colchester – The Batte Lay Tea Room,
The Minories Gallery, 74 High St. CO1 1UE
Billericay - Barleylands Farm,
Barleylands Road CM11 2UD
Heybridge - The View River Café,
Osea Leisure Park, Goldhanger Road CM9 4SA
www.tiptree.com
01621 815407

FOOD LOVERS' GUIDE

Your deliciously indispensable companion to enjoying Essex, edible and otherwise

The Loft - Tea By The Sea, Tollesbury
Woodrolfe Road, Tollesbury near Maldon CM9 8SE
www.thelofttearoom.com
01621 869063

The Tea Barn at Cammas Hall Farm, Dunmow
Needham Green, Hatfield Broad Oak CM22 7JT
www.cammashall.co.uk
01279 718777

Park Fruit Farm, Great Holland
Pork Lane, Great Holland
near Frinton-on-Sea CO13 0ES
www.parkfruitfarm.co.uk
01255 674621

Maria's Vintage Tea Room, East Mersea
Mersea Island Vineyard, Rewsalls Lane,
East Mersea CO5 8SX
www.merseawine.com
01206 385900

Mayfield Farm Bakery Tea Room, Harlow
Sheering Road, Old Harlow CM17 0JP
www.mayfieldfarmbakery.co.uk
01279 411774

Woodlands Tea Rooms, Tiptree
Maldon Road, Tiptree CO5 0QA
www.woodlandstearooms.co.uk
01621 892455

The Salvation Army's, Hadleigh Farm
Castle Lane, Hadleigh, Benfleet SS7 2AP
www.hadleighfarm.org.uk
01702 426268

Tymperley's, Colchester
Trinity Street, Colchester CO1 1JN
www.tymperleys.co.uk
01206 765034

CAFES AND COFFEE SHOPS

Smaller or simpler eating places can make for delicious escapes.

Milly's Deli and Café, Leigh-on-Sea
90 Leigh Road, Leigh-on-Sea SS9 1BU
www.millysdeli.com
01702 474373

The Barnyard Café at Calcott Hall, Brentwood
Ongar Road, Brentwood CM15 9HS
www.calcotthall.com
01277 264164

Spencer's Farm Shop, Wickham St. Paul
Wickham St. Paul near Halstead CO9 2PX
www.spencersfarmshop.co.uk
01787 267977

The Crafty Goat Ice Cream Parlour, Colchester
Butterfly Lodge Dairy, Mersea Road,
Abberton near Colchester CO5 7LG
www.facebook.com/thecraftygoaticecreamparlour
01206 736850

The Art Café, West Mersea & Colchester
2 Coast Road, West Mersea CO5 8QE
01206 385234
7a Trinity Street, Colchester CO1 1JN
01206 577775
www.islandartcafe.co.uk

The Little Kitchen, Epping
180 High Street, Epping CM16 4AQ
www.tlkepping.co.uk
01992 571447

Delicacy, Chigwell
161 Manor Road, Chigwell IG7 5QA
www.facebook.com/delicacychigwell
020 8500 1070

Zoe's Coffee Shop, Great Dunmow
9 High St, Great Dunmow CM6 1AB
01371 878060

The Brentwood Kitchen
2 Wilsons Corner, Ingrave Road,
Brentwood CM15 8AA
www.thebrentwoodkitchen.co.uk
01277 230177

Knead Food Café & Delicatessen, Great Bardfield
The Blue Egg, Braintree Road,
Great Bardfield CM7 4PY
www.kneadfood.com
01371 811801

Angela Reed Café & Bakery, Saffron Walden
5-7 Market Hill, Saffron Walden CB10 1HQ
www.facebook.com/angelareedbakery
01799 520056

Evie's Parlour, Leigh-on-Sea
182 Leigh Road, Leigh-on Sea SS9 1BT
01702 719379
www.facebook.com/eviesparlour

Maison Bleu Café, Chelmsford
10 Meon Close, Chelmsford CM1 7QQ
www.maisonbleustyle.com
07914 248796

Harry's Coffee and Cakes, Clacton
Clacton Factory Outlet, Stephenson Road West,
Clacton-on-Sea CO15 4TL
www.clactonfactoryoutlet.com/tenants/harrys-coffee-and-cakes
01255 220692

Stewart's Deli & Tearoom, Chelmsford
4 Tindal St, Chelmsford CM1 1ER
www.facebook.com/4tindalstreet
01245 265766

Café Deli 37, Billericay
37 High St, Billericay CM12 9BA
01277 653500

8 Rocks Deli & Wine, Loughton
238 High Road, Loughton IG10 1RB
www.8rocks.co.uk
020 8508 7838

Primrose Natural Foods and Juice Bar, Chelmsford
89 Moulsham Street, Chelmsford CM2 0JF
www.primrose-naturalfoods-juicebar.co.uk
01245 258897

Woodlands, Tiptree
Maldon Road, Tiptree CO5 0QA
www.woodlandstearooms.co.uk
01621 892455

Black Horse Café, Earls Colne
Broomfields Farm, Coggeshall Road,
Earls Colne CO6 2JX
www.broomfields-farm.co.uk
01787 224358

Lower Barn Farm, Rayleigh
London Road, Rayleigh SS6 9ET
www.lowerbarnfarm.co.uk
01268 780991

Timbers Restaurant at Blake House, Braintree
Blake End, Rayne near Braintree CM77 6RA
www.timbersrestaurant.co.uk
01376 553146

RHS Garden Hyde Hall, Rettendon
Creephedge Lane, Rettendon
near Chelmsford CM3 8RA
www.rhs.org.uk
01245 400256

Barlow and Fields, Leigh-on-Sea
4 Stirling Hall, rear of Elm Road, Leigh SS9 1HT
www.barlowandfields.co.uk
01702 808982

INFORMAL & UNUSUAL DINING

A new wave of quirky pop-ups and innovative destinations are shaking up how we eat.

The Company Shed, West Mersea
129 Coast Road, West Mersea CO5 8PA
www.thecompanyshed.co
01206 382700

Mehalah's, East Mersea
East Mersea Road, East Mersea CO5 8TQ
www.mehalahs.co.uk
01206 382797

Maldon Smokehouse
Cromwell Lane, Maldon CM9 4LB
www.maldonsmokehouse.vpweb.co.uk
07759 572569

Tom's Salty Shack
festival pop-ups
www.tomssaltyshack.com
07803 828415

Moonbeamers
pop-up outdoor cinema and dining
www.moonbeamers.co.uk
0845 838 0686

Gamekeeper's Daughter
wild food and game pop-up events
www.gamekeepers-daughter.co.uk
07592 400447

Chef Charlie Stocker
pop-up dining events
www.twitter.com/charliejay77

FISH & CHIPS AND TAKE-AWAYS

Eating out for a quick treat can be really tasty at some of these better places.

The Fish House, Southend-on-Sea
11 East St, Southend-on-Sea SS2 6LQ
www.the-fish-house.co.uk
01702 464680

Henleys, Colchester & Braintree
9 Vine Dr, Wivenhoe, Colchester CO7 9HA
01206 820222
18 Queens Road, Braintree CM7 5UA
01376 331006
www.henleysfishandchips.co.uk

Chris' Famous Fish, Rayleigh
81 Grove Road, Rayleigh
near Southend-On-Sea SS6 8RA
www.facebook.com/FamousFish
01268 775856

Louis Fish Bar, Canvey
162 Long Road, Canvey Island SS8 0JP
www.louisfishbar.co.uk
01268 684315

Oldham's of Westcliff
13 West Road, Westcliff SS0 9AU
www.oldhamsofwestcliff.co.uk
01702 346736

Mac's Plaice, Brightlingsea
1 - 3 Church Road, Brightlingsea CO7 0JE
www.facebook.com/macsplaice
01206 306542

PLACES TO STAY

HOTELS & INNS

Six of our featured twenty restaurants not only offer great food but also a comfortable bed for the night.

The Mistley Thorn, Mistley
High St, Mistley CO11 1HE
www.mistleythorn.co.uk
01206 392821

The Sun Inn, Dedham
High Street, Dedham C07 6DF
www.thesuninndedham.com
01206 323351

The Bull and Willow Room, Great Totham
2 Maldon Road, Great Totham CM9 8NH
www.thebullatgreattotham.co.uk
01621 893385

The White Hart, Margaretting Tye
Swan Lane, Margaretting Tye,
Ingatestone CM4 9JX
www.thewhitehart.uk.com
01277 840478

The Cricketers Arms, Rickling Green
Rickling Green, Near Stansted CB11 3YG
www.thecricketersarmsricklinggreen.co.uk
01799 543210

Grain, Colchester
11a North Hill, Colchester CO1 1DZ
www.grain-colchester.co.uk
01206 570005

HOLIDAY HOMES

Get under the skin of Essex staying as welcome guests in a local community.

The Hayloft at Carpenters Farm, Great Bentley
www.carpentersfarmshop.co.uk
01206 255365

Mersea Island Vineyard
www.merseawine.com
01206 385900

Daw Street Farm, Finchingfield
www.essexfarmholiday.co.uk
01371 810315

The Lodge at Oxneys Farm, Felsted
www.felstedholidaycottages.co.uk
01371 820271

Brickwall Farm, Sible Hedingham
www.brickwallfarm.co.uk
01787 460329

Lee Wick Farm, St. Oysth
www.leewickfarm.co.uk
01255 823281

Pond Cottage, St. Osyth
www.earlshallfarm.info
01255 820458

Wakes Hall Lodges, Wakes Colne
www.wakeslodges.co.uk
01206 563222

Rye Farm, Layer-de-la-Haye
www.ryefarm.org.uk
01206 734350

B & B and GUEST ACCOMMODATION

A cosy refuge for the night with a hearty breakfast is one of life's simple pleasures.

Mersea Island Vineyard
www.merseawine.com
01206 385900

Ollivers Farm, Halstead
www.essex-bed-breakfast.co.uk
01787 237642

Bendysh Hall, Radwinter
www.bendyshhallbedandbreakfast.co.uk
01799 599220

Black Bond Hall, Langenhoe
www.blackbondhall.co.uk
01206 735776

Rye Farm, Layer-de-la-Haye
www.ryefarm.org.uk
01206 734350

Puttocks Farm, Great Dunmow
www.puttocksfarm.moonfruit.com
01371 872377

GLAMPING AND CAMPING

Nothing quite like being out under the stars at one with nature.

Barleylands Farm Park, Billericay *camp*
Barleylands Road, Billericay CM11 2UD
www.barleylands.co.uk
01268 288886

Graces Fruit Farm, Wimbish *camp*
Thaxted Road, Wimbish
near Saffron Walden CB10 2XP
01371 830387

Lower Dairy Farm, Nayland *camp*
Water Lane, Nayland near Colchester CO6 4JS
www.lowerdairyfarm.co.uk
01206 262314

Walton Hall Farm, Linford *camp*
Walton's Hall Road, Linford near Stanford SS17 0RH
www.waltonhallfarm.co.uk
01375 644558

Lee Wick Farm, St. Oysth *camp and glamp*
www.leewickfarm.co.uk
01255 823281

Feather Down at Layer Marney Tower, Colchester *glamp*
www.featherdown.co.uk
01420 80804

Lakeland Yurts, Hatfield Peverel *glamp*
www.lakeland-yurts.co.uk
01245 380416

The Shepherd's Hide, Thorrington *glamp*
www.theshepherdshide.co.uk
01206 302964

FUN STUFF

EVENT CATERING

Sometimes we just want to relax and host, leaving it in the hands of the professionals.

Hepburns Butchers *barbecues*
www.hepburnsfood.co.uk
01277 216656

C Johnson Butchers *barbecues and hog roasts*
www.cjohnsonbutchers.co.uk
0208 590 4054

Giggly Pig Company *hog roasts*
www.gigglypig.co.uk
01708 476124

Ashlyns *hog roasts, lamb roasts and barbecues*
www.ashlyns.co.uk
01277 890411

Church's Butchers *hog roasts*
224 High Street, Epping CM16 4AQ
www.churchsbutchers.co.uk
01992 573231

Ellis Catering
www.elliscatering.co.uk
01277 366601

Stock and Bailey Catering
www.stockandbailey.co.uk
01206 616060

Roamers Caterers
www.roamerscaterers.co.uk
01245 353564

Mustard Seed Catering
www.mustardseedcooking.co.uk
01277 363407

Quinnessential Catering
www.quinncatering.co.uk
07803 820606

VINTAGE TEAS

Coming to you, time for tea has never had more class and period charm.

Essex Tea Ladies
www.essextealadies.co.uk
07738160226

Plum Fairy
www.plumfairy.co.uk
07968 280868

Vintage Travelling Tea Party
www.essexafternoontea.co.uk
01245 607087

All The Tea & China
www.allthetea.co.uk
07813 578419

English Rose Vintage Teas
www.englishrosevintageteas.co.uk
07837 428172

WEDDINGS AND PARTIES

Try these for your truly individual Essex wedding or special celebration.

Mersea Island Vineyard
www.merseawine.com
01206 385900

Anne of Cleves Barn at Great Lodge, Great Bardfield
www.greatlodge.co.uk
01371 810776

Layer Marney Tower, Colchester
www.layermarneytower.co.uk
01206 330784

Marks Hall Gardens, Coggeshall
Marks Hall Estate, Coggeshall CO6 1TG
www.markshall.org.uk
01376 563796

Leez Priory, Chelmsford
www.leez-priory.co.uk
01245 362555

Fennes, Braintree
www.fennes.co.uk
01376 324555

Parklands, Quendon
www.quendonhall.co.uk
01799 543800

Prested Hall, Feering
www.prested.co.uk
01376 573300

COOKERY SCHOOLS

If inspired to do more than pick up a good recipe book, learn hands-on from a masterchef.

The Mistley Kitchen, Mistley
High Street, Mistley near Manningtree CO11 1HD
www.mistleykitchen.com
01206 391024

The Cookery School at Braxted Park, Witham
www.braxtedparkcookery.co.uk
01206 255041

Ann's Smart School of Cookery, Danbury
www.annsmartschool.com
01245 227527

Mersea Island Cookery School, East Mersea
www.merseaislandcookeryschool.co.uk
07706 671668

The Green Apron, Coggeshall
www.thegreenapron.co.uk
01206 890387

Baythorne Hall, Halstead
www.baythornehall.co.uk
01440 785680

BakeWell, Dunmow
www.youcanbakewell.co.uk
01371 879679

Delightful Tea Bake School, Southend-on-Sea
www.delightfultea.co.uk
01702 742343

The Gourmet Cake Company, Chelmsford
www.gourmetcupcakes.co.uk
01245 283986

Jo's Blue Aga, Harlow
www.josblueaga.com

Mayfield Farm Bakery *breadmaking courses*
Sheering Road, Old Harlow CM17 0JP
www.mayfieldfarmbakery.co.uk
01279 411774

AlphaBake Cookery, Dunmow *for children*
www.cookiescookingschool.co.uk
07906 158895

Mustard Seed
www.mustardseedcooking.co.uk
01277 363407

EXPERIENCES AND EDUCATION

Getting closer to ingredients, produce and harvest is all part of being a true foodie.

Foragers Feast *guided fungi and wild food foraging*
www.facebook.com/foragersfeast
01206 231660

Forest Foragers *fungi and wild food foraging courses*
www.forestforagers.co.uk
07758 926723

Foraging Adventures *guided wild food adventures*
www.foragingadventures.co.uk
07814 785987

Suffolk Market Events *OTB*
guided wild food walks and cookery demos
www.suffolkmarketevents.co.uk
07704 627973

Essex Bees *beekeeping courses*
www.essexbees.co.uk
07737 942400

Boydells Dairy Farm
open farm and sheep milking parlour
www.boydellsdairy.co.uk
01371 850481

Barleylands Farm Park, Billericay
farm park and retail village
Barleylands Road, Billericay CM11 2UD
www.barleylands.co.uk
01268 288886

The Chappel Chocolate House
chocolate parties and workshops
www.chappelchocolatehouse.co.uk
07787 506846

Slamseys Barn, Great Notley *activities and courses*
www.slamseys.co.uk
01245 361400

FESTIVALS AND EVENTS

No better advert for all that is great about tasty Essex, go explore the artisan vibe.

Essex Fine Food Show, Chelmsford
Chelmsford City Racecourse *mid-May*
www.apteventspro.co.uk
01245 400878

Essex Festival of Food and Drink, Braintree
Cressing Temple Barns *mid-July*
www.apteventspro.co.uk
01245 400878

Barleylands Food Festival, Billericay
Barleylands Road, Billericay *mid-June*
www.livingheritagefoodfestivals.co.uk
01283 820660

Maldon Smoke and Fire Festival
The Promenade, Maldon *late Aug*
www.smokeandfirefestival.com

Coggeshall Food and Drink Festival
West Street Vineyard, Coggeshall *end Sept*
www.facebook.com/coggeshallfoodanddrinkfestival
07795 363398

Cressing Autumn Food Fair, Braintree
Cressing Temple Barns *mid-Oct*
www.oakleighfairs.co.uk
01206 263088

Weald and Essex Country Shows and Food & Drink Markets *late April and mid-Sept*
Weald Country Park, Brentwood
www.classicfestivals.co.uk
01728 685302

Colchester Food and Drink Festival
Lower Castle Park, Colchester *late June*
www.foodanddrinkfestivalsuk.co.uk
07766 056747

Food for Thorpe, Thorpe-le-Soken
Golden Lane, Thorpe-le-Soken *end Aug*
www.thorpefoodfestival.co.uk
07904 313222

Hyde Hall Food Festival, Chelmsford
RHS Hyde Hall, Rettendon *early Oct*
www.rhs.org.uk
01245 400256

Spirit of The Corn Festival, Maldon
Museum of Power, Langford *mid-July*
www.museumofpower.org.uk
01621 843183

Colchester Town and Country Fair
Lower Castle Park, Colchester *early April*
www.oakleighfairs.co.uk
01206 263088

The Tendring Show, Manningtree
Lawford House Park *mid-July*
www.tendringshow.co.uk
01206 231821

Essex Young Farmers Country Show, Chelmsford
Boyton Hall, Roxwell *late May*
www.essexyoungfarmersshow.co.uk
01245 360442

Essex Game and Country Show, Billericay
Barleylands Road, Billericay *early Oct*
www.essexgameandcountryfair.co.uk
01283 820548

Mersea Island Food & Drink Festival
Rewsalls Lane, East Mersea
www.mersea-fdl-festival.com
07973 653873

The Fling Festival
Hylands Estate, Chelmsford *early July*
www.flingfestival.com
01245 606987

Thaxted Festival
Thaxted Parish Church *late June – early July*
www.thaxtedfestival.org.uk
01371 831421

Leigh Folk Festival
across Leigh-on-Sea *late June*
www.leighfolkfestival.com

FOOD LOVERS' GUIDE

Your deliciously indispensable companion to enjoying Essex, edible and otherwise

Brentwood Festival
Brentwood Centre *mid-July*
www.brentwoodfestival.co.uk

NON-FOODIE DELIGHTS

Add a splash of style to match your food.

Aabelard *ultimate kitchen aprons*
www.aabelard.com

PoshLots of Much Hadham *private allotments OTB*
www.poshlots.uk
01279 927030

The Little Beach Hut Company, West Mersea
beach hut hire and seaside chic
www.thelittlebeachhutcompany.co.uk
07817 985514

Abigail's Lifestyle Store, Ingatestone
42 High Street, Ingatestone CM4 9ED
www.abigails.co.uk
01277 354623

The Country Garden Flower Company
bouquets, buttonholes and arrangements
www.thecountrygardenflowercompany.com
01206 330880

The Blue Egg, Great Bardfield *lifestyle store*
Braintree Road, Great Bardfield CM7 4PY
www.kneadfood.com
01371 811801

Maison Bleu, Chelmsford *lifestyle and interiors*
10 Meon Close, Chelmsford CM1 7QQ
www.maisonbleustyle.com
07914 248796

Tides, Brentwood *home and garden*
8 High Street, Brentwood CM14 4AB
www.tideshomeandgarden.co.uk
01277 231799

The Blue Dandelion, Ingatestone
flowers and lifestyle
13 High Street, Ingatestone CM4 9ED
www. thebluedandelion.co.uk
01277 500161

Scape Interiors, Leigh
79 The Broadway, Leigh on Sea SS9 1PE
www.scapeinteriors.co.uk
01702 719253

Life of Riley, Clavering
2 Brice's Yard, Butts Green, Clavering CB11 4RT
www.lifeofrileyonline.co.uk
01799 551813

OUT AND ABOUT

Feeding the soul is just as important as feasting, fill up on eclectic, rustic, local entertainment.

Audley End House & Gardens, Saffron Walden
London Road, Saffron Walden CB11 4JF
www.english-heritage.org.uk
01799 522842

RHS Garden Hyde Hall, Rettendon
Creephedge Lane, Rettendon
near Chelmsford CM3 8RA
www.rhs.org.uk
01245 400256

Colchester Zoo
Maldon Road, Stanway near Colchester CO3 0SL
www.colchester-zoo.com
01206 331292

Essex Outdoors *activity centres*
at Bradwell, Danbury, Harlow and Mersea
www.essexoutdoors.com
0345 200 4220

Rope Runners, Brentwood
Ongar Road, Kelvedon Hatch
near Brentwood CM15 0LA
www.roperunners.co.uk
01277 364470

Royal Gunpowder Mills, Waltham Abbey
Beaulieu Drive, Waltham Abbey EN9 1JY
www.royalgunpowdermills.com
01992 707370

Old MacDonald's Farm, Brentwood
Weald Road, Brentwood CM14 5AY
www.omdfarm.co.uk
01277 375177

Blake House Craft Centre, Braintree
Blake End, Rayne near Braintree CM77 6RA
www.blakehousecraftcentre.co.uk
01376 553146

Christmas Wrapped Up, Dunmow
trees and festive shopping
Easter Hall, Aythorpe Roding
near Dunmow CM6 1PE
www.christmaswrappedup.co.uk
01245 231628

Gardens of Easton Lodge, Great Dunmow
Little Easton near Great Dunmow CM6 2BB
www.eastonlodge.co.uk
01371 876979

The Gibberd Garden, Harlow
Marsh Lane, Harlow CM17 0NA
www.thegibberdgarden.co.uk
01279 442112

Marks Hall Gardens, Coggeshall
Marks Hall Estate, off A120, Coggeshall CO6 1TG
www.markshall.org.uk
01376 563796

Tilbury Fort, Tilbury
The Fort, Fort Road, Tilbury RM18 7NR
www.english-heritage.org.uk
01375 858489

Christmas at Slamseys Barn, Great Notley
festive shopping
Blackley Lane, Great Notley
near Braintree CM77 7QW
www.slamseys.co.uk
01245 361400

GARDEN CENTRES

There is nothing like growing your own, plucking the first crop as it shoots.

Poplar Nurseries, Marks Tey
Coggeshall Road, Marks Tey
near Colchester CO6 1HR
www.poplarnurseries.co.uk
01206 210374

White Elm Garden Centre, Bicknacre
White Elm Road, Bicknacre, Chelmsford CM3 4LR
www.whiteelmgardencentre.com
01245 227829

Wyevale Garden Centres
Chelmsford, Ongar, Braintree, Rayleigh, Upminster and Colchester
www.wyevalegardencentres.co.uk
0844 288 5077

Altons Garden Centre, Wickford
Arterial Road A127, Wickford SS12 9JG
www.alton-gardencentre.co.uk
01268 726421

Summerhill Garden Centre, Billericay
Pipps Hill Road North, Billericay CM11 2UJ
www.summerhillgardencentre.co.uk
01268 280699

Green Island Gardens, Ardleigh
Park Road, Ardleigh near Colchester CO7 7SP
www.greenislandgardens.co.uk
01206 230455

Blenheim Plant & Garden Centre, Colchester
Bromley Road, Colchester CO7 7SF
www.blenheimgardencentre.co.uk
01206 870605

Harlow Garden Centre, Harlow
Canes Lane A414, Hastingwood
near Harlow CM17 9LD
www.bluediamond.gg
01279 419 039

Perrywood, Tiptree
Kelvedon Road, Inworth near Tiptree CO5 9SX
www.perrywood.co.uk
01376 570777

RHS Garden Hyde Hall, Rettendon
Creephedge Lane, Rettendon
near Chelmsford CM3 8RA
www.rhs.org.uk
01245 400256

Meadow Croft Garden Centre, Battlesbridge
Woodham Road, Battlesbridge
near Wickford SS11 7QU
www.meadow-croft.co.uk
01245 320314

Thurrock Garden Centre, Ockendon
South Road, South Ockendon RM15 6DL
www.thurrockgardencentre.co.uk
01708 851991

R & R Saggers, Saffron Walden
Waterloo House, High Street, Newport CB11 3PG
www.facebook.com/randrsaggers
01799 540858

Langthorns Plantery, Dunmow
Little Canfield near Dunmow CM6 1TD
www.langthorns.com
01371 872611

Beeches Nursery, Saffron Walden
Crown Hill, Ashdon Saffron Walden CB10 2HB
www.beechesnursery.co.uk
01799 584362

King & Co. Tree Nursery, Braintree
Dunmow Road, Rayne near Braintree CM77 6WF
www.kingco.co.uk
01376 340469

Chapel End Nursery, Great Dunmow
Chapel End, Broxted near Great Dunmow CM6 2BW
www.chapelendnurserysperry.co.uk
01279 850771

Parker's Garden Company, Frinton-on-Sea
Frinton Road, Kirby Cross near Frinton CO13 0PD
www.parkersgardencompany.com
01255 674838

Woodside Garden Centre, Rayleigh
A127 Arterial Road, Rayleigh SS6 7TZ
www.woodsidegardencentre.co.uk
01268 747888

Webb's Garden Centre, Ilford
609 Green Lane, Ilford IG3 9RP
www.webbsgardencentre.co.uk
020 8597 2684

Rose Cottage Plants, Epping
Bay Tree Farm, Epping Green CM16 6PU
www.rosecottageplants.co.uk
01992 573775

Mill Race Garden Centre, Colchester
New Road, Aldham near Colchester CO6 3QT
www.millracegardencentre.co.uk
01206 242521

Buckhatch Nursery & Garden Centre, Rettendon
Rettendon Common near Chelmsford CM3 8EW
www.bhngardencentre.co.uk
01245 400360

Hearts Delight Garden Centre, Manningtree
Long Road, Lawford near Manningtree CO11 2EF
www.hearts-delight.co.uk
01206 392539

Fillpots, Colchester
52 Straight Road, Boxted near Colchester CO4 5RB
www.fillpots.co.uk
01206 273834

Halstead Garden Centre
Brook Street, Colne Engaine near Halstead CO6 2JH
www.timag.co.uk
01787 473541

Abercorn Plant & Garden Centre, Chelmsford
Beehive Lane, Chelmsford CM2 8LX
www.abercorngc.co.uk
01245 257398

Morley Nurseries, Great Wakering
Southend Road, Great Wakering SS3 0PU
www.morleynurseries.com
01702 585668

Potash Garden Centre, Hawkwell
9 Main Road, Hawkwell near Hockley SS5 4JN
www.gardencentresouthend.co.uk
01702 201120

Riverside Nursery & Garden Centre, Hockley
Lower Road, Hockley SS5 5LE
www.riversidenursery.co.uk
01702 201100

The Barn, Stanway
Turkey Cock Lane, Stanway, Colchester CO3 8ND
www.thebarnstanway.co.uk
01206 211312

Olivers Nurseries, Witham
Maldon Road, Witham CM8 3HY
www.oliversnurseries.co.uk
01376 513239

View Garden Centre, Rayleigh
Old Chelmsford Road, Rayleigh SS11 8SJ
www.viewgardencentre.co.uk
01268 761119

Olivers Plants, Earls Colne
Coggeshall Road, Earls Colne, Colchester CO6 2JX
www.oliversplants.co.uk
01787 220281

The Elms Nursery, Billericay
Hardings Elms Road, Crays Hill, Billericay CM11 2UH
www.theelmsnursery.co.uk
01268 521721

Greenbrook Garden Centre, Chelmsford
Ongar Road A414, Highwood, Chelmsford CM1 3SN
www.greenbrookgardencentre.co.uk
01245 248871

Butts Green Garden Centre, Sandon
Mayes Lane, Sandon CM2 7RW
www.buttsgreen.co.uk
01245 223524

Craft Nurseries, Lawford
34 Harwich Road, Lawford
near Manningtree CO11 2LS
www.craftnurseries.co.uk
01206 230699

Hilltop Garden Centre, Clacton-on-Sea
Clacton Road, Weeley
near Clacton-on-Sea CO16 9DN
www.hilltopgardencentreessex.co.uk
01255 831083

Hanging Gardens, Writtle
Ongar Road, Writtle, Chelmsford CM1 3NT
www.hangingardens.co.uk
0800 970 7661

Writtle Road Nursery, Chelmsford
7 Writtle Road, Chelmsford CM1 3BL
www.writtleroadnursery.co.uk
01245 265655

The Place for Plants, East Bergholt *OTB*
East Bergholt Place, East Bergholt, Suffolk CO7 6UP
www.placeforplants.co.uk
01206 299224

HEALTH SPAS

A proper detox can work wonders for over-indulgence, or for just a little 'me time'.

Lifehouse Spa & Hotel
Frinton Road, Thorpe-le-Soken CO16 0JD
www.lifehouse.co.uk
01255 860050

Aqua Springs, Colchester
Cowdray Avenue, Colchester CO1 1YH
www.aqua-springs.co.uk
01206 282010

Prested Hall, Feering
B1024/A12 junction, Feering CO5 9EE
www.prested.co.uk
01376 572175

KITCHEN DESIGNERS

A great cook and a good meal starts with the perfect culinary surroundings.

Blackstone Kitchens, Earls Colne
3, The Mill Store, Foundry Lane,
Earls Colne CO6 2SB
www.blackstonekitchens.co.uk
01787 275377

Island Furniture Company, West Mersea
2-4 High Street North, West Mersea CO5 8JY
www.islandfurnitureco.co.uk
07970 897032

Lower Barn Farm Design Studio, Rayleigh
London Road Rayleigh SS6 9ET
www.lowerbarnkitchens.com
01268 780991

Luxe Kitchens, Chelmsford
Victoria Court, New Street, Chelmsford CM1 1GP
www.luxekitchens.co.uk
01245 350482

Davonport, Colchester
Peartree Road, Stanway near Colchester CO3 0LQ
www.davonport.com
0845 468 0025

Hutton Kitchens, Billericay
17 Radford Way, Billericay CM12 0AA
www.huttonkitchens.co.uk
01277 633301

Regal Kitchens, Chelmsford & Billericay
2 Navigation Road, Chelmsford CM2 6HX
01245 351151
2 Whitesbridge Retail Park, Crays Hill,
Billericay CM11 2UL
01268 525 922
www.regalkitchens.co.uk

Humphrey Munson Kitchens, Felsted
The Joinery Works, Gransmore Green,
Felsted CM6 3LB
www.humphreymunson.co.uk
01371 821300

Churchill Brothers, Earls Colne
Colne Stoves & Fireplaces,
42 Halstead Road, Earls Colne CO6 2NL
www.churchillbrothers.co.uk
01787 211528

Emerson Interiors, Basildon
8/9 Cranes Industrial Estate, Cranes Close,
Basildon SS14 3JB
www.emersoninteriors.co.uk
01268 525216

Baker & Baker, Stambourne
Greenfield Farm, Yeldham Road,
Stambourne CO9 4ND
www.bakerandbaker.co.uk
01440 788850

De Burgo Pure Bespoke, Chigwell
New Barns Farm, Roding Lane, Chigwell IG7 6BJ
www.deburgo.co.uk
020 8501 4950

Henderson & Redfearn, Beaumont
Lower Barn Farm, Quay Lane, Beaumont near
Clacton-on-Sea CO16 0BB
www.hendersonandredfearn.co.uk
01255 861943

Lewis James Kitchens, Great Baddow
Sandford Mill Lane, Great Baddow
near Chelmsford CM2 7RT
www.lewis-james.co.uk
01245 830813

Simon's Kitchens Ltd., Colchester
40b Crouch Street, Colchester, Essex CO3 3HH
www.simonskitchens.com
01206 766005

Armstrong Jordan Interiors, Matching Green
Kingston Farm, Down Hall Road,
Matching Green CM17 0RB
www.armstrongjordan.co.uk
01279 731220

Harvey Jones Kitchens, Brentwood
4 Ingrave Road, Brentwood CM15 8AT
www.harveyjones.com
01277 280372

Tom Howley Kitchens, Brentwood
3 High Street, Brentwood CM14 4RG
www.tomhowley.co.uk
01277 214587

Crabtree & Hargreeves Bespoke Interiors, Aveley
The Hay Barn, Moorhall Farm,
Romford Road, Aveley RM15 4UU
www.crabtreeandhargreeves.co
01708 864034

Broadway Kitchens, Brentwood
98 High Street, Brentwood CM14 4AP
www.bespokekitchensbybroadway.co.uk
01277 212221

Clive Anderson Bespoke Furniture, Romford
8 Hog Hill Road, Romford RM5 2DH
www.cliveandersonfurniture.co.uk
01708 505528

Claymark Bespoke Furniture, Hawkwell
6 Magees Nurseries, Hawkwell SS5 4LH
www.claymark.co.uk
01702 548609

Cohen & Bryan Interiors, Benfleet
5 Kelvin Road, South Benfleet SS7 4QB
www.cohen-bryan.co.uk
01702 410682

Moylans Design, Leigh-on-Sea
138 Broadway, Leigh-on-Sea SS9 1AA
www.moylans.co.uk
01702 480470

Mulberry Interiors, Loughton
8 Church Hill, Loughton IG10 1LA
www.mulberry-interiors.co.uk
0208 508 1294

Copford Woodcraft Kitchens, Colchester
91 London Road, Copford near Colchester CO6 1LG
www.copfordwoodcraftkitchens.co.uk
01206 210545

Paul Newman Interiors, Hadleigh
136 High Street, Hadleigh SS7 2PB
www.paulnewmaninteriors.co.uk
01702 552868

Recipe index

Starters, sides and light bites

Mains

Puddings

ESSEX FEAST: OUR FAVOURITE PLACES

Where shall we go for lunch? You won't go wrong with one of these twenty places, where the warmest of welcomes and the tastiest of Essex food awaits. Kick back over a relaxed pub meal deep in the timeless Essex countryside, drop in at the well-known spots dotted along the coast, or choose a characterful town or city centre restaurant. In the mood for finer dining? We've got that covered too. The twenty chefs in this book aren't the only ones in Essex of course, but we are particularly fond of them and their restaurants. We know that they will be delighted to welcome you.

The Mistley Thorn
High St, Mistley CO11 1HE
W: mistleythorn.co.uk
T: 01206 392821

The Cricketers Arms
Rickling Green, Near Stansted CB11 3YG
W: thecricketersarmsricklinggreen.co.uk
T: 01799 543210

Haywards Restaurant
111 Bell Common, Epping CM16 4DZ
W: haywardsrestaurant.co.uk
T: 01992 577350

The Sun Inn
High Street, Dedham C07 6DF
W: thesuninndedham.com
T: 01206 323351

The Square & Compasses
Fuller Street near Fairstead CM3 2BB
W: thesquareandcompasses.co.uk
T: 01245 361477

Rubino Kitchen
Chigborough Lodge, Chigborough Farm,
Chigborough Road, Heybridge,
Maldon CM9 4RE
W: rubinokitchen.co.uk
T: 01621 855579

Lucca Enoteca
39-43 High Street,
Manningtree CO11 1AH
W: luccafoods.co.uk
T: 01206 390044

The Spotted Dog
Bishop's Green, Barnston,
Dunmow CM6 1NF
W: the-spotted-dog-bishopsgreen.co.uk
T: 01245 231598

The Magic Mushroom Restaurant
Barleylands Road, Billericay CM11 2UD
W: magicmushroomrestaurant.co.uk
T: 01268 289963

The Bull and Willow Room
2 Maldon Road, Great Totham CM9 8NH
W: thebullatgreattotham.co.uk
T: 01621 893385

The White Hart Inn
Swan Lane, Margaretting Tye,
Ingatestone CM4 9JX
W: thewhitehart.uk.com
T: 01277 840478

Church Street Tavern
3 Church Street, Colchester C01 1NF
W: churchstreettavern.co.uk
T: 01206 564325

The Anchor Riverside Pub & Restaurant
Ferry Road, Hullbridge SS5 6ND
W: theanchorhullbridge.co.uk
T: 01702 230777

The Green Man
Mill End Green, Lindsell,
Dunmow CM6 2DN
W: greenmanlindsell.co.uk
T: 01371 852285

Boathouse Restaurant
Mill Lane, Dedham,
Colchester C07 6DH
W: dedhamboathouse.com
T: 01206 323153

The Creek
Flag Hill, Great Bentley,
Colchester CO7 8RE
W: thecreekgreatbentley.co.uk
T: 01255 317950; 01206 586435

The Hoop
21 High Street, Stock,
Ingatestone CM4 9BD
W: thehoop.co.uk
T: 01277 841137

Grain
11a North Hill, Colchester CO1 1DZ
W: grain-colchester.co.uk
T: 01206 570005

The Vine
Vine St, Great Bardfield,
Braintree CM7 4SR
W: vine-greatbardfield.co.uk
T: 01371 811822

Pig & Whistle Restaurant
Chignal Road, Chignal Smealy,
Chelmsford CM1 4SZ
W: pigandwhistlechelmsford.uk
T: 01245 443186